The Cameron–Clegg Government

Coalition Politics in an Age of Austerity

Edited by

Simon Lee
Senior Lecturer in Politics
University of Hull, UK

and

Matt Beech
Lecturer in Politics
University of Hull, UK

palgrave
macmillan

First published 2011 by
PALGRAVE MACMILLAN

Palgrave Macmillan in the UK is an imprint of Macmillan Publishers Limited,
registered in England, company number 785998, of Houndmills, Basingstoke,
Hampshire RG21 6XS.

Palgrave Macmillan in the US is a division of St Martin's Press LLC,
175 Fifth Avenue, New York, NY 10010.

Palgrave Macmillan is the global academic imprint of the above companies
and has companies and representatives throughout the world.

Palgrave® and Macmillan® are registered trademarks in the United States,
the United Kingdom, Europe and other countries

ISBN: 978-0-230-29071-6   hardback
ISBN: 978-0-230-29644-2   paperback

This book is printed on paper suitable for recycling and made from fully
managed and sustained forest sources. Logging, pulping and manufacturing
processes are expected to conform to the environmental regulations of the
country of origin.

A catalogue record for this book is available from the British Library.

A catalog record for this book is available from the Library of Congress.

10 9 8 7 6 5 4 3 2
20 19 18 17 16 15 14 13 12 11

Printed and bound in Great Britain by
CPI Antony Rowe, Chippenham and Eastbourne

Contents

Foreword

Rt. Hon. Sir Malcolm Rifkind MP

Every once in a while circumstances conspire to produce a distinct, yet unexpected outcome. The formation of the Coalition Government was one such moment. The agreement between the Liberal Democrats and the Conservatives was the product of exceptional developments. Few would have expected, as Tony Blair celebrated his third election win, that the next poll would see his party forced from office by the cooperative efforts of the two opposition parties. Yet a week is a long time in politics, let alone five years. In that time each of the three main political parties changed its leader. The country as a whole plunged into a severe economic malaise, triggered by a financial crisis that few had seen coming. Above all, the electorate produced a political deadlock, ensuring that the job of forming a government fell to the politicians themselves.

As with all major events in politics, the formation of the Coalition proved the importance of individuals. Were one to have replaced any one of the three party leaders with a rival from the same party, and one would almost certainly have seen a different outcome. A less prickly Prime Minister might have been able to tempt the Liberal Democrats to reach a deal with the Labour Party, long considered the home of its ideological cousins. Yet an appealing offer could not be assembled by Gordon Brown, whose command and control style of management had characterized his tenure as both Chancellor of the Exchequer and Prime Minister. Likewise, a Conservative leader lacking David Cameron's pragmatism might have baulked at the idea of offering a compromise on electoral reform in exchange for a working Parliamentary majority. Throughout the campaign Cameron had pushed to secure an outright victory. Yet this was a herculean task given the low base from which his party began the campaign. A lesser man might have been content to settle for what had been achieved, in the hope that a minority Government would eventually come to pass. In turn, the selection of Nick Clegg as party leader by Lib-Dem voters will come to be seen as being of critical importance. Every one of Clegg's predecessors would have struggled to reach an agreement with the Conservatives. Not so the current Deputy Prime Minister, who saw in the deal a once-in-a-lifetime opportunity to prove to the country that Coalition Government could work in practice.

In addition to personality, circumstance played a major role. Over the course of the five days that followed the 2010 General Election, it gradually became clear that a compromise agreement between the Liberal Democrats and Conservatives was the only viable option. The Parliamentary mathematics meant that even a deal between Labour and the Liberal Democrats would have failed to produce a stable administration capable of governing effectively. Even if that had not been the case, the dynamics of the moment favoured a decisive change in Government. Brown had never previously fought an election, and to have remained in office despite major Conservative gains at Labour's expense would have stretched the public's patience to its breaking point. Moreover, the situation in which the country found itself all but forced the hand of those involved. Having seen the Labour Government stave off a deadly financial crisis through an emergency recapitalization of the banking sector 18 months earlier, the would-be Coalition partners found themselves racing the clock to prevent the markets' deep unease about the country's ailing economic situation from spinning out of control. Across the English Channel and the Irish Sea, European partners were seeing severe drops in living standards being forced upon them by the bond markets, to which they had been forced to turn in a final roll of the dice. Neither the Conservatives nor the Liberal Democrats, least of all the civil servants seeking to facilitate a full coalition between the two, could bear to entertain the horror of renewed economic collapse amid a political vacuum.

Indeed, one cannot understand the Coalition Government, or its policy platform, without grasping the scale of the economic challenge. The deficit it now seeks to close is not only the Coalition Government's number one priority, but also its very reason for being. This is in many ways a National Government, more akin to British administrations of wartime than the coalitions that one sees on a regular basis in Europe. Without the economic challenge, it might never have come together.

That is not to say that there were not substantial areas of policy agreement between the two parties, as the bulk of this work makes clear. In the final years of the last decade, Conservative and Liberal Democrats found themselves united in their opposition to the authoritarian and centralizing tendencies of the Labour Government. That common ground is reflected in the Coalition Agreement, which places a tremendous emphasis upon restoring civil liberties, reforming public services and decentralizing power away from Westminster. Indeed, Mark Stuart's analysis of the Liberal Democrats under Nick Clegg is compelling, demonstrating how the party swung from being one that sympathized with the ideals and core aims of the Labour Government to one that considered itself a full opposition party in its own right.

This book helps shed light on all these themes. It explains how events led to the creation of the Liberal Democratic–Conservative Coalition. Yet it also seeks to outline the challenges that the new Government faced upon taking office and to detail how its members have wrestled with a variety of challenges from different ideological perspectives. Matt Beech and Simon Lee have assembled a wide range of contributors to help analyse the Coalition's approach to governance. Each one considers the impact of the Government's austerity drive, which seeks to respond to circumstances that, while not of its making, are now its responsibility. For instance, the acute difficulties faced by the Liberal Democrats in accepting an increase in tuition fees are considered by Simon Griffiths' review of education policy in Chapter 5.

Few will share the conclusions of every contributor. Rajiv Prabhaker rightly cautions against proclaiming the death of 'New Labour', when so many long-serving officials remain within a party that came within a whisker of retaining power. By contrast, I find myself at odds with Chris Martin's pessimistic view of Britain's future international capabilities as a result of the Government's Strategic Defence and Security Review (SDSR). While the Government has had to make substantial savings, it has done so in a way that allows the UK to maintain its short-term commitments, while defending its long-term capabilities. While sacrifices have been made that will impact the UK's defence policy in the medium term, I believe that such efforts are required if the UK is to safeguard its economic stability, the loss of which would have far more serious consequences than any of the measures introduced by the Government. The UK, after these defence cuts, will still have the fourth largest defence budget in the world. The concerns of those who believe Britain is in terminal decline are greatly exaggerated.

Yet different interpretations of the contemporary political scene should not discourage readers from an enjoyment of this important contribution to the public debate. For this is not a book that seeks to provide a definitive historical record of the Coalition's formation or how successful its approach to Government will prove to be. It is rather a guide to the political moment – a snapshot of the political scene as it stands, and how those who observe today's events consider them at this precise point in time. Such a work will be far more valuable to the historians of the future than any speculative work produced without the benefit of hindsight. This is a collection of essays that deserves to be read by both academics and the public at large. Moreover, it deserves to be read now, not in five years' time. By that stage the world will have moved on once more, as it has so many times before.

The Centre for British Politics

The aim of the Centre for British Politics is to combine the research specialisms of Lord Norton, Simon Lee and Matt Beech. Its objectives are to conduct high quality research into aspects of British politics, especially, parties, policies and ideologies, and to reinforce the tradition of teaching and research in the area of British politics that the Department of Politics and International Studies at the University of Hull has developed for over 30 years.

This book is the fourth edited collection, and the third to be published by Palgrave Macmillan since the establishment of the Centre for British Politics in June 2007. As in *Ten Years of New Labour* (2008), *The Conservatives under David Cameron: Built to Last?* (2009), and *The Brown Government: A Policy Evaluation* (2009), a team of contributors has been selected who are united by their previous scholarship in and continuing passion for the study of diverse aspects of British politics, rather than a shared party political affiliation or unified ideological disposition. In that regard, the work of the Centre continues to reflect the spirit of vigorous but friendly academic inquiry and debate fostered by the Department of Politics and International Studies as it approaches its fiftieth anniversary.

It is particularly fitting too that the contributors to this volume should include Professor Arthur Aughey, a Senior Fellow of the Centre, and the author of the Centre for British Politics Norton Lecture 2011, '"With a Shrug of the Shoulders": Is England Becoming a Nation Once More?'

Acknowledgements

The Centre for British Politics would like to thank and acknowledge Matt Beech for assembling the team of contributors to this project and for organizing the symposium on the 3 December 2010 at the University of Hull upon which it was intended to be based. Unfortunately, the intervention of the heaviest snowfall in England for a generation led to the symposium's cancellation. Nevertheless, the editors would like to thank the contributors for their preparedness to travel to Hull and for their willingness to participate in a project for which Simon Lee must assume the responsibility for instigating. Once again this project, like its predecessors, would not have been possible but for the financial support provided by the Department of Politics and International Studies at the University of Hull.

The editors are especially grateful to Sir Malcolm Rifkind for agreeing to write the foreword to the book. They would also like to thank Amber Stone-Galilee for her courage and foresight in commissioning the project. It is unusual for a publisher to be asked to produce a book on a government, whose longevity has continued to be a matter of speculation, after it has served only two months in office. Given that context of great political and economic uncertainty, it is yet more unusual for a publisher to agree to proceed. The editors would also like to acknowledge the work of Liz Blackmore at Palgrave Macmillan on the production of the book and the role of the copy editors for their work in delivering the manuscript.

Finally, Matt, as ever, would like to thank his wife, Claire, for her constant support and love during the production of this book. Simon would like to thank his family for their continued love and support, and Rosie and Sam for their companionship and constant reminders of the world beyond politics.

Notes on Contributors

Arthur Aughey is a Professor of Politics at the School of Criminology, Politics and Social Policy, University of Ulster, and Senior Fellow of the Centre for British Politics, University of Hull. Amongst his published work is *Nationalism, Devolution and the Challenge to the United Kingdom State* (2001), *Politics of Northern Ireland Beyond the Belfast Agreement* (2005) and *The Politics of Englishness* (2007).

Tim Bale is a Professor of Politics at the Department of Politics and Contemporary European Studies, University of Sussex. He is the convener of the PSA's specialist group on Conservatives and Conservatism and is the author of *European Politics* (2008). An updated paperback version of his book, *The Conservative Party from Thatcher to Cameron*, was published in January 2011.

Matt Beech is a Lecturer in Politics and Director of the Centre for British Politics at the Department of Politics and International Studies, University of Hull. His research interests include New Labour, social democracy, the Conservative Party and conservatism. His articles have been published in *Policy Studies*, *The British Journal of Politics and International Relations*, *The Political Quarterly* and *West European Politics*. Amongst others, he is co-editor with Simon Lee of *Ten Years of New Labour* (2008), *The Conservatives under David Cameron: Built to Last?* (2009) and *The Brown Government: A Policy Evaluation* (2009).

John Benyon is a Professor of Political Studies at the University of Leicester and Director of Research in the Institute of Lifelong Learning. As well as lifelong learning issues, his research interests include the politics of law and order, public order, and crime and policing. His articles have been published in a variety of journals and his books include (with C. Bourn) *The Police* (1986), (with John Solomos) *The Roots of Urban Unrest* (1987), and (with Justin Fisher and David Denver) *Central Debates in British Politics* (2002). He is treasurer of the Political Studies Association and chair of the Committee of Learned Societies of the Academy of Social Sciences.

James Connelly is a Professor of Politics at the University of Hull. He teaches political theory, contemporary political philosophy and environmental politics. He has published two editions of his co-authored book *Politics and the Environment: From Theory to Practice* and several articles on the politics and ethics of the environment; he is currently writing a monograph on environmental virtues and citizenship. He also writes on the political philosophy of R.G. Collingwood and the other British Idealists, on the philosophy of history, on electoral systems and political participation.

Stephen Driver is a Principal Lecturer and Head of Social Sciences at Roehampton University. He is a widely published author who has co-written two studies of New Labour with Luke Martell, *New Labour: Politics after Thatcherism* (1998) and *Blair's Britain* (2002). Stephen completed a second edition of *New Labour* in 2006.

Simon Griffiths is a Lecturer in Politics at Goldsmiths, University of London and a Visiting Research Fellow at the Centre for Political Ideologies, Department of Politics and International Relations, University of Oxford. He has also worked as a Senior Policy Adviser at the British Academy, Senior Research Fellow at the Social Market Foundation, a parliamentary researcher and researcher to the sociologist, Anthony Giddens. He is co-editor with Kevin Hickson of *Party Politics and Ideology after New Labour* (Palgrave Macmillan, 2010).

Kevin Hickson is a Senior Lecturer at the Department of Politics, University of Liverpool. Kevin teaches and researches in British politics, with particular research emphasis on political ideologies and political economy. His books include *The IMF Crisis of 1976 and British Politics* (2005), (with Matt Beech) *Labour's Thinkers* (2007) and (with Mark Garnett) *Conservative Thinkers* (2009).

Simon Lee is a Senior Lecturer in Politics and Director of the Centre for Democratic Governance at the University of Hull. His teaching and research interests are principally in the field of political economy, with a particular emphasis on globalization and national economic performance, and the politics and national identity of England. He is the author of *Boom to Bust: The Politics and Legacy of Gordon Brown* (2009) and is working on *The State of England: The Nation We're In*. He is co-editor (with Stephen McBride) of *Neo-Liberalism, State Power and Global* Governance (2007) and (with Matt Beech) *Ten Years of New Labour* (2008), *The Conservatives* *under David Cameron: Built to Last?* (2009) and *The Brown Government: A Policy Evaluation* (2009).

Philip Lynch is a Senior Lecturer in Politics at the Department of Politics and International Relations, University of Leicester. His main research interest is in contemporary British Conservative politics on which he had published a number of books and articles, including the edited volume, *The Conservatives in Crisis* (2003), which examines the fortunes of the Conservative Party under William Hague, and (with Mark Garnett) *Exploring British Politics* (2009).

Chris Martin is a Lecturer and Deputy Director of the Centre for Security Studies at the Department of Politics and International Studies, University of Hull. His principal areas of interest are naval history, the political application of naval force and theories of naval strategy. He is currently engaged in research funded by the British Academy examining the shipbuilding programme of the British Admiralty between 1904 and 1916 and how that programme was influenced by The Hague and London Naval Conferences.

Philip Norton (Lord Norton of Louth) is a Professor of Government and Director of the Centre for Legislative Studies at the University of Hull. He is the author or editor of 29 books covering British politics, the constitution, the Conservative Party, Parliament and legislatures in comparative perspective. He was elevated to the peerage in 1998. He chaired the Conservative Party's commission to strengthen parliament and has served as chairman of the House of Lords Select Committee on the constitution. He is now serving as specialist adviser to the House of Commons Public Accounts Committee.

Robert M. Page is a Reader in Democratic Socialism and Social Policy at the Institute of Applied Social Studies, University of Birmingham. Robert has been a Fellow of the Royal Society of Arts since 1998. He was a Leverhulme Research Fellow at the John F. Kennedy School of Government, Harvard in 2008. His most recent book is *Revisiting the Welfare State* (2007).

Rajiv Prabhakar is a Teaching Fellow in Public Policy Economics and Analysis at the School of Public Policy, University College London. His general research interests cover assets and wealth, public services and welfare policy. His books include *Stakeholding and New Labour* (2003),

Rethinking Public Services (2006) and *The Assets Agenda* (2008). He has recently completed an ESRC-funded project on assets, inequality and education, and has conducted several previous ESRC projects. He is a member of the ESRC's Peer Review College.

The Rt. Hon. Sir Malcolm Rifkind is Member of Parliament for Kensington. He became a member of the Cabinet in 1986 as Secretary of State for Scotland. In 1990 he became Secretary of State for Transport and in 1992 Secretary of State for Defence. From 1995 to 1997 he was Foreign Secretary. He was one of only four ministers to serve throughout the whole prime ministerships of both Margaret Thatcher and John Major. In 1997 he was knighted in recognition of his public service. He served as the Shadow Secretary of State for Work and Pensions and Welfare Reform until December 2005 when he chose to return to the backbenches.

Emma Sanderson-Nash is an Associate Tutor at Sussex University, where she is completing a doctorate on the Liberal Democrats, for whom she worked for fifteen years. She has contributed to *The Liberal Dictionary of Biography*, and is the co-author of 'Sandals to Suits – Professionalization, Coalition and the Liberal Democrats', published in the *British Journal of Politics and International Relations*.

Mark Stuart teaches politics at both Nottingham and Hull Universities, helps to run the revolts website (www.revolts.co.uk) and has written biographies of Douglas Hurd and John Smith. He is a regular political columnist with the *Yorkshire Post*.

Rhiannon Vickers is a Senior Lecturer at the Department of Politics, University of Sheffield. She has research interests in both domestic and international politics, and is especially interested in how the two interact. She is currently writing the second volume of a two-volume study of the political history of the Labour Party's foreign policy. In addition to this she has been developing an interest in public diplomacy and public perceptions of foreign and security policy.

Part One
The Coalition in the Making

1
'We Are All in This Together': The Coalition Agenda for British Modernization

Simon Lee

Introduction

Coalitions have been a relatively infrequent feature of modern British politics. When they have been formed, usually during wartime or major peacetime economic crises, and when they have endured, they have tended to be established in the month of May and, more often than not, led by a Liberal or Conservative politician (Maer, 2010). For example, during the First World War in May 1915, Herbert Asquith formed a Liberal-led Coalition (led from December 1916 by David Lloyd-George), in which the Conservatives provided eight out of 21 Cabinet Ministers, and which endured, despite the interruption of the 1918 General Election, until October 1922 (Morgan, 1978: 25). Similarly, in May 1940 Winston Churchill formed a Coalition National Government, comprising ministers from all three major political parties, which lasted until the landmark General Election of May 1945 (Taylor, 1978: 85). To this extent the formation of a Conservative–Liberal Democrat (hereafter Con–Lib) Government in May 2010, against the backdrop of the worst financial crisis since 1929, following 22 days of frantic negotiations, marked a return to a longstanding British political tradition of forming coalition governments during periods of austerity.

In this introductory chapter to our study of the agenda for British modernization devised by the Cameron–Clegg Government during its first eight months in office, it is suggested that the formation of the

3

Con–Lib Coalition has reflected far more than a pragmatic politics of expediency on behalf of two of the three largest political parties in the United Kingdom. First, the chapter charts the ambivalent relationship between liberalism and social democracy, on the one hand, and liberalism and conservatism, on the other, in debates about British modernization during the twentieth century. Second, the chapter notes the obvious intellectual resonance between David Cameron's liberal conservatism and the economic liberalism of the Liberal Democrats' *Orange Book* (Marshall and Laws, 2004). Third, the chapter notes how the formation of the Coalition has enabled Cameron to engage in an alibi-based politics of deflection to distract attention away from the ultimate failure of his big society-centred agenda to secure a majority Conservative Government for the fourth consecutive General Election. Fourth, the ideological synergy between the two Coalition parties has enabled the formation in only 22 days of a government with a programme possessing, in the view of its principal architects, 'the potential for era-changing, convention-challenging, radical reform' (HM Government, 2010: 7). This has been a Coalition of the willing. Fifth, the chapter summarizes how this book has evaluated this radical partnership government and its implications for domestic and foreign policy, the British constitution and the future of the three major British political parties. The chapter concludes by noting that the very nature of the Coalition's 'era-changing, convention-challenging, radical reform', with its fundamental challenge to the material living standards, interests and expectations of the middle classes, will carry with it the risk of testing to destruction Cameron's signature political mantra for the Coalition: 'We are all in this together'.

The Progressive Dilemma for Liberalism

In modern British politics debates about state-led modernization strategies to remedy the UK's longstanding relative decline, there has long been a battle between social democratic and conservative narratives over which party has been best placed to form a progressive ideological Coalition with liberalism. For English liberalism's greatest political economist and practical thinker, John Maynard Keynes, the Liberal Party remained 'the best instrument of future progress' (Keynes, 1925: 325). On the one hand, Conservatives offered Keynes 'neither food nor drink – neither intellectual nor spiritual consolation', and would promote 'neither my self-interest nor the public good' (Keynes, 1925: 323–4). On the other hand, for Keynes the Labour Party was 'a class party, and the class is not my class'. Keynes did not believe that 'the intellectual elements in the

Labour Party will ever exercise adequate control', which would mean 'too much will always be decided by those who do not know *at all* what they are talking about' (Keynes, 1925: 324).

For the first three-quarters of the twentieth century the battle of ideas in progressive politics for the heart and soul of liberalism appeared to have been won decisively by the forces of social democracy. For example, during the interwar period, despite his doubts about the Labour Party, Keynes was in the forefront of those creating a progressive social democratic agenda to challenge the neoclassical orthodoxy of the Treasury. The Liberal Party had produced the Yellow Book, *Britain's Industrial Future* (1928) and inspired a cross-party report, *The Next Five Years: An Essay in Political Agreement* (1935). Nevertheless, as Keynes had acknowledged in an essay on 'Liberalism and Labour', 'the progressive forces of the country are hopelessly divided between the Liberal Party and the Labour Party' (Keynes, 1926: 339). Moreover, he recognized that 'The Liberal Party is divided between those who, if the choice be forced upon them, would vote Conservative, and those who, in the same circumstances, would vote Labour' (Keynes, 1926: 343).

At that juncture, Keynes did not believe that there was any prospect of the Liberal Party winning even one third of the seats in the House of Commons 'in any probable or foreseeable circumstances' (Keynes, 1936: 339). Indeed, he did not believe that 'Liberalism will ever again be a great party machine in the way in which Conservatism and Labour are great party machines' (Keynes, 1926: 344). However, since 'The brains and character of the Conservative Party have always been recruited from Liberals', it would remain 'right and proper that the Conservative Party should be recruited from the Liberals of the previous generation' (Keynes, 1926: 343–4).

When the liberalism of Keynes and Sir William Beveridge provided the ideological basis for the Attlee Government's pursuit of full employment and expansion of the welfare state it appeared that the battle for a progressive ideological Coalition with liberalism had been won decisively by the social democratic middle ground. However, as Marquand has asserted, British social democracy displayed a failure of political imagination. Its focus on policy and neglect of process meant that modernization programmes were not underpinned by the necessary social and political citizenship. This meant that 'The case for non-statist, decentralist, participatory forms of public intervention was rarely made, and still rarely heard' (Marquand, 1991: 216). In short, social democracy was 'a technocratic philosophy rather than a political one' (Marquand, 1991: 220). Its reductionist individualism and society composed of isolated, atomistic individuals forgot any sense of community and the possibility that 'politics is, or should be, a process through which a political community agrees its common purpose' (Marquand, 1991: 217).

This meant that the progressive ideological coalition between social democracy and liberalism could be judged instrumentally and might only last as long as the resulting political settlement continued to deliver rising living standards, full employment and enhanced individual welfare. When the stagflation and the resulting fiscal crisis of the mid-1970s led the Callaghan Government to the International Monetary Fund and ushered in a turbulent age of austerity, Margaret Thatcher and Sir Keith Joseph seized the opportunity to reclaim economic liberalism for the New Right forces of conservatism. For Thatcher and Joseph, harnessing the Conservative Party to the economic liberalism of Milton Friedman and Friedrich Hayek afforded the opportunity to win the battle of ideas about British modernization. As a champion of political and economic liberalism, Hayek had once explained that he had rejected conservatism on account of its simple adherence to the principle of opposing 'drastic change', which meant that it could not 'offer an alternative to the direction in which we are moving' (Hayek, 1960). By contrast, in 'the great struggle of ideas', liberalism, 'with its advocacy of the free growth, spontaneous association, individual entrepreneurship and self-regulating forces of the market, could offer a politically and morally superior alternative to the rolling forward of the frontiers of the social democratic state' (Lee and McBride, 2007: 4).

Where once British politics had become stranded on a social democratic 'middle ground' exemplified by an 'over-governed, over-spent, over-taxed, over-borrowed and over-manned' declining economy (Joseph, 1976: 19), under Thatcher's leadership the Conservative Party could now reverse the trend towards socialism and harness economic liberalism to conservatism to steer British politics rightwards to occupy the 'common ground'. This political territory would champion the moral and material benefits of the market and remove the obstacles to full employment and prosperity, namely high state spending, high direct taxation, egalitarianism, nationalization, a politicized and Luddite trades union movement and the absence of an entrepreneur-driven enterprise culture (Joseph, 1979: cols. 706–11).

An Ideological Coalition of the Willing

When viewed within the historical context of debates about British modernization, it becomes evident why Cameron should have found it relatively straightforward for his party to form a coalition with the Liberal

Democrats. It was not just a matter of pragmatic electoral arithmetic, with Clegg's 57 Liberal Democrat MPs providing Cameron's 307 Conservative MPs with the opportunity to govern as a majority, rather than a minority, government, while simultaneously providing five Liberal Democrat MPs with the opportunity to be the first serving Liberal politicians in a peacetime Cabinet for 80 years.

It was much more than a matter of the simple personal chemistry between Cameron and Clegg, which had been evident from their inaugural press conference in the garden of 10 Downing Street on that sun-kissed morning in May. It was equally much more than the product of their shared social background as privileged, sharp-suited, upper middle-class, public school- and Oxbridge-educated millionaires. It was also a matter of ideological Coalition.

From the Conservative perspective, in March 2007 Cameron had stated categorically: 'I am liberal Conservative' (Cameron, 2007). He was 'liberal, because I believe in the freedom of individuals to pursue their own happiness, with the minimum of interference from government'. To his liberalism, with its scepticism about the role of the state, its trust in the capacity of people 'to make the most of their lives, and its confidence about 'the possibilities of the future, Cameron had harnessed his conservatism:

I believe that we're all in this together-that there is a historical understanding between past, present and future generations, and that we have a social responsibility to play an active part in the community we live in. (Cameron, 2007)

While Cameron conceded that conservatism and liberalism had frequently been in conflict, as William Gladstone and Benjamin Disraeli had been during the nineteenth century, the two ideologies could be seen to depend on each other 'at a deeper level' (Cameron, 2007). Conservatism's emphasis on communal obligations and institutions could prevent liberalism from becoming 'hollow individualism, a philosophy of selfishness'. By the same token, liberalism's emphasis on individual freedom could prevent conservatism from becoming 'mere conformity, limiting creativity and progress' (Cameron, 2007). Consequently, Cameron was adamant that there could be 'common ground between liberalism and Conservatism', especially in the four crucial policy areas of identity cards, public services, the environment, and localism. In short, Cameron concluded: 'I have a philosophy – liberal Conservatism – which has the answers to the great questions our country faces' (Cameron, 2007).

From the Liberal Democrat perspective, the potential for the party to work closely with a modern Conservative Party, in which the economic liberalism of Hayek and Friedman was more likely to be subscribed to than the one nation conservatism of Disraeli or Harold Macmillan, had been signalled with the publication of *The Orange Book: Reclaiming Liberalism* (Marshall and Laws, 2004). Among the contributors to this collection of essays, whom the then Liberal Democrat leader Charles Kennedy had described as 'hard-headed in their economic liberalism' (Kennedy, 2004), had been a number of eminent Liberal Democrat politicians who would play a leading role in both the negotiation of the Con–Lib Coalition and the staffing of its inaugural Cabinet, notably Nick Clegg, David Laws, Vince Cable and Chris Huhne.

In their respective contributions to the *Orange Book*, there was little that Cameron, George Osborne or the ranks of the quintessentially Thatcherite MPs populating the contemporary Conservative Party might have taken issue with. For example, in his attempt to reclaim liberalism, the Con–Lib Coalition's future (albeit, short-lived) Chief Secretary to the Treasury, David Laws, defined liberalism in terms of four strands – personal, political, economic and social – three of which few Conservative MPs would have cause to dissent from. Indeed, they would likely have cheered to the rafters Laws' advocacy of economic liberalism –'the belief in the value of free trade, open competition, market mechanisms, consumer power, and the effectiveness of the private sector' – and his call to 'resist a nanny-state liberalism' (Laws, 2004: 42). Similarly, the Conservatives would have found much to admire in Cable's assertion that 'whenever possible, "command and control" regulation should be replaced by self-regulation reinforced by statute', and reform of the public services informed by a vision 'in which a mixture of public sector, private and mutually owned enterprises compete to provide mainstream services' (Cable, 2004: 153, 161).

Admittedly, a rival edited collection, *Reinventing the State: Social Liberalism for the 21st Century* (Brack, Grayson and Howarth, 2007), had been published subsequently, during the tenure of Menzies Campbell as Liberal Democrat party leader (with contributions from both Clegg and Huhne, but neither Laws nor Cable). *Reinventing the State* made the case for why social liberalism, rather than the *Orange Book*'s 'hard-headed' economic liberalism, should be to the fore in Liberal Democrat thinking and policy. However, the victory of Clegg over Huhne for the right to succeed Campbell as party leader had symbolized the hegemony of economic and political liberalism over social liberalism within the party's thinking and policy. Moreover, social liberalism had become associated principally with Kennedy and Campbell, who had both failed to deliver an electoral breakthrough at successive General Elections. Furthermore, unlike their four 'hard-headed' English colleagues representing English constituencies, both Kennedy and Campbell represented constituencies in Scotland. In the post-devolution UK political settlement, where British governments would increasingly focus on reforms to public policy and services in England alone, the authority and capacity of social liberalism's two most eminent advocates to influence policy development affecting England would likely be diminished.

Viewed in the light of the economic liberalism of the *Orange Book*, both the willingness of the Liberal Democrats to negotiate a coalition with the Conservative Party rather than the Labour Party and the acquiescence of the five Liberal Democrat Con–Lib Coalition Cabinet members in the face of the cuts to public spending and the introduction of radical, market-based reforms of public services in England, becomes more readily comprehensible. Furthermore, the formation of the Coalition offered the Liberal Democrats the opportunity to end 80 years of British political history during which the party and its predecessor, the Liberal Party, had 'found itself confined for most of the twentieth century to, at best, influence, not power' (Marshall, 2004: 2). For example, Laws was able to become 'the first Liberal Treasury minister since 1931', and then, following his resignation over allegations about his private life, sexuality and parliamentary expenses, 'the shortest-lived holder of a Cabinet Office for 200 years' (Laws, 2010: 8–10). It also offered Clegg the opportunity to become the most powerful Deputy Prime Minister to serve in a British Cabinet since the appointment of Attlee to that role in the wartime National Government.

The Politics of Deflection and the Big Society

For a party leader who had spent so much of his tenure since December 2005 attempting to persuade the Conservative Party to heed the wake-up call from the electorate at three consecutive General Elections to 'smell the coffee' (Ashcroft, 2005), by detoxifying the Conservative Party's organization, image, ideas and policy from the worst excesses of the 'nasty' party (May, 2002), the Coalition with the Liberal Democrats offered Cameron the perfect political alibi to implement a new politics of deflection. First, Cameron could now deflect the blame onto the Coalition for having to drop those policies and marginalize those parts of his parliamentary party which had led the majority of voters in key marginal seats to think the Conservative Party was 'out of touch, had failed to learn from its mistakes, cared more about the well-off than have-nots, and did not stand for opportunity for all' (Ashcroft, 2005: 3). Second, Cameron could now deflect the blame on to the Liberal Democrats and his own Deputy Prime Minister for the very painful political choices necessitated by the transition from New Labour's 'age of irresponsibility' to 'the age of austerity' (Cameron, 2009a) and the onset of fiscal conservatism. Third, and most importantly, Cameron could use the Coalition, and the fact that it had provided him with a route to avoid minority government, to deflect attention from the Conservative Party's failure under his leadership to win a parliamentary majority at a fourth consecutive General Election.

It should not be forgotten that Cameron had attributed his party's recent electoral defeats to its failure to recognize that it had actually won the battle of ideas in British politics. The proof of that victory was the creation of the New Labour project, the electoral triumphs of Tony Blair and the fact that New Labour's 'Social justice and economic efficiency' had become 'the new common ground in British Politics' (Cameron, 2006). However, Cameron equally knew from the evidence of Thatcher's unceremonious removal from office by her own party, and the three subsequent General Election defeats under John Major, William Hague and Michael Howard, that a simple appeal to Thatcherite economic liberalism and the political narrative of the 'nasty' party era would be sufficient only to rally the party's core voters. He needed an alternative political narrative.

Cameron had concluded that 'towards the end of the 1980s we had become too much the economics party' (Cameron, cited in Jones, 2008: 288). The problem had been that 'no one knew what we thought about the health service, or the environment or society' (Cameron, cited in Jones, 2009: 290). As a consequence, where Thatcher had 'mended the broken economy in the 1980s', so now Cameron wished 'to mend Britain's broken society in the early decades of the twenty-first century' (cited in Jones, 2008: 308–9). The challenge was to convince the electorate that such 'real change is not delivered by government on its own, it's delivered by everyone playing their part in a responsible society'; but this in turn would mean convincing the British people that the agents of social change should be individuals, families and businesses, all acting as social entrepreneurs, rather than the customary top-down initiatives engineered by institutions of the British state (Cameron cited in Jones, 2008: 308).

How this major political and electoral challenge was to be met was not explained until Cameron delivered the 2009 Hugo Young Lecture on 10 November 2009. Here, he asserted that the 'trend of continuous central state expansion was not politically inevitable'. The role of the state could be reimagined so that it could be used 'to remake society' (Cameron, 2009b). To this end, he once again sought to harness conservatism to liberalism by identifying 'a strong liberal, civic tradition within Conservative thinking, stretching back from Edmund Burke through to Michael Oakeshott, that celebrates the small and local over the big and central' (Cameron, 2009b). Big government had failed. The expenditure by New Labour of £473 billion on welfare payments since 1997, and the rolling forward of the frontiers of 'more redistribution, means-tested benefits and tax credits', had not only failed to reduce, but actually had witnessed increased inequality and youth unemployment:

> The paradox at the heart of big government is that by taking power and responsibility away from the individual, it has only served to individuate them. What is seen in principle as an act of social solidarity, has in practice led to the greatest atomization of our society. The once natural bonds that existed between people-of duty and responsibility-have been replaced with the synthetic bonds of the state-regulation and bureaucracy. (Cameron, 2009b)

Citing the work of Philip Blond, director of the newly created think tank ResPublica, and the subsequent author of *Red Tory*, a book which had sought to combine economic equity with social conservatism (Blond, 2010), Cameron noted how the centralization of power had made people more passive and cynical, when they should actually be active and idealistic.

The Conservative alternative to the failure of the big state would not be 'no government – some reheated version of ideological laissez-faire. Nor is it just smarter government.' Instead, the alternative platform and big idea on which Cameron's Conservatives would fight the 2010 General Election would be 'the big society' (Cameron, 2009b). In the view of his Shadow Chancellor, the politics of prosperity had now given way to the politics of austerity (Osborne, 2009). But rather than engaging with the traditional electoral staples of the economy, health and education, and law and order, and clarifying the Conservative agenda for dealing with the budget deficit and the threat of recession, Cameron had chosen to focus on a strategy for social action. His party's focus would be on the social entrepreneurs possessing 'the capacity to run successful social programmes in communities with the greatest needs', community activists and, above all, the majority of the population, because 'The big society demands mass engagement: a broad culture of responsibility, mutuality and obligation' (Cameron, 2009b). Existing civic institutions, 'like shops, the post office and the town hall', would be strengthened (Cameron, 2009b).

At no point did Cameron acknowledge that the future spending cuts necessitated by his fiscal conservatism might undermine the social action and constituent community organizations of his 'big society'. Nor did he contemplate that the bonds of duty and responsibility, whose loss he had lamented, might owe as much to the creative destruction of liberalized markets, especially for employment, as to an over-mighty state. From the perspective of his own much diminished ranks of party activists, it was difficult to see how the idea of the 'big society', with its roots in theology and academic political philosophy, could be comprehended, let alone sold on the doorstep during a General Election campaign.

In the event, the Conservative Party did succeed in adding almost 22 per cent and nearly two million votes to its June 2005 General Election total. This translated into a gain of 97 seats, more than at any General Election since 1931, and a swing from Labour to the Conservatives of 5.1 per cent (second only to the 5.3 per cent swing to Thatcher's Conservatives in May 1979). However, while the Conservatives' 36.1 per cent share of the vote was an improvement on the party's performance in the three previous elections, 'it was lower than at any other election since the war' (Ashcroft, 2010: 100) and left Cameron 19 seats short of an overall parliamentary majority. Given that the Labour Party could muster only 29 per cent of the vote, Gordon Brown had become a hugely unpopular Prime Minister and had presided over the worst financial crisis since the 1930s, an explanation had to be sought for why the Conservatives' double-digit opinion poll lead during the two years prior to the May 2010 General Election had evaporated.

Extensive polling organized and funded by Michael Ashcroft, Deputy Chairman of the Conservative Party, suggested that the party had neither completed the transformation of the Conservative Party brand nor established itself as 'a party of real change' (Ashcroft, 2010: 113). Three months prior to the election, while 82 per cent of voters had agreed with the statement 'It is time for change', only 40 per cent had intended to vote Conservative. On 6 April 2010, the date the General Election was called, these doubts in the electorate's mind were repeated. While more than three-quarters thought it time to change from Labour, only 34 per cent thought it time to change to the Conservatives. Moreover, 72 per cent indicated that they were not convinced the Conservative Party put ordinary people first (Ashcroft, 2010: 110). Seen in the light of this electoral failure, in which the Liberal Democrats had shared with a net loss of five seats and a meagre 1 per cent increase in their share of the popular vote, it is evident why Cameron and Clegg should have shown such enthusiasm for joining in a Coalition of the willing. Not only would the Coalition govern with 56 per cent of the seats at Westminster, and a combined 59.1 per cent of the votes cast. The formation of the Coalition would provide an opportunity to assemble a bold programme for government to put their respective electoral failures behind them.

An Historic Programme for Partnership Government

In the foreword to their Coalition's programme for government, Cameron and Clegg ventured a series of very bold and ambitious claims which sought to demonstrate that their partnership was born out of genuine political conviction rather than an expedient marriage of convenience. First, they began by asserting:

> This is an historic document in British politics: the first time in over half a century two parties have come together to put forward a programme for partnership government. (HM Government, 2010: 7)

Second, they claimed that the Coalition would be greater than the sum of its constituent parties and that because their respective visions would be strengthened and enhanced rather than compromised by working together, the Coalition would have 'the potential for era-changing, convention-challenging, radical reform' (HM Government, 2010: 7). Third, that radical reform would translate into economic renewal in the form of 'a new economy from the rubble of the old', social renewal in 'a Britain where social mobility is unlocked' and political renewal, through a commitment 'to turning old thinking on its head and developing new approaches to government' (HM Government, 2010: 7). In so stating, the Coalition was repeating the three prerequisites for British national renewal identified by previous state-led modernization programmes.

Fourth, Cameron and Clegg claimed that in every part of their agreed programme the Coalition had been able to go 'further than simply adopting those policies where we previously overlapped'. This in turn had been possible because of their discovery that 'a combination of our parties' best ideas and attitudes has produced a programme for government that is more radical and comprehensive than our individual manifestos' (HM Government, 2010: 8). As a consequence, it had been possible, for example, to fashion 'a Big Society matched by big citizens' from a combination of 'Conservative plans to strengthen families and encourage social responsibility' and 'the Liberal Democrat passion for protecting our civil liberties and stopping the relentless incursion of the state into the lives of individuals' (HM Government, 2010: 8). Indeed, it was claimed there was potential for nothing less than a complete recasting of the relationship between people and the state.

Fifth, the political dividend of greater strength derived from the combination of Conservative and Liberal Democrat ideas had extended to 'the crucial area of public service reform', and in particular the area of the National Health Service (NHS). Indeed, 'Conservative thinking on markets, choice and competition' had been added to 'the Liberal Democrat belief in advancing democracy at a much more local level' to fashion:

> a united vision for the NHS that is truly radical: GPs with authority over commissioning; patients with much more control; elections for your local NHS health board. Together, our ideas will bring an emphatic end to the bureaucracy, top-down control and centralization that has so diminished our NHS. (HM Government, 2010: 8)

Following the precedent of the Blair and Brown governments there was no acknowledgement that these reforms would apply to England only. It was also evident that after 13 years of permanent revolution and reorganization of England's public services, the pace of reform would not slacken in the face of the fiscal challenges confronting the Coalition. Indeed, if anything, the pace of reform would accelerate.

Finally, Cameron and Clegg acknowledged that 'Three weeks ago we could never have predicted the publication of this document' (HM Government, 2010: 8). The option of minority government had been available following the General Election, but both leaders had been 'uninspired by it' given the alternative of seizing 'the option of a Coalition in the national interest'. Although both parties had begun with only 'some policies in common and a shared desire to work in the national interest', they had arrived at the programme for government as 'a strong, progressive Coalition inspired by the values of freedom, fairness and responsibility' (HM Government, 2010: 8). Moreover, this programme would yield 'five years of partnership government driven by those values', in the belief that in turn it could deliver nothing less than

> radical, reforming government, a stronger society, a smaller state, and power and responsibility in the hands of every citizen. Great change and real progress lie ahead. (HM Government, 2010: 8)

The ambitious claims made on behalf of the Coalition by its Prime Minister and his Deputy have been matched during the Cameron–Clegg Government's first nine months in office by the frenetic tempo of its reforms. First, the initial agreement arising from the Conservative–Liberal Democrat (Con–Lib hereafter) Coalition negotiations had promised that 'a plan for deficit reduction should be set out in an emergency budget within 50 days of the signing of any agreement' (Conservative Party/ Liberal Democrat Party, 2010). That pledge was fulfilled on 22 June with the delivery of an emergency budget, which identified an additional £40 billion of fiscal consolidation by 2014–15 to that planned by the Brown Government, of which 80 per cent would be accounted for by cuts in public expenditure (HM Treasury, 2010a: 15). Second, both the Con–Lib Coalition Agreement and programme for government had committed the parties to 'a full Spending Review reporting this autumn, following a fully consultative process involving all tiers of government and the private sector' (Conservative Party and Liberal Democrat Party, 2010; HM Government, 2010: 16). That commitment was delivered on 20 October with the publication of a spending review which envisaged the tightest squeeze on overall public expenditure since 1945; the tightest settlement for spending on public services since the age of austerity which lasted from April 1975 to March 1980; and the tightest squeeze on NHS spending since the period from April 1951 to March 1956 (Crawford, 2010).

The Coalition presented its agenda for tackling the challenges posed by the age of austerity as 'Britain's unavoidable deficit reduction plan', a political *fait accompli* necessitated by its inheritance from the Brown Government of a gaping hole in the UK's public finances amounting to 'the largest in its peacetime history' (HM Treasury 2010b: 5). In order to secure economic stability, the Treasury claimed that 'The Spending Review makes choices', but unavoidable choices born out of necessity (HM Treasury, 2010b: 5). However, many of these choices had not appeared in either of the Coalition parties' General Election manifestos. Some choices, most notably the proposed increases in tuition fees for students attending universities in England, contradicted both manifestos' commitments and signed undertakings to oppose such fees. Others, most significantly the Coalition's plans for the reform of the NHS in England, not only had not appeared in either party's manifesto, but had not been clearly specified in either the initial Coalition Agreement or the subsequent programme for government.

Many of these policy choices, not least Michael Gove's nationalization of the funding for schools in England and Andrew Lansley's GP-centric NHS reforms in England, flatly contradicted Cameron and Clegg's promise to bring about 'an emphatic end to the bureaucracy, top-down control and centralization that has so diminished our NHS' (HM Government, 2010: 8). They also threatened to make a mockery of the Coalition's claim to believe it to be 'time for a fundamental shift of power from Westminster to people', through the promotion of 'decentralization and democratic engagement' and an end to 'the era of top-down government' by 'the radical devolution of power and greater financial autonomy to local government and community groups' (HM Government, 2010: 11). Such a powerful commitment to devolution appeared highly suspect at best, and openly mendacious at worst, when the spending review delivered a 27 per cent cut in real terms in funding for local government in England between 2010–11 and 2014–15 (HM Treasury, 2010b: 10), and when the Coalition's flagship Localism Bill for local government in England incorporated 126 new powers for ministers over local authorities – a further centralization of power dismissed as 'entirely the norm' by Eric Pickles, the Secretary of State for Communities and Local Government (Pickles, 2011: col. 558).

The Coalition's 'unavoidable' choices have also been underpinned by the three themes of freedom, fairness and responsibility, and by Cameron's repeated big society mantra that 'We are all in this together'. However, Cameron's attempts to portray the age of austerity as an inclusive, collective struggle undertaken in the national interest have not been assisted by the fact that his Cabinet has appeared to be the most privileged and unrepresentative of wider British society for at least a political generation. With only four women, one (unelected) member of the ethnic minorities and no openly gay members among the 29 people entitled to attend Cabinet meetings, the majority of the Cabinet has also been drawn from the ranks of millionaires, educated at private schools and Oxbridge colleges (most notably, Cameron, Clegg and Chancellor of the Exchequer, George Osborne).

While the Coalition's political narrative had been one of austerity necessitating expenditure cuts of such scale and urgency as to risk major public squalor, the emergency budget and spending review had been conducted, in vivid contrast, against the context of relative government inaction in the face of spectacular private affluence. Multi-billion pound bonuses had continued to be paid out to unapologetic bankers less than two years after UK taxpayers had provided some £850 billion of guarantees, shares and loans (including £117 billion of cash invested by the Treasury in the banks) as a reward for their irresponsible and imprudent risk-taking (National Audit Office, 2010: 5). The notion of the British people being 'all in it together' in an age of austerity would become even harder for the Coalition to sustain once research from the Bureau of Investigative Journalism revealed that the City of London's financiers had donated no less than £42.76 million to the Conservative Party since Cameron had become its leader, with £11.4 million or 50.8 per cent of donations during 2010, compared with only £2.75 million or 25 per cent during 2005 (Bureau of Investigative Journalism, 2010).

The Structure of Our Book

The promise of 'era-changing, convention-challenging, radical reform' (HM Government, 2010: 7), delivered by the first peacetime Coalition Government since the National Government of 1931–40, inspired the Centre for British Politics at Hull University to assemble a team of 17 academics drawn from 11 universities to analyse and evaluate the Cameron–Clegg Government's agenda for economic, social and political renewal. This book constitutes the first of two studies which will undertake that task. At the conclusion of its tenure, a second detailed study will be published evaluating the Coalition's record in office and the effectiveness of the implementation and outcome of its programme for government. This first study provides an analysis of the Coalition's agenda for British modernization. It is presented in four parts.

In Part One: The Coalition in the Making, three chapters are devoted to a brief analysis of the role of liberalism in British modernization programmes; the legacy of New Labour for the Coalition; and the actual process of the formation of the Coalition. In Part Two: Coalition Politics in Perspective, the implications of the Coalition's programme for government and spending review for major areas of domestic economic and social policy, constitutional reform and the nations of the United Kingdom beyond England are explored. Following an initial contextual analysis of the Coalition's agenda for reducing the deficit and rebalancing the economy, three chapters explore the coalition agenda for education policy, health policy and welfare reform. Two further chapters are devoted to the Coalition's agenda for environment and transport policy, and home affairs. Part Two concludes with studies of the Con–Lib agenda for constitutional reform and its impact in Scotland, Wales and Northern Ireland.

In Part Three: Coalition Policies Abroad, a critical evaluation of the agenda for national security and strategy is followed by an exploration of the agenda for foreign policy and international development. The book concludes in Part Four: A Coalition Built to Last? with three chapters devoted to exploring the Coalition's impact on the three major UK political parties and the battle of ideas in British politics. An analysis of the impact of coalition politics on the Conservative Party and Liberal Democrats is followed by an evaluation of the prospects for the Labour Party. Finally, the implications of the Coalition for British liberalism are examined.

In his chapter on the legacy of New Labour Rajiv Prabhakar explores the different meanings of New Labour in terms of its association with Blair and his allies, Gordon Brown, and its definition as an approach to policy, before analysing the continuities and changes between New Labour and the Coalition, New Labour's impact on the Labour Party itself and whether the Coalition's big society rhetoric constitutes a departure from New Labour. Mark Stuart completes Part One by providing an explanation as to why the Liberal Democrats were more predisposed to join a coalition with the Conservatives than has previously been appreciated, and an overall assessment of the factors which led to the formation of the Coalition.

Part Two begins with my analysis of the Coalition's economic policies. While the focal point of the Coalition's strategy has been its fiscal conservatism and the reduction of the budget deficit, it is argued that there is little prospect or evidence that a 'rebalancing' of the economy will occur. Indeed, a key weakness of the Coalition is the absence of a strategy to support manufacturing industry commensurate with the past and on-going state support of the City of London. Simon Griffiths' evaluation of the Con–Lib agenda for education policy shows how, more than any other area of policy, it has revealed an underlying tension between the Coalition partners, especially in the area of higher education policy. In his analysis of the Coalition's agenda for health policy, Robert Page examines the development of the Coalition's health strategy from the respective General Election manifestos to the major structural reforms of the NHS in England, to establish whether a new direction in health policy is being pursued.

Stephen Driver's analysis of welfare policy under the Coalition shows how, if reform proved to be tough-going during the era of 'non-inflationary consistent expansion', it will be even harder in the 'age of austerity'. The chapter explores the continuity and changes in welfare policy compared with those implemented by its Labour predecessors, and also questions whether the Coalition has been offered the opportunity to establish the longer-term settlement for welfare desperately needed in the UK. In his analysis of coalition policy for the environment and transport, James Connelly notes how Cameron pledged, three days after the formation of the Coalition, that 'This will be the greenest government ever'. In the light of this bold claim the chapter considers both the shape and direction of Coalition environment policy, and also the tensions and compromises which are an inevitable consequence of coalition formation and practice. John Benyon's exploration of the Coalition's home affairs agenda for law and order notes how in Opposition the Coalition parties were united in their common opposition to what they perceived to be New Labour's illiberal policies. The chapter therefore analyses the extent to which this unanimity has been maintained by the Coalition partners in government in their development of the principal policy areas of home affairs, such as crime and criminal justice, punishment and imprisonment, policing, security and public order, immigration and civil liberties and equalities.

The formation of a Coalition Government heralded a new form of politics in that the parties to the Coalition adhered to the terms of a published agreement. Philip Norton's analysis of the 'new politics' examines how the clear ideological divide between the Conservatives and Liberal Democrats has been addressed in the Coalition's agenda for constitutional reform. Part Two concludes with Arthur Aughey's evaluation of the Coalition's agenda for Scotland, Wales and Northern Ireland. Following an analysis of the Coalition's inheritance from New Labour, the chapter examines the formation of coalition policy and its implications for each of the three nations.

Chris Martin opens Part Three by analysing the Coalition's agenda for national security and strategy, including its Strategic Defence and Security Review and its National Security Strategy. Despite differences in the Coalition partners' respective manifestos, this chapter highlights how coalition policy has not altered the UK's self-perception of its role in global security. In her evaluation of its agenda for foreign policy and international development, Rhiannon Vickers notes how the Coalition Government has signalled its intention to implement a foreign policy distinct from its Labour predecessor's. Having highlighted the renewed focus on the 'national interest', the chapter examines the new National Security Strategy and Strategic Defence and Security Review, before evaluating the Government's approach to international development. Part Three concludes with Philip Lynch's analysis of the Coalition's agenda for Europe, an area where ideological differences between the Conservatives and Liberal Democrats are starker than in most other policy areas. Lynch explores how Cameron's instinctive Euroscepticism and Clegg's commitment to European integration have been reconciled in the early months of the Coalition and in the development of the programme for government.

Part Four commences with Tim Bale and Emma Sanderson-Nash's analysis of the impact of the Coalition on the Conservatives and Liberal Democrats. Following an outline of where the two parties stood at the time of the May 2010 General Election, the chapter addresses how they have, more or less, adapted to the advent of the Coalition Government. Using the conceptual framework furnished by Richard Katz and Peter Mair's seminal comparative project on political parties, the impact of the Coalition for both parties is explored in terms of 'the party in public office', 'the party in central office' and 'the party on the ground'. Kevin Hickson explores the future for the Labour Party by assessing the impact on it of the Coalition. Hickson suggests that there is cause for optimism for the Labour Party because its political and electoral position is much better than first appeared to be the case. He then analyses the party's leadership contest and the ways in which Ed Miliband has responded to the Coalition. The book concludes with Matt Beech's explanation of how the Con–Lib Government represents a new period in British politics. An accord between two political parties espousing two types of liberalism: liberal conservatism and *Orange Book* liberalism. The chapter explores these two liberalisms and demonstrates how they contain both similarities as well as stark differences, which have implications for the Coalition's future prospects.

Conclusion: A Risk-based Politics

Many of the policy choices to be implemented by the Cameron–Clegg Coalition Government have been deemed to be necessitated by the toxic fiscal legacy bequeathed by Brown's British model of political economy, with its ill-advised, 'risk-based' approach to the governance of liberalized financial markets (Lee, 2009). It may also be said of the Con–Lib Coalition that its programme for government and wider agenda for British modernization are equally risk-based. Much more is at risk than the fate of the UK's three major political parties and the political fortunes of their respective leaderships. The very future of the UK itself could be threatened if the consequences of cuts to funding and tax increases provoke a major political backlash.

The Coalition is attempting a fiscal retrenchment far more ambitious than anything attempted by any British Government since 1945. Even the Thatcher Government's ambitions to roll back the frontiers of the state and roll forward the frontiers of enterprise and entrepreneur-led innovation took more than a decade and nearly three full terms of office to cut total managed expenditure from an inheritance of 45.1 per cent in 1978–79 to 39.2 per cent in 1989–90, and even then expenditure was allowed to climb as high as 48.1 per cent in 1982–83 and to remain above 47 per cent of GDP for five consecutive years (HM Treasury, 2010c: 59), as Thatcher's hard-line rhetoric disguised political and fiscal pragmatism. The Coalition's spending review is attempting a larger fiscal retrenchment than that attempted or achieved by Thatcher, and in a single parliamentary term.

While it may have felt able to blame New Labour in general, and Brown's fiscal imprudence in particular (Lee, 2009), for having to make difficult but 'unavoidable' political choices, the nature of those choices has been solely the responsibility of the Coalition itself. If those choices prove to have been wrong or fundamentally flawed, and driven more by ideological zeal rather than pragmatic statesmanship, the political and electoral price to be paid at the next General Election is likely to be substantial for one or both of the Coalition partners.

The economic, fiscal and social burden of the age of austerity will fall primarily neither on the shoulders of the rich, whose wealth will remain largely untouched by the Coalition's proposals, nor on the shoulders of the poor, who lack the income and wealth to make the most substantial fiscal contribution to the elimination of the budget deficit. The greatest danger to the Coalition is the fact that its programme of spending cuts, welfare reforms and tax increases will impact most heavily on middle-income individuals and families. As has already been demonstrated in relation to university tuition fees in England and the aborted privatization of England's forests, Middle England is unlikely to take the Coalition's programme for government lying down. Once that essential political truth becomes apparent, and a generation accustomed only to credit-fuelled, instant gratification and ever-rising living standards comes to terms with the prospect of an era of austerity and diminished availability of personal credit, cheap mortgages and increased personal wealth from rising property values, the personal and political mettle of the Con–Lib Coalition will be tested to the full.

What is certain is that such is the radical ambition and scale of the Con–Lib Coalition's agenda, as set out and analysed in this book, very few parts of the UK are likely to be left untouched by its political, economic and social consequences. To that extent, at the very least, we can be said to be all in this together.

References

Ashcroft, M. (2005) *Smell the Coffee: A Wake-up Call for the Conservative Party* (London: Michael Ashcroft).

Ashcroft, M. (2010) *Minority Verdict: The Conservative Party, the Voters and the 2010 Election* (London: Biteback).

Blond, P. (2010) *Red Tory: How Left and Right Have Broken Britain and How We Can Fix It* (London: Faber and Faber).

Brack, D., Grayson, R. and Howarth, D. (eds.) (2007) *Reinventing the State: Social Liberalism for the 21st Century* (London: Politico's).

Bureau of Investigative Journalism (2011) City Financing of the Conservative Party Doubles under Cameron. Press release, 9 February. www.thebureauinvestigates. com/2011/02/08/city-financing-of-the-conservative-party-... (accessed 9 February 2011).

Cable, V. (2004) Liberal Economics and Social Justice. In P. Marshall and D. Laws (eds.), *The Orange Book: Reclaiming Liberalism* (London: Profile Books).

Cameron, D. (2006) Modern Conservatism. Speech, Demos, London, 30 January.

Cameron, D. (2007) A Liberal Conservative Consensus to Restore Trust in Politics. Speech, Bath, 22 March.

Cameron, D. (2009a) The Age of Austerity. Speech, Conservative Spring Forum, Cheltenham, 26 April.

Cameron, D. (2009b) The Big Society. Hugo Young Lecture, London, 10 November.

Conservative Party and Liberal Democrat Party (2010) *Conservative–Liberal Democrat Coalition Negotiations Agreements Reached*, 11 May (London: Conservative Party and Liberal Democrats).

Crawford, R. (2010) *Where Did the Axe Fall?* (London: Institute for Fiscal Studies).

Hayek, F.A. (1960) *The Constitution of Liberty* (Chicago, IL: University of Chicago Press).

HM Government (2010) *The Coalition: Our Programme for Government* (London: The Cabinet Office).

HM Treasury (2010a) *Budget 2010*, HC 61 (London: The Stationery Office).

HM Treasury (2010b) *Spending Review 2010*, Cm. 7942 (London: The Stationery Office).

HM Treasury (2010c) *Public Expenditure Statistical Analyses 2010*, Cm.7890 (London: The Stationery Office).

Jones, D. (2008) *Cameron on Cameron: Conversations with Dylan Jones* (London: Fourth Estate).

Joseph, K. (1976) *Monetarism is not Enough* (London: Rose).

Joseph, K. (1979) Debate on The Address, *Hansard*, 21 May, cols. 706–11.

Kennedy, C. (2004) Foreword. In P. Marshall and D. Laws (eds.), *The Orange Book: Reclaiming Liberalism* (London: Profile Books).

Keynes, J.M. (1925) Am I a Liberal? In J.M. Keynes, *Essays in Question* (New York: W.W. Norton, 1963 edition).

Keynes, J.M. (1926) Liberalism and Labour. In J.M. Keynes, *Essays in Question* (New York: W.W. Norton, 1963 edition).

Laws, D. (2004) Reclaiming Liberalism: A Liberal Agenda for the Liberal Democrats. In P. Marshall and D. Laws (eds.), *The Orange Book: Reclaiming Liberalism* (London: Profile Books).

Laws, D. (2010) *22 Days in May: The Birth of the Lib Dem–Conservative Coalition* (London: Biteback).

Lee, S. (2009) *Boom and Bust: The Politics and Legacy of Gordon Brown* (Oxford: Oneworld).

Lee, S. and McBride, S. (eds.) (2007) Introduction: Neo-liberalism, State Power and Global Governance in the Twenty-First Century. In S. Lee and S. McBride (eds.), *Neo-Liberalism, State Power and Global Governance* (Dordrecht: Springer).

Maer, L. (2010) *Hung Parliaments* (London: House of Commons Library).

Marquand, D. (1991) *The Progressive Dilemma* (London: Heinemann).

Marshall, P. (2004) Introduction. In P. Marshall and D. Laws (eds.), *The Orange Book: Reclaiming Liberalism* (London: Profile Books).

Marshall, P. and Laws, D. (eds.) (2004) *The Orange Book: Reclaiming Liberalism* (London: Profile Books).

May, T. (2002) Speech to the Conservative party conference, Bournemouth, 7 October.

Morgan, K. (1978) 1902–1924. In D. Butler (ed.), *Coalitions in British Politics* (London: Macmillan).

National Audit Office (2010) *The Asset Protection Scheme*. Report by The Comptroller and Auditor General, HC.567, Session 2010–2011, 21 December (London: National Audit Office).

Osborne, G. (2009) Policy Making after the Crash. Speech, Royal Society of Arts, London, 8 April.

Pickles, E. (2011) Localism Bill. *Hansard*, 17 January.

Taylor, A.J.P. (1978) 1945–1977. In D. Butler (ed.), *Coalitions in British Politics* (London: Macmillan).

2
What is the Legacy of New Labour?

Rajiv Prabhakar

Introduction

The 2010 General Election ended Labour's 13 years in office. Tony Blair led Labour to victory in 1997, and he had been at the helm when Labour was re-elected to government in the 2001 and 2005 General Elections. Labour's victory in 1997 had followed a period of 18 years of Conservative rule. A key part of Blair's electoral strategy was the creation of a 'New Labour' project that would convince voters that the Labour Party had changed. Blair resigned as Prime Minister in 2007 and was replaced by his long-standing colleague and rival Gordon Brown. Under Brown, Labour polled 29.7 per cent of the vote at the 2010 General Election. After 1983, this was the worst Labour result at a General Election since 1918 (Curtice, Fisher and Ford, 2010). A Conservative–Liberal Democrat Coalition Government was formed and has begun implementing a programme of spending cuts that promises to cut the budget deficit (HM Treasury, 2010).

Since the 2010 General Election, politicians have been keen to distance themselves from New Labour. Brown resigned the leadership of the party after the election. All the candidates for the Labour leadership sought in different ways to go beyond New Labour. In a speech launching his bid, the initial favourite, David Miliband, stated: 'New Labour did fantastic things for the country. But now we are out of power, what counts is next Labour' (Miliband, 2010). The eventual winner of the contest, his brother Ed Miliband, declared: 'The era of New Labour has passed. A new generation has taken over' (reported in Porter and Winnett, 2010). These sentiments have been echoed within the Coalition Government. At the Conservative Party conference on 3 October 2010, Foreign Secretary William Hague stated: 'But now New Labour is dead' (Hague, 2010). Did the 2010 General Election then mark the end of the New Labour experiment? Was New Labour, as Ed Miliband and Hague suggest, consigned to the grave? In this chapter I examine the legacy of New Labour. Although things will only become clearer with time, I suggest that parts of New Labour have survived the General Election. New Labour may be wounded but it is not yet buried. I argue that New Labour can be detected in some of the ideas and policies influencing the Coalition Government. Indeed, New Labour was an early source of ideas for the present Conservative leadership. At a dinner at the 2005 Conservative party conference, Cameron reported that he was the genuine heir to Blair (Pierce, 2005). Although Cameron later regretted that remark because of concern that it upset Conservative grassroots support (Shipman, 2010), he nevertheless foreshadowed the influence of New Labour ideas for the Coalition Government. Politicians closely associated with New Labour have taken various advisory roads for the new government. Lord Hutton, Frank Field and Alan Milburn are advising the Coalition on pensions, welfare and social mobility. Similarly, former special advisers to New Labour have taken posts in the Coalition Government. For example, one of Field's former advisers when he was Minister for Welfare Reform, Richard Reeves, is now special adviser to Deputy Prime Minister Nick Clegg.

Of course, the fact that these individuals give advice does not mean that the Coalition Government will accept their recommendations. However, there are also signs that New Labour is being felt at the level of policy as well as ideas. In areas such as education and health the Coalition Government is arguably extending Blair's approach to the reform of public services. Blair's autobiography, *A Journey*, hints that he too backs the Coalition Government's policy on cutting public spending (Blair, 2010). This is not to claim that the Coalition Government is simply New Labour by another name. In areas such as civil liberties the Coalition Government is arguably breaking with an authoritarian streak in New Labour. This covers the scrapping of identity cards, as well as some anti-terror legislation. The overall picture is therefore mixed. Furthermore, New Labour's legacy might be diluted depending on how coalition policy unfolds.

This chapter is organized as follows. First, I consider what is meant by New Labour. One view is that it is best understood as a small group of people who tried to change the party after successive defeats to the Conservative Party from 1979. This part of the chapter looks at whether

New Labour here is associated only with Blair and his allies or if it extends to cover Brown. Second, I sketch whether New Labour might be better seen as an approach to policy. If New Labour is understood only as being associated with a group of people, then when these people left government New Labour would presumably have died. However, contributors to New Labour talked of a 'project' that would outlast their personal involvement. Furthermore, Miliband and Hague commented on the death of New Labour after 2010, several years after its chief architect Tony Blair had left office. The third section looks at overlaps between New Labour and the Coalition Government, looking at the areas of education, health and welfare reform. The fourth section considers New Labour and the Labour Party. The fifth section looks at how different parties may be breaking with New Labour with their current rhetoric about the big society. A conclusion summarizes the ground covered in this chapter.

What is New Labour?

Any assessment of the legacy of New Labour must start by defining what is meant by this label. The term is both vague and controversial. One starting point is to try to associate it with a group of individuals. New Labour was the creation of a specific set of people at a particular time. Blair is perhaps the pre-eminent New Labour figure. He is probably the person most comfortable using the term and remains a true believer. In an interview with the BBC journalist Andrew Marr in September 2010, Blair declared that he thought the best strategy for the Labour Party is not to 'move a millimetre from New Labour'. Similarly, perhaps his closest political ally, Peter Mandelson, warned that Brown's successor as leader should not establish a 'pre-New Labour' party (BBC News, 2010). Blair, Mandelson and Blair's press secretary, Alastair Campbell, are probably at the heart of New Labour. Alongside this inner core were politicians such as Alan Milburn, John Reid and John Hutton.

This group omits Blair's colleague and rival Gordon Brown. Peter Mandelson's (2010) memoir, *The Third Man*, alludes to the fact that he, alongside Blair and Brown, is crucial for understanding the Labour governments from 1997. Most recent accounts of the Labour Party highlight a fraught relationship between Blair and his Chancellor. This was the central fault-line in the Labour governments elected since 1997 (Blair, 2010; Mandelson, 2010; Rawnsley, 2010). However, in the early 1990s, Blair and Brown tended to be allies rather than competitors. Both wanted to reposition the party after successive defeats to the Conservative

Party. Also both were nurtured by the previous Labour leader, John Smith. In this way, both can be implicated in the creation of New Labour.

The seeds of discontent between Blair and Brown were sown after the death of John Smith in 1994. Brown decided not to stand for leadership to allow a clear path for Blair. However, Brown believed that Blair then reneged on a promise to stand aside later to allow Brown to take the leadership (Rawnsley, 2010). Although the nature of any pact is disputed, I suggest that any account that focuses on Blair alone will be partial. Brown was also significant for the creation of New Labour. This view suggests that New Labour covered a disparate set of people. The conflicts between Blair and Brown mean there were tensions between the different people associated with New Labour. Furthermore, people's relationships to New Labour shifted over time. For example, during the 2010 Labour leadership campaign David Miliband was keen not to be seen as the creature of New Labour. As noted above, while he wanted to recognize New Labour's achievements, he was also keen to go beyond this and avoid being cast as the 'New Labour' candidate in the leadership election.

New Labour as a Project

A particular set of people were then crucial for the creation of New Labour. However, New Labour should perhaps not be reduced simply to these individuals. As highlighted in the introduction, the creators of New Labour discussed a project that would outlive their influence. New Labour might then be associated with a particular approach to governing or policy. This can be seen perhaps by efforts to make a 'third way' key to the identity of New Labour. Blair, supported by academics such as Anthony Giddens, claimed he was developing an approach to public policy that differed from both free markets and state-centred social democracy (Blair, 1998; Giddens, 1998).

The third way prompts controversy. Some commentators regard New Labour as little more than a catch-up to the ideas and policies associated with Thatcher's Conservative Party. On this view, New Labour was the bending of social democracy to meet the demands of the market (Hay, 1998). More sympathetic observers see New Labour as involving a distinct set of ideas, although there is disagreement about the content of these ideas (Finlayson, 2008). The various individuals involved in New Labour mean that this was never a fully consistent set of ideas and policies. Different people had different emphases. Blair's approach to public services differs from those favoured by Brown. In this sense, it is more accurate to refer to the presence of 'New Labours' rather than a single New Labour project. Also, New Labour blended together electoral concerns as well as policy ideas. Part of New Labour aimed at developing policies that would appeal to swing voters in marginal constituencies. New Labour, then, refers to a diverse set of ideas and policies. It is not my aim here to outline the main strands associated with New Labour. I focus only on those themes that can be detected in current politics. The diversity of New Labour means that different strands can have varying legacies for the future.

Coalition Government

In this section I look at the legacy of New Labour for the Conservative–Liberal Democrat Government. I suggest that a Blairite strain is probably the most important legacy of New Labour for the Coalition Government. The Conservative Secretary of State for Education, Michael Gove, alludes to the influence of a Blairite approach to education when he cites previous Labour Minister David Blunkett as one of the four Education Secretaries that he most admires since the end of the Second World War (Beckett, 2010).

Gove praises Blunkett for introducing academy schools. These are publicly funded schools that have freedoms from central government or local authority control over how they deliver the national curriculum as well as the pay they offer to staff. Freeing such schools from these controls is thought to be a spur for innovation, which is aimed at helping to drive up standards in education. The former Schools Minister Andrew Adonis, who was a key Blair adviser, probably played an important role in this policy as it drew on his long-standing views in supporting local freedoms for schools (Adonis and Pollard, 1997). In March 2000 Blunkett stated he would be introducing a set of 'city academies'. These schools would be aimed at underperforming schools and would be able to attract sponsorship from businesses, religious organizations and voluntary groups (Carvel, 2000). In September 2000, Blunkett announced the introduction of the first three city academies in England (Department for Children, Schools and Families, 2000). Labour's Education Act 2002 renamed these academy schools and allowed academies to be set up anywhere in England and to be able to provide primary as well as secondary education.

The academy programme provokes controversy within Labour ranks. One concern is that academies contribute to a 'two-tier' education system in which academies are dominated by children from better-off backgrounds, while their less well-off peers would go to inferior schools. In this way, academies undermine equality. For example, former Labour Education Secretary Estelle Morris asks: 'In five years' time, whose children will be going to these new academies? Will choice and market forces once again squeeze out the children of the disadvantaged?' (BBC News, 2005). In the run-up to becoming party leader, Brown said that he would continue the academy programme, although there were hopes among teaching unions and some Labour MPs that he would drop them. Education Secretary Alan Johnson, though, said they would be limited to 400 schools.

Conservatives are in favour of academy schools. In a speech to the Confederation of British Industry on 16 May 2007, Conservative Shadow Education Secretary David Willetts stated: 'Academies are very popular with parents and doing better than the schools they have replaced . . . They show that proper academic rigour should never just be reserved for the leafy suburbs and for prosperous families. We in the Conservative Party back them wholeheartedly' (reported on BBC News, 2007b). The academy programme was itself anticipated by a previous Conservative government's policy on city technology colleges (CTCs). This highlights how New Labour itself drew on previous Conservative governments, and so part of the legacy of New Labour reflects longer trends in public policy. The Coalition Government is committed to extend the academy programme. This is underlined by the fact that this is one of the first new pieces of legislation introduced by the new government. The Academies Act was placed on the statute book in July 2010. The Coalition Government can be thought of as extending a Blairite approach to education insofar as Blair wanted to turn all schools ultimately into academies. This might lend weight to Cameron's claim that he is the true heir to Blair. There is continuity between the Coalition Government's plans on education and the previous Labour administration policy on academy schools.

Health Reform

A second area in which the Coalition Government shows continuity with New Labour is in its policy towards health. The Coalition Government plans will be explored in greater depth in a different chapter. In this chapter I just signal some of the ways that the Conservative–Liberal Democrat administration is building on the decisions of the previous Labour Government. Julian Le Grand, a former health policy adviser to Tony Blair, highlights this when he argues that the decisions of the Coalition Government represent evolution not revolution. He says: 'many of Andrew Lansley's key proposals have their origin in policy reforms initiated by John Major's Conservative government in the 1990s and subsequently developed by Tony Blair's Labour government (to which I served as an adviser in 10 Downing Street)' (Le Grand, 2010). As with education policy, Le Grand points to the longer continuities in British public policy. General Practitioners (GPs) are part of 'primary care' and are often a patient's first point of contact with health services. Successive health reforms have tried to make GPs the gatekeepers to health services. Le Grand (2010) notes that in the early 1990s the Conservative Government introduced GP fundholding. This gave GPs control over some budgets and allowed them to commission elective surgery. He comments that the Labour Party was sceptical of the benefits of GP fundholding, but that Blair tried to revive this when he sought to introduce 'practice-based commissioning' in his later time in office. This provided GPs with indicative budgets and tried to get GPs to work together in consortia to commission services. However, Le Grand continues that GPs did not have access to real budgets under practice-based commissioning and so this policy step had mixed success.

The Conservative–Liberal Democrat Government is extending this GP commissioning model in their proposals for health reform. This would devolve the bulk of the National Health Service (NHS) budget to GPs. Previously, Primary Care Trusts (PCTs) were in charge of commissioning health services for local populations. Under Coalition plans, GPs would have control of budgets and work together in consortia to commission services from hospitals or other providers (Department of Health, 2010). The Coalition Government plans to allow GPs greater authority over what medicines to prescribe to patients. Previously, the National Institute of Clinical Excellence (NICE) made decisions about what drugs to license. Under the new plans, NICE's role will be to advise only and GPs will have the final decision.

Welfare Reform

One might expect to find a legacy of New Labour in those areas in which figures associated with New Labour are advising the Coalition Government. This points to the area of welfare reform. Part of New Labour's approach to welfare stressed the importance of the duties as well as rights of individuals. The emphasis here was on the obligations that individuals have to the wider political community. 'No rights without responsibilities' became a New Labour mantra. New Labour also emphasized that work is the most important route out of poverty, and this helped shape their welfare-to-work policies.

Former Labour Minister Frank Field plays a role for the Coalition Government. Field had a short spell as Minister for Welfare Reform when Labour won the General Election in 1997. Field says that Blair asked him to develop a programme of reform, often dubbed 'thinking the unthinkable', but he was ultimately frustrated from opposition from the Treasury headed by Gordon Brown (Field, 2000). In June 2010, Prime Minister Cameron commissioned Field to review current approaches to poverty. Field has had a long-standing interest in tackling poverty. His work is influenced by neoconservative arguments about welfare dependency. This sees poverty as not simply about lack of money but also a culture of dependency. Benefit payments, while providing immediate relief, also can encourage people to become dependent on the state and fail to take the steps to break a cycle of dependency. This means that any policy towards the poor should go beyond income payments (Field, 2000). Field draws on the above in his report for the Coalition Government. In the document published on 3 December 2010 he writes:

> We have found overwhelming evidence that children's life chances are most heavily predicated on their development in the first five years of life. It is family background, parental education, good parenting and the opportunities for learning and development in those crucial years that together matter more to children than money, in determining whether their potential is realized in adult life. (Field, 2010: 5)

The report says that the early years are crucial for child development, and calls for policy to be aimed at these 'foundation years'. This involves the services aimed at young children, such as Children Centres, as well as recognizing the role perhaps for classes for good parenting.

David Freud provides another example of continuity between New Labour and the Coalition Government. Freud was an adviser to the previous Labour Government on welfare reform. In December 2009 he defected to the Conservatives and was eventually made a Conservative peer. He is now a Minister for Welfare Reform in the Coalition Government. His advice to the previous Labour Government involved reforms to incapacity benefit. In this report he noted that the 'Government has made a commitment to rights and responsibilities a central feature of policy . . . Recent evidence suggests that expecting more from those on incapacity and lone parent benefits, alongside the right support, can deliver greatly improved outcomes' (Freud, 2007: 8). Freud draws on these ideas in his role in the Coalition Government. In a speech made to welfare providers he stated that coalition reforms are based on a simple premise: 're-establishing responsibility and fairness as the cornerstone of our society' (Freud 2010: 1).

Former Conservative leader Iain Duncan Smith is leading the welfare reform programme in his role as Secretary of State for Work and Pensions.

He highlights the significance of responsibility in a speech on welfare for the twenty-first century delivered on 27 May 2010: 'some of the most difficult challenges will be cultural . . . for too long we have discouraged people from taking up their responsibilities as the Welfare State has pushed in to fill the gap where family and society used to function far more effectively' (Duncan Smith, 2010). One of his central reforms is for the payment of a universal credit. Pleas for this have been outlined in the Welfare Reform Bill (Department of Welfare and Pensions, 2011). The universal credit aims to simplify the benefit system by rolling together all the different range of benefits that can be paid out into a single universal credit. To encourage people to move into work, the plan is that no one will be better off on a universal credit than in work (Department for Work and Pensions, 2010).

This continues an emphasis on work as the best route out of poverty (notwithstanding the possibility of the 'working poor') and that people have responsibilities to take employment. Changes to existing benefits will occur because of this universal credit. The universal credit is likely to involve changes to incapacity benefit, which will mean that many of those in receipt of this benefit will now be expected to find work. This will represent a shift to stressing what they are capable of doing rather than highlighting the ways in which they are incapable of working.

The Labour Party Perspective

I have noted above how the newly elected Labour leader Ed Miliband insisted that it is time to go beyond New Labour. He repeated this at a speech in Gillingham on 27 November 2010 announcing a two-year review of Labour Party policy: 'we've got to move beyond New Labour' (Miliband, 2010). Given that the Labour Party has been home to New Labour, one might nevertheless expect New Labour to have a legacy for the Labour Party. The extent of this legacy is likely to be shaped by the outcome of these policy reviews. The reviews might be used to rethink the assumptions that guided New Labour. However, this will not necessarily be the case. Even if the policy reviews recommend a break with New Labour, the party leadership may decide to reject these suggestions. This might be done to compromise with those sections of the party and broader labour movement that remain sympathetic to New Labour.

New Labour themes are likely to feed into current party discussions. For example, Blairite voices can be heard in debates about the appropriate stance to the Coalition Government's plans to cut the budget deficit. Blair suggests in his recent autobiography that Labour should oppose the composition but not the direction of the Coalition Government's plans to cut the budget deficit (Blair, 2010). Former Labour Chancellor Alistair Darling had plans to halve the deficit over the lifetime of a Parliament if Labour had been re-elected in 2010. Ed Balls, the former Schools Secretary and close ally of Brown, argues that the thrust of both the Coalition and Darling deficit plans are too deep and too fast (Wintour, 2010). Ed Miliband could have given credence to this alternative economic view by immediately appointing Balls as Shadow Chancellor. However, perhaps to avoid reviving a division between Blairites and Brownites, he chose to appoint Alan Johnson, who gave early indications that he supported Darling's position over the deficit (Watt, 2010). By appointing Balls in the wake of Johnson's resignation in January 2011, Miliband has altered Labour's emphasis on the balance between reducing expenditure and securing future growth.

One sign of tension between Ed Miliband and his former Shadow Chancellor was over the 50 per cent income tax rate. In 2010 the Labour Government introduced a 50 per cent rate for those earning over £150,000 a year. This was imposed in the aftermath of the financial crisis of 2008 and was justified as part of a series of measures to address the deficit. The measure broke with New Labour's electoral strategy of avoiding raising income taxes on high earners. Since Ed Miliband's election there had been reports of disagreements between Johnson and Miliband about whether or not to keep this tax. While Miliband appears to favour the 50 per cent tax rate as a matter of social justice, Johnson seemed to chime with a New Labour view and suggested the rate should be seen as a temporary measure (Porter, 2010). It seems that with the appointment of Balls, Miliband has a Shadow Chancellor who views the top rate of income tax in a similar manner to himself.

Ed Miliband also seems to agree with some New Labour themes. For example, in his acceptance speech as leader he declared: 'The new generation in my party understands the fundamental New Labour lesson that we must build prosperity as well as redistributing it' (Miliband, 2010b). One theme of New Labour is that it is possible to combine prosperity with redistribution. This was expressed in various ways, such as the idea that markets and social justice go together. Although the crisis in financial markets in 2008 may have shaken faith in this assumption, it still has a hold over the party leadership. What this means is that New Labour ideas are likely to inform 'next generation' thinking. While the Labour Party may draw on social democratic traditions arguably neglected during the New Labour years, for example those strands that focus on cooperatives or mutuals, one might still expect to find the imprint of New Labour on party debates.

The Big Society

The legacy of New Labour has so far been understood as the continuity the Coalition Government has with the previous Labour government. However, the word legacy can also be understood in an opposite sense in which it prompted later politicians to break with New Labour. Part of the legacy to New Labour therefore might be reaction to New Labour. One example of this is recent interest in the 'big society'. The attention to the big society is contrasted with the emphasis New Labour placed on using central direction, seen in policies such as national targets, for reforming public services.

The Conservative Party made the big society a key part of their 2010 General Election manifesto. This document declared: 'Big Society runs consistently through our policy programme. Our plans to reform public services, mend our broken society, and rebuild trust in politics are all part of our Big Society agenda' (Conservative Party, 2010: 37). During the election campaign Conservative activists were worried that the big society did not mean much to voters. Tim Montgomerie, editor of the website conservativehome, writes: '[the] Big Society message was never poll tested or properly focus grouped and failed to cut through on the doorstep' (Montgomerie, 2010). Although Cameron moderated references to the big society during his campaigning, for example during the televised debates between the party leaders, he has nevertheless returned to this theme as Prime Minister. In a speech in Liverpool on 19 July 2010 he declared: 'my great passion is building the big society . . . for a long time the way government has worked – top-down, top-heavy, controlling – has frequently had the effect of sapping responsibility, local innovation and civic action' (Cameron, 2010: 1–2).

Cameron sees the big society as a bottom-up alternative to top-down government by New Labour. At present what this idea implies in policy is fairly thin. Arguably, some of the proposed reforms to schools might overlap with big society themes. Insofar as there is continuity with 'New Labour' education policy, then arguably New Labour also had a big society theme. However, Cameron suggests a more thoroughgoing reaction against central government. So far perhaps the most detailed government proposals are about 'big society' finance. The fuller Coalition Agreement between the Conservatives and Liberal Democrats outlines plans for a big society bank that will fund neighbourhood groups, social enterprises and charities (HM Government, 2010).

It is too early to say whether the big society will be a passing fad. However, at present it helps shape the ways that different parties might try to break with New Labour. Ed Miliband highlights how the policy review should be used to wrest the big society idea from the Conservatives: 'we need to think really hard in our policy review about how we are the people who stand up for strong communities and strong society and I tell you this, we've got to take that term 'Big Society' back off David Cameron' (Miliband, E. 2010). The big society may go the way of previous political slogans in promising much but delivering little. However, the big society might also point to the way in which the political parties rethink the role of the state. This might amount to greater pluralism in public policy and a greater break with the central state. A legacy of New Labour may be the extent to which it triggered this shift away from the central state.

Conclusion

This chapter has looked at the legacy of New Labour. Although politicians from different parties are keen to declare the death of New Labour, the reality is likely to be otherwise. However, any attempt to assess the legacy of New Labour is bound to be a thorny task. Most obviously, not enough time has passed to make any judgement on this issue. This task is further complicated by ambiguities about the term New Labour as well as the different ways that legacy might be understood. I have suggested that New Labour was the creation of a specific set of people at a particular time; it nevertheless went beyond this involvement. However, the ideas and policies associated with New Labour were never fully consistent and there were contradictory strands. Education, health and welfare are areas in which the Coalition Government is arguably extending a Blairite approach to the reform of public services. However, these Blairite reforms also show the impact of previous Conservative policy, and so New Labour has mixed parents.

One of the legacies of New Labour might also be the extent to which it prompted parties to react to New Labour. This can be seen in the current rhetoric surrounding the big society. As noted above, Ed Miliband is keen to develop his own version of the big society. As the Labour Party's policy review has just started and will last two years, it is perhaps more difficult to predict the impact of New Labour for the Labour Party than the Coalition Government. For the latter one can point to government policy for evidence of a legacy of New Labour. Ed Miliband may succeed in creating a next generation. If that happens, then the Coalition

Government might ultimately prove to be a better carrier for New Labour than the Labour Party.

References

Adonis, A. and Pollard, S. (1997) *A Class Act: the myth of Britain's classless society* (London: Hamish Hamilton).

BBC News (2005) *Parents Back Academies Say Blair.* news.bbc.co.uk/1/hi/education/4236354.stm, 12 September, accessed 18 November 2010.

BBC News (2007a) *Cameron Hits Back over Grammars*, 16 May. news.bbc.co.uk/1/hi/education/6658613.stm, accessed 18 November 2010.

BBC News (2007b) *In Full: Willetts' speech.* news.bbc.co.uk/1/hi/uk_politics/6662219.stm, 17 May, accessed 18 November 2010.

BBC News (2010) *Shift from New Labour Backed by Poll Findings.* www.bbc.co.uk/news/uk-politics-11185576, accessed 11 November 2010.

Beckett, F. (2010) *What We Can Learn from Michael Gove's Educational Heroes.* www.guardian.co.uk/politics/2010/oct/03/michael-gove-education-secretary, accessed 12 November 2010.

Blair, T. (1998), *The Third Way: New Politics for a New Century*, Fabian pamphlet 588 (London: Fabian Society).

Blair, T. (2010), *A Journey* (London: Hutchinson).

Cameron, D. (2010) *Big Society Speech.* www.number10.gov.uk/news/speeches-and-transcripts/2010/07/big-society-speech-53572, accessed 9 December 2010.

Carvel, J. (2000) Blunkett Plans Network of City Academies. *The Guardian*, 15 March. www.guardian.co.uk/uk/2000/mar/15/schools.news, accessed 18 November 2010.

Conservative Party (2010) *Invitation to Join the Government of Britain.* media.conservatives.s3.amazonaws.com/manifesto/cpmanifesto2010_lowres.pdf, accessed 2 December 2010.

Curtice, J., Fisher, J. and Ford, R. (2010) Appendix 2: An Analysis of the Results. In D. Kavanagh and P. Cowley, *The British General Election of 2010* (Basingstoke: Palgrave Macmillan), pp. 385–426.

Department for Children, Schools and Families (2000) *Blunkett Announces Locations for First Three City Academies*, www.dcsf.gov.uk/pns/DisplayPN.cgi?pn_id=2000_0396, accessed 18 November 2010.

Department of Health (2010) *Equity and Excellence: Liberating the NHS.* www.dh.gov.uk/prod_consum_dh/groups/dh_digitalassets/@dh/@en/@ps/documents/digitalasset/dh_117794.pdf, accessed 2 December 2010.

Department for Work and Pensions (2010) *Universal Credit: Welfare that Works.* www.dwp.gov.uk/docs/universal-credit-full-document.pdf, accessed 3 December 2010.

Duncan Smith, I. (2010) *Welfare for the 21st Century.* www.dwp.gov.uk/newsroom/ministers-speeches/2010/27-05-10.shtml, accessed 9 December 2010.

Field, F. (2000) *The State of Dependency. Welfare under Labour* (London: Social Market Foundation).

Field, F. (2010) *The Foundation Years: Preventing Poor Children Becoming Poor Adults. The Report of the Independent Review of Poverty and Life Chances.* povertyreview.independent.gov.uk/media/20254/poverty-report.pdf, accessed 3 December 2010.

Freud, D. (2007) *Reducing Dependency, Increasing Opportunity: Options for the Future of Welfare to Work. An Independent Report for the Department for Work and Pensions.* www.dwp.gov.uk/docs/welfarereview.pdf, accessed 3 December 2010.

Freud, D. (2010) *Address to Welfare Providers.* www.dwp.gov.uk/newsroom/ministers-speeches/2010/02-06-10.shtml, accessed 9 December 2010.

Giddens, A. (1998) *The Third Way: The Renewal of Social Democracy* (Cambridge: Polity).

Hague, W. (2010), *New Labour is Dead.* Speech, Conservative party conference, 3 October. www.conservatives.com/News/Speeches/2010/10/William_Hague_New_Labour_is_dead.aspx, accessed 8 November 2010.

Hay, C. (1999) *The Political Economy of New Labour: Labouring under False Pretences* (Manchester: Manchester University Press).

HM Government (2010) *The Coalition: Our Programme for Government.* www.cabinetoffice.gov.uk/media/409088/pfg_coalition.pdf, accessed 2 December 2010.

HM Treasury (2010), *Comprehensive Spending Review 2010.* cdn.hm-treasury.gov.uk/sr2010_completereport.pdf, accessed 9 November 2010.

Le Grand, J. (2010) *Greater Choice and Competition in the NHS Now Provides a Mature Set of Solutions Whose Time Has Come,* 15 July. blogs.lse.ac.uk/politicsandpolicy/?p=3372, accessed 26 November 2010.

Mandelson, P. (2010) *The Third Man: Life at the Heart of New Labour* (London: HarperPress).

Miliband, D. (2010) *Next Labour: Winning the Battle of Ideas,* Speech, South Shields, 17 May. www.davidmiliband.info/speeches/speeches_010_05.htm, accessed 9 November 2010.

Milband, E. (2010a) *Speech to the National Policy Forum.* www2.labour.org.uk/ed-milibands-speech-to-labours-npf,2010-11-27, accessed 9 December 2010.

Miliband, E. (2010b) *Acceptance Speech,* 28 September. www.guardian.co.uk/politics/2010/sep/28/ed-miliband-labour-conference-speech, accessed 14 December 2010.

Montgomerie, T. (2010) *Executive Summary.* conservativehome.blogs.com/generalelectionreview/2010/05/executive-summary.html, accessed 9 December 2010.

Pierce, A. (2005) *Horror as Cameron Brandishes the B Word.* www.timesonline.co.uk/tol/news/politics/article574814.ece, accessed 9 November 2010.

Porter, A. (2010) Johnson Rebuffs Miliband over 50p Tax Rate. www.telegraph.co.uk/news/newstopics/politics/ed-miliband/8135584/Miliband-rebuffs-Johnson-over-cut-to-50p-tax-rate.html, accessed 13 December 2010.

Porter, A. and Winnett, R. (2010) *Ed Miliband: New Labour is Dead,* 26 September. www.telegraph.co.uk/news/newstopics/politics/labour/8026708/Ed-Miliband-New-Labour-is-dead.html, accessed 8 November 2010.

Rawnsley, A. (2010), *The End of the Party. The Rise and Fall of New Labour* (London: Viking).

Shipman, T. (2010) *I Should Never Have Called Myself 'The Heir To Blair', Admits Cameron.* www.dailymail.co.uk/news/election/article-1272398/GENERAL-ELECTION-2010-David-Cameron-admits-heir-Blair-branding-mistake.html, accessed 9 November 2010.

Watt, N. (2010) *Alan Johnson Backs Alistair Darling's Deficit Reduction Plan,* 8 October. www.guardian.co.uk/politics/2010/oct/08/alan-johnson-backs-darling-timetable, accessed 18 December 2010.

Wintour, P. (2010) *Darling and Balls Clash over Labour's Deficit Plans,* 27 September. www.guardian.co.uk/politics/2010/sep/26/darling-balls-labour-deficit-clash, accessed 18 December 2010.

3
The Formation of the Coalition

Mark Stuart

The purpose of this chapter is not to give a blow-by-blow account of the British General Election of 2010, nor to provide a chronological account of the formation of the Coalition between the Conservatives and the Liberal Democrats. That task has already been performed commendably (Fox, 2010; Kavanagh and Cowley, 2010; Laws, 2010; Norton, 2010; Snowdon, 2010). Instead, the twin objectives here are first, to provide a longer-term explanation as to why the Liberal Democrats were more predisposed to link up with the Conservatives than has previously been appreciated, and second, to provide an overall assessment of the variety of factors which led to the formation of the Coalition between the Liberal Democrats and the Conservatives in May 2010.

The Election Outcome

That the 2010 General Election should have produced a hung Parliament for the first time in 26 years with no party enjoying an overall majority came as no surprise to many academic observers. Assessing the Conservatives' chances in mid-2009 – the nadir of Gordon Brown's Government – John Curtice sagely pointed out:

> Thanks to the operation of the electoral system, the Conservatives face a formidable challenge if they are to secure office after the next election. They are likely not simply to have to outpoll Labour, but to do so by some considerable margin, even just to become the largest party in a hung parliament. (Curtice, 2009: 182)

Members of David Cameron's election team also knew that the Conservatives had never won a General Election from as weak a starting point as the one they faced in 2010. Stephen Gilbert, co-director of the Tories' key seats strategy, gave a slide presentation in September 2009 during which he revealed the sheer scale of the Conservatives' electoral challenge: the party needed to win an additional 117 seats just to achieve an overall majority of one. That would have represented the biggest number of Conservative gains at a General Election since 1931, when the party gained 214 seats. In the postwar period, only Blair's victory in 1997 had produced as many or more seats (in Blair's case 147) as the Conservatives needed to secure victory (Gilbert, 2009). Put another way, the Conservatives required a 6.9 per cent uniform swing from Labour to the Conservatives to produce an overall majority, greater than the swings that had propelled Edward Heath to power in 1970 and Margaret Thatcher in 1979.

What changed expectations about the final result, however, was the remarkable public reaction to Nick Clegg's performance in the first ever televised Leaders' debate[1] in a British General Election campaign. Instant polls showed Clegg to be the clear winner against David Cameron and Gordon Brown, and within four days the Liberal Democrats had increased their support by 50 per cent, something which had never happened in UK polling history. Some opinion polls briefly showed the Liberal Democrats in the lead. And although the Liberal Democrat bandwagon was clawed back to some extent by Cameron's better performances in the second and third television debates, none of the final polls predicted the outcome accurately, all of them overestimating, to varying degrees, the extent of Liberal Democrat support.

It therefore came as a huge shock to everyone when the exit polls were broadcast at 10 pm on election night, 6 May. That they predicted a hung parliament was not a surprise, but the precise seat shares – Conservatives 307, Labour 255, Liberal Democrats 59 and Others 29 – produced disbelief. Surely the Liberal Democrats could not have lost three seats on their 2005 performance? However, the exit polls proved remarkably accurate, coming within one of the Conservative final tally of 306 seats, within three of Labour's haul of 258 seats and within two of the Liberal Democrat overall yield of just 57.

Instead of toasting his party's expected breakthrough with champagne, Clegg was forced to endure a long night in his Sheffield Hallam constituency watching his hopes of making gains evaporate on television screens, while his own count was delayed into the early hours of Friday morning because the polling stations had been unable to cope with a fairly modest rise in turnout (Electoral Commission, 2010). Clegg now headed a party that had achieved its historic aim – holding the balance of power in the House of Commons after a General Election – but not in the circumstances that he had imagined. Had Clegg been able to realize his dream scenario of winning 100 seats, finishing second in terms of the share of the vote ahead of Labour, with all the popular legitimacy that that would have brought, he would have been able to dominate the negotiations with the other two main parties; now he was left with far fewer cards to play, having boxed himself in during the election campaign.

Which Horse to Back

Clegg had come under increasing pressure during the campaign to reveal which party he would support in the event of a hung Parliament, especially after the first Leaders' debate when the opinion polls consistently showed Labour trailing in third place. The Liberal Democrat leader had begun the campaign by stating that he would open negotiations with the party that won the most votes and the most seats. But maintaining that line became increasingly difficult because the Liberal Democrat surge meant that it was now possible that the Conservatives could win most votes, with Labour finishing third in the popular vote and yet gaining most seats. On 25 April 2010, Clegg made it clear both in an interview with the *Sunday Times* and later on *The Andrew Marr Show* that if Labour ended up with the largest number of MPs, but came third in the popular vote, he would not allow Brown to continue to 'squat' as Prime Minister in Number 10. It was hoped that this new line would blunt the Conservative message that a vote for the Liberal Democrats would help keep Brown in Downing Street. In fact, Clegg's revised set of post-election preconditions served only to intensify media interest in every single permutation of the election outcome. In the event, on 6 May Labour finished a comfortable second in the popular vote, but with considerably fewer seats than the Conservatives. Therefore, on the Friday morning after the election, speaking outside Liberal Democrat headquarters in Cowley Street, Clegg was able to deliver on his original pledge to begin negotiations with the party that had won the most votes and the most seats: the Conservatives.

An Accident of Arithmetic?

In many respects the arithmetic of the election outcome in terms of seats won set the framework within which all three main parties had to operate. In the event of failing to win an overall majority, the

Conservatives' Plan B had involved reaching an agreement with the Democratic Unionist Party's eight MPs, but the post-election tallies of both parties combined still left them ten short of an overall majority. The Labour Party would have preferred a Coalition with the Liberal Democrats, but that too left Labour short of a majority by a margin of ten. Even a 'rainbow' Coalition combining Labour, the Liberal Democrats, the Scottish National Party, Plaid Cymru, the SDLP (closely connected to Labour), one Alliance MP (a sister party of the Liberal Democrats) and the one Green MP, still only produced a tiny overall majority. It appears that Brown was even considering a Coalition involving all the Northern Ireland parties, including the DUP (Laws, 2010: 7 May). However, any broad-based combination of parties was always going to be very difficult to put together; as Peter Hennessy commented on *Channel 4 News* on the Monday after the election, a rainbow Coalition had 'too many moving parts'.

Only one combination in the excruciating post-election scenario made arithmetic sense – a coalition between the Liberal Democrats and the Conservatives – which eventually produced an overall working majority of 83.[2] Robert Axelrod's minimum connected winning coalition model – that political parties will form a coalition with the minimum possible number of parties in order to ensure a working majority – seemed to be proved correct (Axelrod, 1970). But the other component of Axelrod's theory – that parties will link up with partners that are closest ideologically to their own viewpoint – appears, at first sight at least, not to have been fulfilled. Surely the Liberal Democrats' natural bedfellows were Labour. Taking this narrative to its natural conclusion, it can be argued that it was only an accident of arithmetic that forced the Liberal Democrats to consider a deal with the Conservatives. Shortly after the Coalition Agreement had been reached, former Liberal Democrat leader Paddy Ashdown seemed to give credence to this theory, remarking ruefully, 'Our heads went one way, but the arithmetic went the other way' (BBC2, 2010).

Falling out of Love with Labour

Despite the crucial importance that the post-election arithmetic played in the outcome of the Coalition talks, Ashdown's interpretation flies in the face of a longer-term trend which had seen the Liberal Democrats progressively fall out of love with Labour in the decade since Ashdown had stood down as leader. In May 1995, he formally abandoned equidistance between the two main parties, shifting the Liberal Democrats firmly in an anti-Conservative direction (Ashdown, 2000: 595–7). Ashdown was merely reflecting reality: during the 1992 Parliament, Liberal Democrat MPs voted with the Labour Party in nearly 80 per cent of House of Commons divisions (Cowley et al., 2003: 115). When Labour entered Government in 1997, the Liberal Democrats supported much of the Blair's administration's agenda, even participating in a Cabinet Committee on constitutional reform. Although relations had cooled slightly with Labour from about 1999 onwards, by the end of the first Blair Parliament on whipped votes the Liberal Democrat MPs still divided their favours roughly evenly between the Conservatives and the Labour Party (Cowley and Stuart, 2003). However, that position changed dramatically by the end of the 2001 Parliament, with the Liberal Democrats only voting with Labour on 25 per cent of whipped votes and against Labour 75 per cent of the time (Cowley and Stuart, 2004). It is important to note here that these trends occurred long before Clegg was elected Liberal Democrat leader in December 2007. By the end of the 2005 Parliament, the Liberal Democrats had voted with Labour only 21 per cent of the time and against it 79 per cent of the time. Thus, over the space of roughly 20 years, the Liberal Democrats had gone from being 80 per cent in favour of Labour to nearly 80 per cent against it. That is not to suggest that they had *necessarily* become ideologically closer to the Conservatives (although, as we shall see, that may have been occurring), merely that they had fallen out of love with Labour.

Much significance has been made of the publication of the *Orange Book* in 2004 (Marshall and Laws, 2004) in which a series of Liberal Democrat authors made a conscious effort to reclaim both economic and political liberalism for the twenty-first century (Randall, 2007). Of greater importance was a discernible shift away from traditional left-of-centre policies under the leaderships of both Sir Menzies Campbell (2006–7) and Nick Clegg. Charles Kennedy's flagship promise to introduce a top rate of tax of 50 pence in the pound was abandoned after a major struggle with the more left-leaning grass roots of the party at the Liberal Democrat conference in 2006 (Denham and Dorey, 2007). Throughout 2009, Clegg sought to water down his party's pre-election spending commitments: in January, the Federal Policy Committee (FPC) voted by a margin of 18 to 5 against dropping the commitment to abolish fees, with Clegg voting with the minority; in July, the FPC engaged in a heated debate over what to trim in terms of the party's spending commitments; at the Bournemouth conference in September, Clegg surprised Liberal Democrat activists when referring to the need for 'savage cuts' in public expenditure and once again sought to dilute the party's commitment to tuition fees: 'There is no question mark over the policy of the Liberal Democrats to scrap tuition fees. The only question mark is about when we can afford to scrap tuition fees' (Kavanagh and Cowley, 2010: 109–10).

Less perceptively, the cumulative effect of facing 13 years of Labour rule (particularly a government that had, in their view, engaged in an illegal war over Iraq) gradually chipped away at the previously accepted orthodoxy that the Liberal Democrats were the natural bedfellows of Labour. On the contrary, issues ranging from the erosion of civil liberties and the relentless centralization of government at the expense of localism found the Liberal Democrats making common cause with the Conservatives. Indeed, in April 2009, the two parties combined to defeat the Government over the settlement rights of the Gurkhas, inflicting a first Commons defeat on Brown (Cowley and Stuart, 2009).

Meanwhile, Cameron, a self-styled 'liberal Conservative', had started moving his own party closer to the centre ground. In the run-up to the election campaign, Cameron highlighted the similarities rather than the differences between the Conservatives and the Liberal Democrats, claiming that 'Britain needs a strong Coalition for progressive change in our politics'. Whilst he was engaging in mischievous 'love-bombing' of Liberal Democrat voters rather than directly courting Clegg, the Conservative leader was right to point out that there was 'barely a cigarette paper between us' on a range of issues (Cameron, 2009).

So, it seems that long before the 2010 General Election, the Liberal Democrats had progressively fallen out of love with the Labour Party and were far more favourably predisposed towards the Conservatives than the current narrative suggests. This state of affairs had important consequences for the Coalition talks. For a start, it meant that the possibility of the Liberal Democrats and the Conservatives entering a Coalition together was a far less stomach-turning possibility that it might have seemed only five years earlier under Kennedy's leadership. Moreover, the Labour hierarchy (with the sole exception of Andrew Adonis) seemed almost wholly unaware of these shifts in the political landscape, preferring to rely on their close contacts with the old guard of Liberal Democrat leaders, apparently not realizing that a new, younger generation of movers and shakers now made up the Liberal Democrat leadership. As Kavanagh and Cowley argue, Labour 'underestimated the extent to which there had been a generational shift at the top of the Liberal Democrats' (Kavanagh and Cowley, 2010: 210).

The Formation of the Coalition

In order to understand the approach of the Liberal Democrats in the five days after the election, it is necessary to realize that they were the best prepared of the three main parties, and that, unlike the other two, they had the clearest idea of what they wanted to achieve from the negotiations.

It is clear that not only had the Liberal Democrats taken a tremendous amount of care over the precise personnel of their negotiating team – comprising Danny Alexander, Chris Huhne, David Laws and Andrew Stunell – but that they also had engaged in months of preparation covering every possible scenario, including that of entering a full coalition either with the Conservatives or with Labour. When undertaking that formidable task, the Liberal Democrats could draw on the prior experience of seasoned coalition negotiators, including Lord Wallace of Tankerness, who, as Jim Wallace, had played a pivotal role in forging a coalition between the Liberal Democrats and Labour following the first Scottish Parliamentary elections in 1999. It is also significant that Laws had played a key role in drawing up the first draft coalition agreement with Labour in Scotland during his stint as the Liberal Democrats' Director of Policy and Research from 1997 to 1999 (Kavanagh and Cowley, 2010: 227).

But what distinguished the Liberal Democrats most from the other two main parties was their absolute clarity about what they wanted to gain from the talks. Basically, they adopted a policy-based approach, using the four main aims in their 2010 election manifesto – based around the central theme of fairness – as their four objectives in the Coalition talks: fair taxes (raising the income tax threshold for lower earners to £10,000); fair chances (introducing a pupil premium for underprivileged children); a fair future (breaking up the banks and creating jobs in the green economy); and a fair deal (cleaning up politics, including electoral reform). These four planks would all later be incorporated into the heart of the Coalition Agreement, while the central idea of the manifesto – that of fairness – would be bolted onto almost every subsequent Coalition policy.

It was also clear from the Friday morning onwards that the Liberal Democrats favoured a twin-track approach, courting both Labour and the Conservatives. Although Clegg stated that it was right that negotiations began first with the Conservatives, simultaneously Danny Alexander contacted Andrew Adonis, a member of Labour's negotiating team, to reassure him that Clegg's statement didn't mean the Liberal Democrats were only interested in talking to the Tories (Mandelson, 2010: 543).

What is also evident is that the Liberal Democrats negotiating team regarded a loose agreement with a minority Conservative Government to support the Queen's Speech and Budget ('confidence and supply') as 'sub-optimal' (private information), and from an early stage their strong preference was for a full Coalition. Not only was this view held by the party leadership, it was also shared by the Liberal Democrat MPs, who were not interested in brokering a watered-down deal with the Conservatives (Laws, 2010: 10 May; Mandelson, 2010: 552).

In sharp contrast, the Labour Party was badly prepared for the negotiations. The election campaign had already begun before Nick Pearce, Labour's Head of Policy, was asked to draft a ten-page document, outlining seven potential areas of agreement with the Liberal Democrats (Kavanagh and Cowley, 2010: 206). Labour's initial negotiating team comprised Mandelson, Adonis, Darling and Ed Miliband. However, its composition varied as Brown attempted to keep all potential malcontents in his party happy.[3] Worse still, members of the Cabinet had differing views about whether a deal with the Liberal Democrats was appropriate. Adonis, the Transport Secretary, himself a former Liberal Democrat, was by far the keenest on making a deal with his old party. Both Alan Johnson and Ed Miliband were in favour of a coalition, but this was not a view shared by his elder brother David, who, like Darling, was deeply sceptical. In the end, only three members of the Cabinet – Andy Burnham, Liam Byrne and Jack Straw – dissented against opening formal talks with the Liberal Democrats on the Monday night (Kavanagh and Cowley, 2010: 213). However, what mattered was the negative impression the Labour negotiators created with their Liberal Democrat counterparts. As one of them remarked: 'We appeared to be negotiating with two separate Labour teams. One wanted a deal, the other didn't' (Laws, 2010: 10 May).

In the immediate hours after the election, the picture gained of Brown is of a deeply tribal politician, clinging on to the wreckage, trying to keep the Conservatives out of power at all costs. For the next few days, the Prime Minister's tunnel vision kicked in as he tried to concoct a deal with the Liberal Democrats, deploying his strong friendships with both Vince Cable and Menzies Campbell, pestering them with early morning calls. When Brown allowed himself to get into such a mode of thought, it proved very difficult for others in his own party, and in the Liberal Democrat negotiating team, to get him to listen. In his first telephone conversation with Clegg on the Friday after the election, Brown set out the broad parameters of a deal: agreements on public expenditure and economic recovery, possible electoral reform and fixed-term parliaments. Mandelson, listening to the conversation on another telephone, felt afterwards that Brown 'might have come across too heavily, telling Nick what he should think, rather than asking him what he thought' (Mandelson, 2010: 545). We also know that Brown's overbearing personality grated with Clegg; as he put down the telephone at the end of the conversation outlined above, the Liberal Democrat leader apparently said, 'That man!' (Laws, 2010: 7 May).

More importantly, the continued presence of Brown as Prime Minister – what Danny Alexander referred to as 'personnel' – formed a formidable obstacle to any deal between Labour and the Liberal Democrats (Mandelson, 2010: 550). Once described by the Conservatives as the 'roadblock' to reform of the public services, Brown was very much seen by the Liberal Democrats as the roadblock to a coalition deal. On the Sunday night, at a clandestine meeting between Clegg, Alexander, Brown and Mandelson in Brown's House of Commons office, Clegg told the Prime Minister that it was important that he should step down in a dignified way. Brown appeared to set fresh conditions, saying he wanted to ensure that both a referendum on the Alternative Vote and economic recovery were in place by the time he departed, but in response, Clegg emphasized the 'massive political risk' the Liberal Democrats were taking in being seen to keep Brown in Number 10 after the election result had so clearly shown him to be defeated (Mandelson, 2010: 548). By the Monday morning, several prominent Liberal Democrats, including Ashdown, reinforced the message to Brown that he would have to step down as Prime Minister by mid-October at the latest. Later that same day, after another private conversation between Clegg and Brown in the House of Commons, Brown agreed to step down, allowing for a new Labour leader to be in place by October. This deal facilitated Brown's dramatic announcement late on the Monday afternoon that he would be stepping down, opening the way for formal talks to begin between Labour and the Liberal Democrats on the Monday night.

Those talks, however, began badly, with both sides exchanging sharp differences of view on a range of issues. Mandelson noted 'a new attitude of prickliness, even truculence' from the Liberal Democrats (Mandelson, 2010: 552). It appears that the Liberal Democrat and Conservative negotiators had made a breakthrough in their negotiations on the Monday night – moves which led the Liberal Democrats to find excuses for not doing a deal with Labour.

Ultimately, however, the opportunity to forge a coalition between Labour and the Liberal Democrats foundered with the refusal of several leading Labour figures to countenance the idea of creating a coalition of losers. Most notably, two former Labour Home Secretaries, David Blunkett and John Reid, publicly spoke out against a deal, arguing that Labour had lost the election and that it was embarrassing itself in trying to secure a deal. This was a view widely shared in the wider parliamentary Labour Party. In private chats with Mandelson, Blair also expressed his fear that Labour would do long-term damage to its image with the voters if it was seen to cling on to power in such a desperate way (Mandelson, 2010: 549–50). A potential deal with Labour also had an element of the unknown about it, given that the Liberal Democrats had no idea who would emerge victorious in the forthcoming Labour leadership contest. The very fact of a leadership contest (and therefore one for the Prime Ministership) would have provided for an unsettling first few months of a coalition, to say the very least. Moreover, in one of the last of several phone calls between Clegg and Brown on the Tuesday afternoon, Clegg hit the mark when he told Brown that his party could not deliver on a coalition agreement (Mandelson, 2010: 552).

The Conservatives' role in the negotiations remains the most opaque of the three main parties. What we do know, however, is that Oliver Letwin, the key policy guru inside Team Cameron, played a central role in both the preparation and the detail of the Conservatives' approach to the coalition talks. Moreover, his predilection for policy-based negotiations ended up chiming neatly with the Liberal Democrats' similar obsession with policy minutiae (Kavanagh and Cowley, 2010: 227).

By breakfast time on the Friday morning, Cameron was very firmly in favour of a full coalition with the Liberal Democrats. The historian is left wondering why he wasn't bolder in the early hours of Friday morning in insisting that the Conservatives were by far the largest party and had secured the most votes and that therefore he was perfectly entitled to seek to form either a minority government or a 'confidence and supply' agreement with the Liberal Democrats. Supporters of Cameron would claim that, far from showing timidity, his 'big, open and comprehensive offer' of a full coalition with the Liberal Democrats was the ultimate act of decontamination, creating a progressive alliance on the centre-right of British politics. Leading Tory modernizers such as Steve Hilton, Oliver Letwin and Ed Llewellyn, agreed with Cameron that the formation of the Coalition provided 'the opportunity to accelerate decontamination of our party in government' (Snowdon, 2010: 415).

However, it is worth questioning Cameron's real motivation for embracing the Liberal Democrats so swiftly and so warmly in the immediate post-election period. Like Clegg, Cameron's party had performed disappointingly. The Tory leader would have been well aware that the knives were out for him in the immediate days after the election.

The chilling and unexpected appearance of Lord Ashcroft on the BBC election night programme had sent an early warning to Cameron that he faced an inquest – from the right of the party especially – into his failure to secure an overall majority.[4] By making a bold offer to the Liberal Democrats, Cameron was able to deflect attention away from the election outcome. Ever the consummate actor, the Tory leader was able to pull that trick off with aplomb. As Fraser Nelson later commented: '[Cameron] has the air of a winner, and certainly behaves like that.' Paradoxically, Nelson argues, the outcome of the election with the Conservatives as the largest single party but bereft of an overall majority left Cameron in a stronger position to modernize the Conservative Party with the aid of Liberal Democrats MPs than if he had won a slim majority, when he would have been held to ransom by a powerful group of his 'notoriously regicidal backbenchers' (Nelson, 2010).

Doubts have persisted since the formation of the Coalition about the degree to which the emerging financial crisis in Greece impinged upon the decision of Cameron to opt for a full coalition or whether the European financial crisis was used as a justification, particularly by the Liberal Democrats, for securing a coalition deal. Cable, the Liberal Democrats' Treasury spokesperson (and subsequent Business Secretary in the Coalition), maintains that the severity of the European sovereign debt crisis during the coalition negotiations led him to change his mind about the need to make immediate and deep cuts in the Budget for 2010–11, something that he had vehemently opposed throughout the election campaign. In reality, Britain was not on the verge of economic collapse during the coalition talks. Lord Turnbull, the former Cabinet Secretary, has since challenged Osborne's claim in his Commons statement on the Comprehensive Spending Review (CSR) that Britain had been 'on the brink of bankruptcy' in May 2010. Nor, it turns out, was the UK in the position of Ireland or Greece, facing a sovereign debt crisis, provided that some form of deficit reduction plan had been put in place after the election (Treasury Select Committee, 2010). Leaving these arguments to one side, it must have dawned on the prospective Chancellor that he needed the maximum degree of parliamentary support possible for the tough decisions on public spending that were to follow, and that the best means of securing that was through a strong and stable coalition with the Liberal Democrats. These political calculations seem to explain Osborne's firm backing for Cameron's stance in trying to cut a deal with the Liberal Democrats.

What is surprising about the Conservative stance vis-à-vis talks with the Liberal Democrats is that, from an early stage, they were prepared to be so open-minded and flexible about the contours of a full coalition. This had the effect of endearing them to the Liberal Democrat negotiating team and creating the right 'mood music' between the two teams of negotiators. Added to this was the good personal chemistry that developed between Clegg and Cameron, something which continued to flourish long after the Coalition agreement was signed.[5]

Sophistry over the Alternative Vote?

The major sticking point in the negotiations between the Conservatives and the Liberal Democrats centred on the extent to which the Tories were willing to make concessions on electoral reform for future Westminster General Elections. For the Liberal Democrat negotiators 'the reality was that electoral reform, of some sort *was* a deal breaker' (Kavanagh and Cowley, 2010: 225). So it came as no surprise when the Liberal Democrats rejected Cameron's initial offer of an all-party committee of inquiry on electoral reform. Although the Liberal Democrats harboured the long-term aim of securing the single transferable vote for Westminster elections, they were realistic enough to see that they were not in a position to secure that from either of the major parties in the Coalition negotiations;[6] they sought instead to secure the alternative vote (AV), either with or, intriguingly, without a referendum.

The first known mention of the possibility of AV without a referendum appears to have come from Liberal Democrat negotiator Danny Alexander in a conversation with Mandelson on the Saturday morning after the election. According to Mandelson, the Liberal Democrats were worried that a referendum on AV would be lost (Mandelson, 2010: 546). But at no point did Labour offer the Liberal Democrats AV without a referendum, either formally or informally. Besides, as Straw later pointed out in the House of Commons, there were real doubts about the deliverability of such a proposal within the parliamentary Labour Party given that 'a significant proportion of Labour Members, including myself, would never have accepted such a proposition had it been put forward' (HC Debates, 7 June 2010, col. 29). In reply to a hostile parliamentary question from the Conservative MP Dr Julian Lewis, Clegg (now Deputy Prime Minister) denied that Labour had formally offered AV without a referendum (HC Debates, 7 June 2010, col. 44). And yet someone clearly convinced Cameron that such an offer had been made because the Tory leader mentioned it both to his Shadow Cabinet in the late afternoon of Monday and at a crucial meeting of his parliamentary party held in Committee Room 14 later that same night. We also know that Hague – one of the four Conservative negotiators – was convinced that Labour had made the offer (Newsnight website, 26 July 2010). It is worth recalling the pivotal state of negotiations on that Monday night. Brown had just sacrificed his own position to facilitate formal talks with the Liberal Democrats. That bold move had thrown the Conservatives into a spin and must have been the key determinant in forcing Cameron into a better 'final' offer on electoral reform – promising AV with a referendum.

While Kavanagh and Cowley provide a comprehensive account of the AV without a referendum episode, their final assessment that Cameron's use of that point 'may have helped put pressure on Conservative backbenchers' (Kavanagh and Cowley, 2010: 215) is something of an understatement. Here was a Tory leader who had been forced throughout his years in Opposition to trim his liberal Conservative message to appease his right wing (Bale, 2010) now putting that argument to those very same Tory MPs, many of whom were extremely uneasy about entering into a coalition deal with the Liberal Democrats. Cameron had indicated that he *thought* that Labour *might* have offered the Liberal Democrats AV without a referendum, but exactly who was responsible for putting about that particular message remains unclear.

The most likely people to have mentioned the possibility of AV without a referendum to Cameron were the Liberal Democrat negotiators, or persons closely connected with them. It was in the interests of the leading Liberal Democrats to gain the best deal possible: after all, they were engaged in a bidding war between Labour and the Conservatives. One means of raising the stakes may have involved presenting to the Conservative negotiators an exaggerated version of what Labour was prepared to offer. According to Clegg's reply to the House of Commons, he played no part in this alleged sophistry.

Alternatively, Cameron's team was just as anxious as the Liberal Democrat negotiators to cut a full coalition deal as soon as possible. We know from Laws' account of the negotiations that Conservative whips had been ordered by the party leadership to sound out their backbenchers as to what was the maximum deal on electoral reform that they would be prepared to accept (Laws, 2010, 10 May). In such a sounding-out process, it is remarkable how quickly Chinese whispers can turn an innocuous mention of a negotiating gambit that never became airborne into a mistaken belief that such a firm offer had been made by Labour. Such a sequence of events might explain why Hague told Michael Crick so adamantly that Labour had offered AV without a referendum (Newsnight website, 26 July 2010). Whatever the final truth, there is no denying that Cameron's use of the argument that the Labour Party was prepared to offer AV *without* a referendum was a decisive factor in persuading his doubting parliamentary party to concede the lesser, but still distasteful option of AV *with* a referendum. We know from Laws that on the Monday night, Tory MPs were 'thawing on voting reform' (Laws, 2010, 10 May): learning the erroneous information that Labour's team was ready with a better deal is bound to have had a decisive effect on wavering Conservative backbenchers. Kavanagh and Cowley may indeed be correct to claim that the debate over whether Conservative MPs were deceived is somewhat 'academic' in the sense that Cameron simply had to make a higher offer on electoral reform in order to secure a deal with the Liberal Democrats whether or not Labour had offered AV without a referendum (Kavanagh and Cowley, 2010: 215). However, they do not appear to appreciate fully that Cameron would have faced a much tougher time in persuading his backbenchers of the merits of his increased offer of AV without a referendum had he not been able to deploy the very powerful argument that Labour had already put a more attractive offer on the table. What is clear is that no such Labour offer ever existed.

Conclusion

Whatever the rights and wrongs of the Coalition deal, what has not been fully appreciated until now is the extent to which the Liberal Democrats had, during the course of the previous two Parliaments, fallen out of love with their traditional Labour bedfellows. Less obviously, the party had begun to move closer ideologically in the direction of their former sworn enemy, the Conservatives, making the outcome of the May 2010 Coalition talks less of a surprise than it seemed at the time.

It appears that the Liberal Democrats entered into the Coalition with the Conservatives for two main reasons. First, they genuinely believed that entering into a deal with Labour carried too many risks. It would be seen by a majority of voters as a 'coalition of losers' and would have kept Brown, the party leader who had lost the most seats at the election, however briefly in Number 10. Laws put it much more bluntly: 'It was clear that if we went into a Coalition with Labour, we would not be establishing a new government, we would be chaining ourselves to a decaying corpse' (Laws, 2010: 11 May). It would also have involved too much uncertainty, not just because of Brown's characteristic prevarication over the timing of his departure, but also because of the four months of uncertainty that would have ensued during a Labour leadership contest, the final outcome of which they could neither influence nor predict. In any event, the arithmetic wasn't there for a Liberal Democrat–Labour coalition to be viable, and there were serious doubts about Labour's ability to deliver on their side of any draft agreement because of divisions within Brown's negotiating team and within the parliamentary Labour Party. As so often happens in life, the Liberal Democrat negotiators preferred the certainties of a deal with the Conservatives to the multitude of uncertainties that a deal with Labour would have presented.

The second reason for the Liberal Democrats signing up to the coalition deal with the Conservatives is that it was the least worst option. Here we need to re-emphasize the earlier point that Clegg's party had not achieved the election outcome that they had hoped for: the Liberal Democrats had not won 100 seāts and were not in a position to boss the Coalition talks. But they did hold the balance of power and there was a strong sense among the party leadership that they simply could not be seen to duck that opportunity, however unfavourable the economic and political circumstances. Clegg was determined to kill forever the British myth (ironically propounded by the Conservatives during the election campaign) that hung parliaments automatically lead to instability. Perhaps Clegg's party was still scarred by their negative experiences of the short-lived Lib-Lab pact in the late 1970s, in which they had taken much of the blame for the failure of Callaghan's Labour Government. This factor may help explain why Clegg's negotiators had apparently planned for quite some time to embrace the idea of a full coalition with either of the two parties. It also may explain why at no point in the coalition talks did it occur to the Liberal Democrat negotiators that it might be in their party's long-terms interests *not* to do a deal with *either* main party. There was a feeling that if they did not enter into a full Coalition Government, then the Liberal Democrats would never be taken seriously again.

What is more curious, however, is the observation that the vast majority of Liberal Democrat MPs thought they had gained a good deal from the Conservatives.[7] In many respects they *had* struck a good deal. As one Liberal Democrat negotiator commented, the Conservatives had 'given us virtually the whole Lib Dem manifesto' (Kavanagh and Cowley, 2010: 216). And during the Liberal Democrats' key Tuesday meeting at which they voted to accept the Conservative deal, even Ashdown, the most pro-Labour person in his party, on reading the draft Coalition Agreement commented:

> I'm not happy with where we've arrived. I'm not happy at the death of the realignment of the left. But I can see the logic of where we are. I've looked at this document. It's amazing. (*Sunday Times*, 16 May 2010)

The Liberal Democrats became too fixated on the minutiae of what they had gained in terms of policy concessions from the Conservatives, particularly their long-term obsession with electoral reform. What they seemed unable to realize at the time was that their central concession to the Conservatives on the economy – agreeing to cut the deficit further and faster than Labour – trumped all their anorak manifesto commitments put together. Nor were they able to foresee that they would take nearly all of the blame and gain virtually none of the political credit for taking the tough decisions on spending within the Coalition. The irony was that while behind the scenes the Liberal Democrats were realizing Cable's aim of being 'quite influential if we go with the Tories' (*Sunday Times*, 16 May 2010), to the wider electorate they were merely breaking a series of solemn election promises, most notably on tuition fees.

Thus far, by entering into the Coalition with the Conservatives, the Liberal Democrats have borne the brunt of the blame from the voters for the failings of the new government. No amount of effort on the part of Liberal Democrat ministers to bolt 'fairness' artificially onto each and every cut in public expenditure seems to be working with the electorate. The Liberal Democrats now face a slow and painful death at the hands of the voters, beginning with the local and devolved elections during 2011. Despite such electoral pressure, the parliamentary party will probably cling even tighter to their Coalition partners at a national level, while locally they are forced to watch as the Liberal Democrat membership and support base crumbles before their eyes.

Back in April 1924, Lloyd George made a speech at Llanfairfechan in Wales, in which he predicted:

> Liberals are to be the oxen to drag the Labour wain over the rough roads of Parliament for two or three years, goaded along, and at the end of the journey, when there is no further use for them, they are to be slaughtered. That is the Labour idea of co-operation.

While the Liberal leader's prediction of the survival of Ramsay MacDonald's first government in 1924 proved inaccurate (it lasted less than nine months), if we were to insert the word 'Conservative' instead of 'Labour' in his words, then we have a chilling summary of the likely fate of the Liberal Democrats in the present Coalition.

Notes

1. On 2 March 2010, the 'Leaders' debates' were renamed the 'Prime Ministerial debates'.

2. This figure is arrived at by excluding the Speaker and the Deputy Speakers (none of whom vote, except in the event of a tie), as well as the Sinn Fein MPs who do not sit or vote in the House of Commons.
3. By the time of Saturday morning talks with the Liberal Democrats, Ed Balls and Harriet Harman were added, while Alistair Darling, as Chancellor of the Exchequer, wholly preoccupied in talks with other European finance ministers about the growing financial crisis in Europe, was not included. And by the time formal talks with the Liberal Democrats began on the Monday night, Labour's team was bereft of Harman, and now comprised Balls, Adonis, Miliband and Mandelson.
4. In the event, Lord Ashcroft's subsequent analysis of the failings of the Conservatives' election campaign was remarkably anodyne (Ashcroft, 2010).
5. The good personal chemistry between Clegg and Cameron had been forged to some extent as a result of an extended 45-minute impromptu chat during the launch of the New Supreme Court building in October 2009, after which they knew they could do business together (BBC2, 29 July 2010).
6. Labour may have aired the idea of putting the STV option on the ballot paper of a multi-option referendum, but there are real doubts about whether the parliamentary Labour Party would have accepted such a major concession.
7. In a joint meeting of the Liberal Democrat parliamentary party, peers and Federal Executive on the Tuesday night, 50 Liberal Democrat MPs voted in favour of a deal, with only Charles Kennedy and a few others abstaining. The peers voted 31-0, while the Federal Executive voted 27-1 in favour, with only former Lib Dem MP, David Rendel voting against (Kavanagh and Cowley, 2010: 220; 228).

References

Ashcroft, M. (2010) *Minority Verdict* (London: Biteback).

Ashdown, P. (2000) *The Ashdown Diaries, Volume One, 1988–1997* (London: Allen Lane).

Axelrod, R. (1970) *Conflict of Interest* (Chicago, IL: Markham).

BBC2 (2010) *Five Days That Changed Britain* (29 July).

Bale, T. (2010) *The Conservative Party from Cameron to Thatcher* (Cambridge: Polity).

Cameron, D. (2009) A Lib Dem–Tory Alliance Will Vanquish Labour. *The Observer*, 20 September.

Cowley, P., Darcy, D., Mellors, C., Neal, J .and Stuart, M. (2000) Mr. Blair's Loyal Opposition? The Liberal Democrats in Parliament. *British Elections and Parties Review*, 10: 100–16.

Cowley, P. and Stuart, M. (2003) Labour in Disguise? Liberal Democrat MPs, 1997–2001. *British Journal of Politics & International Relations*, 5: 393–404.

Cowley, P. and Stuart, M. (2004) From Labour Love-In to Bona Fide Party of Opposition. *Journal of Liberal History*, 43: 18–19.

Cowley, P. and Stuart, M. (2009) *Dissension amongst the Parliamentary Labour Party, 2008–2009. A Data Handbook* (Nottingham: University of Nottingham).

Crick, M. (2010) Was the Coalition Built on a Lie? *BBC Newsnight* blog (26 July).

Curtice, J. (2009) Back in Contention? The Conservatives' Electoral Prospects. *Political Quarterly*, 80: 172–83.

Denham, A. and Dorey, P. (2007) 'Meeting the Challenge?' The Liberal Democrats' Policy Review of 2005–2006, *Political Quarterly*, 78: 68–77.

Electoral Commission (2010) *Interim Report: Review of Problems at Polling Stations at Close of Poll on 6 May 2010*.

Fox, R. (2010) Five Days in May: A New Political Order Emerges. In A. Geddes and J. Tonge (eds.), *Britain Votes 2010* (Oxford: Oxford University Press), pp. 25–40.

Gilbert, S. (2009) *Uphill Challenge* (London: Conservative Party).

Kavanagh, D. and Cowley, P. (2010) *The British General Election of 2010* (Basingstoke: Palgrave Macmillan).

Laws, D. (2010) *22 Days in May* (London: Biteback).

Liberal Democrats (2010) *Liberal Democrat Manifesto 2010* (London: Liberal Democrat Party).

Mandelson, P. (2010) *The Third Man. Life at the Heart of New Labour* (London: HarperPress).

Marshall, P. and Laws, D. (eds.) (2004) *The Orange Book: Reclaiming Liberalism* (London: Profile Books).

Nelson, F. (2010) What to Do after a Three-Way Car Crash. *The Observer*, 31 October.

Norton, P. (2010) The Politics of Coalition. In N. Allen and J. Bartle (eds.), *Britain at the Polls* (London: Sage), ch. 9.

Oakeshott I., Woolf, M. and Oliver, J. (2010) Against the Wall. *Sunday Times*, 16 May.

Randall, E. (2007) Yellow versus Orange – Never a Fair Fight: An Assessment of Two Contributions to Liberal Politics Separated by Three-Quarters of a Century. *Political Quarterly*, 78: 40–9.

Snowdon, P. (2010) *Back from the Brink: The Extraordinary Fall and Rise of the Conservative Party* (London: HarperPress).

Treasury Select Committee (2010) Oral Evidence: Lord Turnbull (transcript), 28.

Part Two

Coalition Politics in Perspective

4
No Plan B: The Coalition Agenda for Cutting the Deficit and Rebalancing the Economy

Simon Lee

Introduction: Back to the Future, the Quest for a New Economic Model

In its 1979 White Paper *Government Expenditure Plans 1979–84*, the first Thatcher Government (in)famously asserted: 'Public expenditure is at the heart of Britain's present economic difficulties.' Indeed, the White Paper further stated: 'Over the past five years output has grown less than half as fast as it did over the previous 20 years, and a little over a third as fast as in other industrialised countries' (HM Treasury, 1979: 1). The inference of the latter statement was that public spending was the cause of Britain's 'economic difficulties' by crowding out private investment, innovation and enterprise. However, as the Treasury's own public spending statistics have subsequently shown, total managed expenditure between 1975–76 and 1979–80 had actually declined from 49.7 per cent to 44.6 per cent of GDP (HM Treasury, 2010a: 59). The more than halving in output growth appeared to be a result of the accompanying decline of public sector net investment during this period from 5.6 per cent to 2.3 per cent of GDP. Rather than crowding out the private sector, the state's intervention had been serving as a necessary corrective to a longstanding market failure to invest.

Thirty-one years after the previous occasion on which Conservative economic policy had embraced the 'crowding-out' thesis, the

Conservative–Liberal Democrat Coalition's *Spending Review 2010* document noted:

> Over the last decade, the UK's economy became unbalanced, and relied on unsustainable public spending and rising levels of public debt. For economic growth to be sustainable in the medium-term, it must be based on a broad-based economy supporting private sector jobs, exports, investment and enterprise. (HM Treasury, 2010b: 6)

As Chancellor of the Exchequer, George Osborne has asserted that this rebalancing would require a wholesale departure from the failed economic policy framework of the last decade which 'promised stability, prudence and an end to the [economic] cycle' but 'delivered instability, imprudence and the biggest boom followed by the deepest bust' (Osborne, 2010a). Indeed, rebalancing will require nothing less than a move away from 'an economic model based on unsustainable private and public debt' to 'a new model of economic growth that is rooted in more investment, more savings and higher exports' (Osborne, 2010a). In 1979, on the last occasion that the Conservative Party confronted an age of austerity and the seeming inevitability of the United Kingdom's relative economic decline, Sir Keith Joseph had argued that solving the union problem would be the key to Britain's recovery (Joseph, 1979). The union problem was duly solved, in Joseph's terms, but decline was not reversed. In union militancy, Joseph had mistaken the reaction to the decline of living standards and the social wage, for the principal cause of national decline. Thirty-two years later, solving the banking problem had become the key to national recovery.

The size of the task should not be underestimated. Osborne correctly suggested that 'rebalancing' the UK economy in these terms would require 'new policies and new institutions' (Osborne, 2010a). However, during its first eight months of office, the Coalition had shown little evidence that it had either the political imagination or the political ambition to bring about such a radical political economy. It would not be a straightforward matter of centralized, top-down, technocratic manipulation. In that respect, it would not constitute comfortable political territory for the British political and administrative elite, and would take it firmly out of its metropolitan comfort zone. In practice, it constituted not only the greatest policy challenge and political risk confronting the Coalition, but potentially the greatest challenge for a peacetime British government since the quest for full employment for the demobilizing armed forces in the immediate aftermath of the Second World War.

In the light of the scale of this challenge, this chapter explores the Cameron–Clegg Government's agenda for cutting the UK's budget deficit and rebalancing the economy. It contrasts the great urgency with which Osborne delivered both an 'emergency' budget and the spending review, with the relaxed attitude which the Coalition adopted towards the possible reform of the UK's banks and the bonuses which they have paid to their staff. It argues that in pledging 'I'll cut the deficit, not the NHS' (Conservative Party, 2010), David Cameron focused on only one of several key deficits which affect and reflect upon the UK's economic performance. Aside from the deficit in the public finances, there are also vital balance of payments' deficits in the trade in goods (especially manufactures) and the current account. This chapter concludes that the Coalition greatly underestimated the political, ideological and institutional prerequisites for 'rebalancing' the economy. However, this misjudgement is shared by the wider political elite. For world markets to be re-entered, or entered for the first time, by companies based in the UK, to close the deficit in trade in manufactures and accentuate the surplus in trade in service sufficiently to generate a current account surplus would require a very different sort of political economy and a very different set of political priorities. In the interim, with the UK facing falling living standards and the greatest squeeze on incomes since the 1920s, the principal danger facing the economy has been seen to be a return to the stagflation of the mid-1970s.

The New British Economic Model: Fiscal Conservatism and Rebalancing

Economic policy during the tenure of Cameron as leader of the Conservative Party, and Osborne as Shadow Chancellor (and now Chancellor of the Exchequer) has evolved through four phases. The new economic model implemented by the Coalition has constituted the fourth phase. The evolution of policy has often appeared to owe more to pragmatism and political expediency than deeply held conviction. During the first phase, from Cameron's election as party leader in December 2005 until the demise of Northern Rock in September 2007, Conservative economic policy had converged towards New Labour by agreeing that the proceeds of growth should be divided between additional resources for public services and higher private incomes. During the second phase of the evolution of Conservative economic policy, with the onset of a series of major financial crises in the UK's banking sector, Cameron and Osborne moved from convergence towards

New Labour to a critique of the huge levels of imprudent private and public debt crippling the British economy. With the onset of recession during the autumn of 2008, a third phase of economic policy developed during which fiscal conservatism was embraced and strenuous efforts were made to personalize the responsibility for the UK's economic malaise by identifying it with Gordon Brown and the Labour Party. Thus, it was asserted that 'Britain's economy is in a debt crisis: Labour's debt crisis' (Conservative Party, 2009).

The fourth phase of development of Conservative economic policy under Cameron and Osborne began in February 2010 with the sketching in Osborne's 2010 Mais Lecture of the outlines of a new economic model. This model would incorporate three elements: 'a new approach to macroeconomic and financial policy, where we seek to contain credit cycles as well as target price stability'; 'a new fiscal policy framework, with an Independent Office for Budget Responsibility to ensure that public debt is sustainable'; and 'a supply side revolution that releases the pent up enterprise and wealth creation of our country, encourages a nation of savers, and addresses the long term structural weaknesses that no government has ever properly tackled-like poor education and a welfare system that traps people in workless poverty' (Osborne, 2010a).

To deliver this new economic model, the Coalition Agreement identified 'deficit reduction and continuing to ensure economic recovery' as 'the most urgent issue facing Britain' (Conservative Party/Liberal Democrat Party, 2010). Honouring the pledge to introduce an emergency budget within 50 days of any coalition agreement to govern, Osborne's 22 June Budget statement asserted that the objective would be 'a new, balanced economy where we save, invest and export'; where 'the state does not take almost all our national income, crowding out private endeavour'; and where 'prosperity is shared among all sections and all parts of the country' (Osborne, 2010b). He also made some characteristically bold claims about his budget, maintaining it was 'a progressive Budget', delivered on behalf of 'a progressive alliance governing in the national interest'. It had paid for the past, planned for the future, supported a strong enterprise-led recovery, rewarded work and protected the most vulnerable in society (Osborne, 2010b).

To replace 'the intrinsic weakness in backward-looking fiscal rules', which New Labour had bequeathed and which Osborne claimed would mean that Brown's golden rule would be missed by £485 billion over the current economic cycle, Osborne would implement a fiscal mandate which would be forward-looking and composed of three elements. The mandate would be 'Structural – to give us flexibility to respond to external shocks'; 'Current – to protect the most productive public investment'; and 'Credible – because the Office for Budget Responsibility, not the Chancellor, will decide the output gap'. These elements would in turn be supplemented by 'a fixed target for debt, which in this Parliament is to ensure that debt is falling as a share of GDP by 2015–16' (Osborne, 2010b). Osborne's thesis was that 'The country has overspent; it has not been under-taxed' (Osborne, 2010b). Under his fiscal conservatism, net borrowing would fall from £149 billion or 10.1 per cent of GDP in 2010–11 to £60 billion in 2013–14, and to £20 billion or 1.1 per cent of GDP by 2015–16. During this period, public sector net debt would rise from 62 per cent of GDP in 2010–11 to 69 per cent in 2014–15, before falling to 67 per cent in 2015–16 (Osborne, 2010b). Osborne's budget measures would mean that 77 per cent of the fiscal consolidation would be achieved by spending cuts and 23 per cent through tax increases. By 2014–15, with the exception for the protected budgets for the NHS and international development, departmental budgets would have been cut by an average of 25 per cent in real terms over four years, compared to the Brown Government's planned average real reduction of 20 per cent for unprotected departments (Osborne, 2010b). To redress the 45 per cent real terms increase in welfare spending under New Labour to £192 billion, there would be cuts in welfare programmes delivering a saving of £11 billion a year by 2014–15. Furthermore, to promote 'a sustained, job-creating recovery', corporation tax would be cut by 1 per cent per annum over a four-year period to 24 per cent, 'the lowest rate of any major Western economy, one of the lowest rates in the G20, and the lowest rate this country has ever known'. Instead of implementing the Brown Government's proposed increase in small companies' tax from 21 to 22 per cent, it would instead be cut to 20 per cent (Osborne, 2010b). These tax cuts would be financed in large measure by an increase in VAT from 17.5 per cent to 20 per cent. In effect, Osborne was cutting taxes for enterprise by increasing taxation on consumption.

To deliver the Coalition's new, 'balanced' and market-led growth model, on 22 October, the spending review detailed Britain's 'unavoidable deficit reduction plan', forecast by the Institute for Fiscal Studies to be the 'tightest squeeze on total spending since the end of World War II' (Crawford, 2010). The review envisaged a total of £80.5 billion of expenditure savings by 2014–15, with Total Managed Expenditure planned to fall from 47.3 per cent of GDP in 2010–11 to 41 per cent of GDP in 2014–15. Allied to tax increases of £29.8 billion by 2014–15, this implied a total fiscal tightening of £110.3 billion by 2014–15 composed of 73 per cent in spending cuts and 27 per cent in tax rises (HM Treasury,

2010b). Given that the UK economy was forecast to grow by 2.7 per cent in 2014–15, but the state was planned to contract by around 6.3 per cent of GDP, the Coalition's plans assumed a 'crowding in' of investment and growth by the private sector equivalent to 9 per cent of GDP, or around £180 billion of output by 2015. This appeared at best highly optimistic and at worst a barely credible forecast.

The forecasts for future employment seemed equally incredible. The Government forecast that these cuts would result in the loss of 490,000 public sector jobs (later downsized to 330,000). Previous leaks from the Government had suggested that the Coalition believed cuts in public spending might result in up to 700,000 jobs being lost in the private sector. However, the Office for Budget Responsibility forecast that total employment would increase by 1.3 million jobs between 2010 and 2015. That meant the Coalition expected the private sector to create a net total of around 2.3 million jobs by the end of 2015. Jobs had not been created at this pace during the non-inflationary continual expansion of the economic boom from 1997 to 2007. It was hard to imagine why the private sector would now invest to create employment in such large numbers during an age of austerity.

This further dividend from 'balanced' growth seemed implausible given the past and recent performance of the UK economy, the parlous state of major export markets, and the evidence cited by Osborne himself of how long it had taken output and employment to recover from past financial crises (Reinhart and Rogoff, 2009). In the week before the spending review was published, the Office for National Statistics released the UK's trade statistics for August 2010. These revealed that, in the three months to August, the UK's deficit on trade in goods alone had been £24.434 billion, the worst figure since records began in 1697. The deficit on trade in goods and services had been £13.692 billion, the worst quarterly performance since such records were first kept in 1955 (Office for National Statistics, 2010a: 1).

The blame for having to embrace austerity through fiscal conservatism was laid firmly at the door of Brown and New Labour's mismanagement of the public finances. The Coalition contended that there was no alternative to fiscal retrenchment and public expectations of the future collective provision of welfare by the state should be reduced. However, the choices about public spending were quintessentially political choices, and not an unavoidable economic necessity. First, UK net public debt as a percentage of national income had rarely been as low during the past two centuries, and the long-term interest rates charged on government debt had rarely been lower. At the height of the Great Depression of the 1930s, net public debt had reached 177 per cent of GDP, and at the end of the Second World War, the UK had been indebted to the tune of 252 per cent of GDP in 1946–47. At a peak of 70.3 per cent of GDP in 2013–14 (HM Treasury, 2010c: 100), the UK would still be well below its annual average during most of the nineteenth and twentieth centuries. Second, the Coalition had emphasized the urgency of having to make £6.2 billion of immediate cuts during 2010–11 to restore the confidence of credit rating agencies and other financial traders. Within six months, Osborne would be announcing at Westminster the Coalition's willingness to provide billions of pounds of financial assistance to Ireland. This assistance to a 'friend in need' was deemed to be in the national interest (Osborne, 2010c: c.40). Only five years earlier, Osborne had written of the Irish economy: 'They have much to teach us, if only we are willing to learn' (Osborne, 2006). The sole lesson to be learnt from Ireland was of the danger that the irresponsible risk-taking and lending fostered by liberalized financial markets might pose to a generation of taxpayers when they were presented with the bill to pay for such spectacular market failures. Moreover, within eight months, in its supplementary estimates for public spending during 2010–11, the Treasury would announce that it would be seeking an extra £8.1 billion from Parliament (HM Treasury, 2011a: 3), more than eliminating the savings delivered by the June 2010 Budget.

Third, the Coalition had highlighted repeatedly the £43 billion annual cost of debt repayment, which had arisen from the growth in government borrowing. However, almost unnoticed, Her Majesty's Revenue and Customs was soon to admit that the government's overall tax gap ('the difference in tax collected and the tax that should be collected') had been estimated to be £42 billion in 2008–9, following deficits totalling £151 billion in the previous four financial years (Her Majesty's Revenue and Customs, 2010: 9). In these circumstances, and given the importance attached by Osborne to cutting the budget deficit, it was perhaps surprising that the Coalition had allocated only an additional £900 million over the duration of the spending review to bring in extra tax revenue of £7 billion a year by 2014–15, given that on current trends, more than £160 billion of tax would not have been paid or collected in that time. Fourth, Osborne had argued that the UK had overspent, but not been under-taxed. The truth, however, was that, on the revenue side, despite the spending review's planned tax increases, current tax receipts in 2014–15 at 38.8 per cent of GDP would still be only 1.6 per cent of GDP or £29 billion higher than in 2010–11 (HM Treasury, 2010b: 100). During the 18 years of Conservative government between May 1979 and May 1997, the average annual tax burden had been 1.4 per cent of GDP higher at 40.2 per cent of GDP (Chote, Crawford, Emmerson and Tetlow, 2010: 1).

Facing the Political Realities: Learning the Lessons of the 1980s

In its wider approach to macroeconomic policy and strategy for sustainable growth, the Conservative–Liberal Democrat Coalition Government has revived the same flawed 'crowding-out' thesis which had been implemented, and failed, during the first Thatcher Government. There was no place for industrial policy in Osborne's new economic model. Indeed, he had claimed that 'We all know that Government can't pick winners or transform the economy overnight', but nevertheless the state can work with the private sector 'to identify the impediments to growth' (Osborne, 2010a). Thus, Osborne had further asserted that 'We have learnt the mistakes of the past', but this had been belied by the fact that his new model had been based on the assumption that if the frontiers of the state investment and intervention were simply rolled back, the frontiers of the market, enterprise and entrepreneurship would spontaneously roll forward to fill the vacuum. It hadn't worked during the 1980s, and it would not work now.

At this juncture, Cameron and Osborne would do well to remember that for Thatcher necessity became the mother of intervention. As she recollected in her memoirs, in the face of a deep recession 'the political realities had to be faced' (Thatcher, 1993: 121). Her government had intervened on a massive scale, providing £990 million to save the state-owned car manufacturer BL from liquidation, writing off £3.5 billion of the state-owned British Steel's capital and allowing it to borrow an additional £1.5 billion. As a result, government spending on trade, industry and energy had actually doubled in real terms from £5.5 billion in 1978–79 to £11 billion in 1982–83. Thereafter, a series of state-owned industries, including BAE, Amersham International, ICL, British Telecom, INMOS, Jaguar, Rolls-Royce, Ferranti, British Shipbuilders and the Royal Ordnance Factories, had been restructured and had their balance sheets reordered, all at the taxpayers' expense, in preparation for privatization, which was to become one of the principal instruments of the Thatcher government's industrial policies (Lee, 1997). These interventions had been accompanied by the provision of major fiscal incentives for foreign manufacturers to direct their investment to the UK in order to enable it to re-enter world markets for manufactures. This pattern of intervention had been most conspicuous in the motor vehicle industry with the construction of new factories in Sunderland (Nissan), Burnaston (Toyota) and Swindon (Honda). Allied to the continuing and extensive taxpayer support for the military industries of the warfare state, most notably aerospace, the purportedly non-interventionist Thatcher Government had continued to pick winners throughout the 1980s.

There was an equally valuable lesson to be learnt from the Thatcher Government's policy towards the most dynamic markets in the private sector. Rather than allowing the City of London's financial markets to regenerate themselves through the Hayekian discovery process of market innovation and entrepreneurial risk-taking, the Thatcher Governments had intervened on an heroic scale, orchestrating a huge programme of liberalization and deregulation, culminating in the 'Big Bang' of 1986. Between 1981 and 1988, the state had also established and funded the London Docklands Development Corporation to channel more than £4 billion of taxpayers' subsidies into the creation of the Isle of Dogs' Enterprise Zone and allied projects. Together with a further £4 billion of state investment in the London Docklands Light Railway and Jubilee Line Tube extension, and billions of additional tax subsidies to private sector property developers, this dirigisme would eventually spawn the new Canary Wharf financial district. Osborne had only to look to the taxpayers' £1.2 trillion support for the City to witness the very same industrial policy in practice.

Bankers' Bonuses: The Political Contradictions of Capitalism

The speed with which the Coalition acted to tackle public debt and the deficit in the UK's public finances, as potential threats to financial stability and economic recovery, stood in vivid contrast to its relative inactivity in relationship to private debt and the potentially destabilizing deficit in the finances of the UK's banks, arising from their irresponsible risk-taking. Osborne contended that, 'while private sector was the cause of this crisis, public sector debt is likely to be the cause of the next one' (Osborne, 2010b). However, given the fact that the Coalition has acted so quickly to curb public debt, but had done so little to prevent a repetition of a private debt-led crisis, and also given that the burden of private corporate and individual debt exceeds public debt, that contention was highly dubious.

At the end of December 2010, public sector net debt in the UK stood at £889.1 billion or 59.3 per cent of GDP. However, with the effects of the taxpayers' rescue of UK banks included, net debt stood at £2,322.7 billion or 154.9 per cent. Thus, rescuing the banks had added £1,433.6

billion or 95.6 per cent of GDP to the national debt (Office for National Statistics, 2011a: 1). By contrast, during Brown's tenure as Chancellor, he had allowed public sector net debt to increase from a low of £307.1 billion or 29.1 per cent of GDP in February 2002 to £512.9 billion or 36.5 per cent of GDP by the end of May 2007, the point at which Brown succeeded Tony Blair as Prime Minister (Office for National Statistics, 2010b: 1–2). This meant that, during the period when Osborne had accused Brown of borrowing recklessly and failing to fix the roof while the sun was shining, the national debt had increased by 7.4 per cent of GDP, a relatively small price to pay for Brown's alleged political failures compared with the subsequent cost of rescuing the banks and dealing with a massive market failure.

Paradoxically, the scale of the financial services sector's dependency on the taxpayer, and the City of London's subsidy addition, has become ever more evident during the Coalition's tenure. The National Audit Office reported that by December 2010 the taxpayer had invested £124 billion in the banks, and was still liable for up to £512 billion through the various schemes of support which had been provided by the state. Furthermore, the paper loss on the 83 per cent of shares in Royal Bank of Scotland and the 41 per cent of shares in Lloyds owned by the taxpayer was £12.5 billion, with the state having to pay 'some £5 billion a year (£10 billion so far) on the Government borrowing raised to finance the purchase of shares and loans to banks' – a cost only partly offset by the £9.91 billion in fees and interest received by the Treasury (National Audit Office, 2010: 6). Beyond the bailout of UK banks, Andrew Haldane, Executive Director of the Bank of England, noted that the taxpayer-supported banks enjoyed a £177 billion subsidy from 2007 to 2009 (equivalent to an annual average subsidy of £59 billion), compared to 'standalone' banks, because their support meant that their stronger credit rating by agencies allowed them to fund their borrowing at a significantly lower cost (Haldane, 2010: 25). The New Economics Foundation calculated this annual subsidy for the five biggest UK banks as 'in the range of £30 billion', but has identified much wider 'feather-bedding of financial services' (New Economics Foundation, 2011: 3).

During the 1970s, at a time of fiscal retrenchment during a previous age of austerity, Samuel Brittan had identified what he termed the economic contradictions of democracy where 'the generation of excessive expectations' and 'the disruptive effects of the pursuit of group self-interest in the market place' had resulted in an excessive burden being placed on 'the "sharing out" function of government' (Brittan, 1976: 98). By contrast, one of the principal features of the contemporary age of austerity has been what might be termed the political contradictions of capitalism. On the one hand, the taxpayer has expected the state to take decisive action to ensure that there is no future repetition of the fiscal and economic austerity inflicted on a generation of workers, consumers and savers by the irresponsible risk-taking made possible by liberalized markets and their ineffectual, risk-based regulation. The taxpayer has also expected the state to tax those responsible for causing the crisis so that they take full fiscal responsibility for paying a much greater percentage of the economic costs (if not the social and political costs) of the financial crisis they precipitated. On the other hand, the state has found itself confronting a scenario where the banks have resisted steadfastly the demands for greater and more effective regulation and taxation. The result has been that under the Coalition, it appears that the proceeds of banking profit have been largely privatized, and the risks and costs of financial market failure socialized.

In the initial Agreement and subsequent Programme for Government, the Coalition had affirmed that it would 'reform the banking system to avoid repeat of the financial crisis'; bring forward 'detailed proposals for robust action to tackle unacceptable bonuses in the financial sector' which would in turn reduce risk (HM Government, 2010: 9). In his June emergency budget statement, Osborne had suggested: 'In putting in order the nation's finances, we must remember that this was a crisis that started in the banking sector.' Indeed, he argued, 'The failures of the banks imposed a huge cost on the rest of society.' Osborne believed that it was 'fair and it is right that in future banks should make a more appropriate contribution, which reflects the many risks they generate' (Osborne, 2010b). Paradoxically, when Osborne announced an increase in the bank levy to be introduced in 2011, it was only by £800 million to £2.5 billion (HM Treasury, 2011b). This was an insignificant sum when set against the £1,200 billion which the taxpayer had found to support the banks, and anticipated bank profits for 2011 of more than £25 billion.

During its first eight months in office, the Coalition failed to deliver the promised 'robust action'. The Coalition's prevarication and weakness was demonstrated when the details of Project Merlin, the accord between the major UK banks and the Cameron–Clegg Government, were published on the 9 February 2011. Bank lending to UK businesses during 2009 had actually contracted by 1.8 per cent, and then by a further 9.3 per cent and 8.2 per cent during the first two quarters of 2010 (Bank of England, 2011: 4). Under Project Merlin, the banks agreed to gross lending of £190 billion in 2011 to UK businesses (compared to £179 billion in 2010), including £76 billion for small and medium-sized enterprises

(SMEs) (compared to £66 billion in 2010). However, this agreement was accompanied by a series of major qualifications, including that lending would proceed only 'should sufficient demand materialize' and with each bank's 'lending expectations, capacity and willingness' to be 'subject to its normal commercial objectives, credit standards and processes and regulatory obligations, as well as the availability of the required funding' (Project Merlin, 2011: 2–3). Given that the Bank of England had estimated that UK banks would need to refinance 'around £400 billion to £500 billion of wholesale debt' at the end of 2012 (Bank of England, 2010: 8), the availability of funding could not be taken as a given.

Project Merlin did not incorporate a single sanction should the banks fail to deliver the agreed gross lending. At the same time, while the banks agreed that 'the aggregate 2010 bonus pool (including deferrals) for their UK-based staff will be lower than that of 2009' (Project Merlin, 2011: 4), this would not extend to the more than 350,000 bankers employed overseas by these banks. Furthermore, the banks would undertake this very limited action only because of their understanding of 'the public mood' and their desire to respond to it (Project Merlin, 2011: 4), rather than any acceptance of the dubious morality of the epic scale of their rewards, during an era of austerity brought about by their collective failure. The banks' seeming indifference to the Coalition's threats of 'robust action' was demonstrated less than a week after the publication of the accord when Barclays reported pre-tax profits of £6.07 billion, announced group performance-related pay down 7 per cent to £3.4 billion (including a 12 per cent decline for staff at Barclays Capital, the bank's investment banking arm). Barclays also announced that it would no longer be providing loans for equipment to SMEs with a turnover of less than £5 million. It was tantamount to the confiscation of Merlin's magic wand and the rewarding of the banking knights of the Round Table with large bonuses for mortgaging Camelot. Vince Cable, the Business Secretary, who had been a trenchant critic of the banks in Opposition, described these 'enormous' bank bonuses as 'offensive' (Cable, 2011), but, having previously threatened to 'bring the government down' (Cable, 2010), simply acquiesced. The only act of dissent came from Cable's Liberal Democrat colleague, former City financier and spokesman in the House of Lords, Lord Oakeshott, who stood down from his role, describing Treasury negotiators for Project Merlin as 'an awful combination of arrogance and incompetence' (BBC, 2011). It appeared Oakeshott had the courage of Cable's convictions.

Conclusion: April is The Cruellest Month

The publication of the major UK banks' annual results, and attendant bonuses, occurred against the backdrop of a developing picture of austerity for the vast majority of the British people, with the looming threat of a return to the combination of economic stagnation and inflation not witnessed since the 1970s. January 2011's inflation figures witnessed consumer price inflation rising to 4 per cent, twice the Coalition's 2 per cent inflation target. Aside from Osborne's January increase in Value Added Tax (VAT) from 17.5 per cent to 20 per cent, the principal source of inflation had been imported goods, with gas prices having risen by over 15 per cent and food prices by about 20 per cent during the past three months (Office for National Statistics, 2011b: 1). By contrast, average weekly earnings (including bonuses) had risen by only 1.8 per cent between October–December 2009 and October–December 2010. Unemployment for October to December 2010 had also risen by 44,000 to reach 2.49 million, with the unemployment rate for people aged 16 to 24 having increased by 1.5 per cent of 66,000 to reach 965,000, the highest figure since comparable records had begun in 1992 (Office for National Statistics, 2011c: 2).

The Governor of the Bank of England, Mervyn King, warned that real take-home pay had been squeezed by around 12 per cent by higher import and energy prices and taxes, which meant that during 2010 real wages had fallen 'sharply' despite rising productivity. Moreover, real wages would be likely to fall during 2011, because of inflation and the rise in VAT, meaning that they would be 'likely to be no higher than they were in 2005'. Indeed, King noted that 'One has to go back to the 1920s to find a time when real wages fell over a period of six years' (King, 2011: 4). By contrast to this age of austerity, King's own pension pot had recently been topped up by more than one third from £3.95 million to £5.36 million by the Court of the Bank of England, enabling him on retirement in 2013 to draw an annual income equivalent to £198,200 (Aldrick, 2011).

Output still remained 4 per cent below the level it had reached prior to the financial crisis, and close to 10 per cent below a continuation of its pre-crisis trend (King, 2011: 6). There remained little sign of Osborne's 'rebalancing' and an investment-, export- and private sector-led recovery. During the third quarter of 2010, total business investment, in seasonally adjusted terms, had risen by only 3.1 per cent to £30.2 billion when compared with the previous quarter, but total manufacturing investment had actually fallen by 2.5 per cent to a paltry £2.6 billion (Office for National Statistics, 2010c 1). Despite the continuing weakness of sterling after its 25 per cent depreciation since 2007, in December 2010, the UK's seasonally adjusted deficit on trade in goods and services had actually risen to £4.8 billion, while the deficit for 2010 had also widened to £46.2 billion, compared with only £29.7 billion in 2009. The deficit on goods alone for 2010 had soared by £14.8 billion to £97.2 billion, more than wiping out the £51 billion on trade in services, a small decline from the £52.7 billion in 2009 (Office for National Statistics, 2011d: 2).

When millions of workers receive their pay slips in April 2011, and the full fiscal consequences of increases in employee national insurance and cuts in welfare benefits for their already diminishing living standards become evident, following the revelation of billions of pounds of lightly taxed bonuses, Cameron's mantra of 'We're all in this together' will never have sounded so hollow. With a clear majority of the Coalition's Cabinet members already enjoying millionaire status, and her Majesty's Revenue and Custom projecting that during the tax year 2010–11, 275,000 individuals would pay £41.4 billion in tax – no less than 25.7 per cent of the total income tax paid (Wallop, 2011) – the evidence of growing inequalities in income and wealth were becoming more evident after less than a year of Coalition Government.

Rebalancing the economy will require a much larger political project than fiscal conservatism and simply rolling back the frontiers of state expenditure in the hope that the market will spontaneously fill the resulting vacuum. The choice facing the Cameron–Clegg Government is not whether to intervene or to have an industrial policy. For more than 300 years, since the establishment of the Bank of England, the British developmental state has intervened almost continually to nurture the international competitiveness of defence industries and the City of London. This longstanding pattern of intervention will have to be extended to other sectors of the economy if the UK's balance of payments' deficit is not to reach such destabilizing proportions that it triggers a new crisis.

In 1985, a House of Lords' Select Committee report forecast that the UK's poor performance in manufacturing undoubtedly contained 'the seeds of a major political and economic crisis in the foreseeable future' (House of Lords, 1985: 56). This prediction was reiterated to the Major Government in 1991 when another House of Lords' Select Committee report warned, in the face of a declining manufacturing base, that 'The implications for our future prosperity are grave' (House of Lords, 1991: 29). That major political and economic crisis has now manifested itself for the Coalition. The implications for the future prosperity of the UK, and its political and social cohesion, are indeed grave. For more than

30 years, the implications of deindustrialization for prosperity had been hidden by increases in consumer spending, fuelled initially by North Sea oil and privatization receipts, and latterly by the financial innovations which enabled unprecedented levels of consumer borrowing and the resulting £1.45 trillion of personal debt to maintain artificially high, but ultimately unsustainable living standards. Those policy options are no longer available (Lee, 2010). The Government urgently needs to develop an Economic Plan B or the image of the UK presented to the world at the 2012 Olympics will be of a broken economy in decline and a broken society in turmoil, rather than a nation at ease with itself.

References

Aldrick, P. (2011) Bank of England Boosts Mervyn King's Pension by £1.4m. *The Daily Telegraph*, 31 January.

Bank of England (2010) *Financial Stability Report*, Issue No. 28, December (London: Bank of England).

Bank of England (2011) *Trends in Lending: January 2011* (London: Bank of England).

BBC (2011) Lib Dem Lord Oakeshott Resigns after Attack on Banks. *BBC News*, 9 February. bbc.co.uk/news/uk-politics-12411664 (accessed 9 February 2011).

Brittan, S. (1976) The Economic Contradictions of Democracy. In A. King (ed.), *Why is Britain Becoming Harder to Govern?* (London: British Broadcasting Corporation).

Chote, R., Crawford, R., Emmerson, C. and Tetlow, G. (2010) *The Tax Burden under Labour: 2010 Election Briefing Note No. 4* (London: Institute for Fiscal Studies).

Cable, V. (2010) I Could Bring Down the Coalition If I'm Pushed. *The Daily Telegraph*, 20 December.

Cable, V. (2011) Interview, *Andrew Marr Show*, BBC1, 13 February. www.bbc.co.uk/news/entertainment-arts-12443223 (accessed 13 February 2011).

Conservative Party (2009) *Labour's Debt Crisis* (London: Conservative Party).

Conservative Party (2010) I'll Cut the Deficit, not the NHS. Speech to launch the Conservative Party's draft health manifesto, London, 4 January.

Conservative Party/Liberal Democrat Party (2010) *Conservative Liberal Democrat Coalition Negotiations Agreements Reached*, 11 May (London: Conservative Party/Liberal Democrats).

Crawford, R. (2010) *Where Did the Axe Fall?* (London: Institute for Fiscal Studies).

Haldane, A. (2010) *The $100 Billion Question*. Comments given by the Executive Director, Financial Stability, Bank of England, Institute of Regulation and Risk, Hong Kong, 30 March.

Her Majesty's Revenue and Customs (2010) *Measuring Tax Gaps 2010* (London: Her Majesty's Revenue and Customs).

HM Government (2010) *The Coalition: Our Programme for Government* (London: The Cabinet Office).

HM Treasury (1979) *The Government's Expenditure Plans 1980/81*, Cmnd 7746 (London: The Stationery Office).

HM Treasury (2010a) *Public Expenditure Statistical Analyses 2010*, Cm 7890 (London: The Stationery Office).

HM Treasury (2010b) *Spending Review 2010, Cm. 7942* (London: The Stationery Office).

HM Treasury (2010c) *Budget 2010, HC61* (London: The Stationery Office).

HM Treasury (2011) *Central Government Supply Estimates 2010–11, HC 790* (London: The Stationery Office).

HM Treasury (2011) Bank Levy Rates to Be Increased Raising £800m more in 2011. HM Treasury press release 14/11, 8 February.

House of Lords (1985) *Overseas Trade*, Report of the House of Lords' Select Committee, HL 238-I (London: Her Majesty's Stationery Office).

House of Lords (1991) *Innovation in Manufacturing Industry*, Report of the House of Lords' Select Committee on Science and Technology, HL18-I, 1990-91 (London: Her Majesty's Stationery Office).

Joseph, Sir K. (1979) *Solving the Union Problem is the Key to Britain's Recovery* (London: Centre for Policy Studies).

King, M. (2011) Speech given by the Governor of the Bank of England, Civic Centre, Newcastle, 25 January.

Lee, S. (1997) Industrial Policy and British Decline. In A. Cox, S. Lee and J. Sanderson, *The Political Economy of Modern Britain* (Cheltenham: Edward Elgar).

Lee, S. (2010) Necessity as the Mother of Intervention: The Industrial Policy Debate in England. *Local Economy*, 25(8), December: 622–30.

National Audit Office (2010) *Maintaining the Financial Stability of UK Banks: Update on the Support Schemes, Report by the Comptroller and Auditor General, HC 676, Session 2010–2011* (London: National Audit Office).

New Economics Foundation (2011) *Feather-bedding Financial Services: Are British Banks Getting Hidden Subsidies?* (London: The New Economics Foundation).

Office for National Statistics (2010a) *Balance of Payments: 3rd Quarter 2010* (Newport: Office for National Statistics).

Office for National Statistics (2010b) *UK Trade: September 2010* (Newport: Office for National Statistics).

Office for National Statistics (2010c) *Business Investment Revised Results: 3rd Quarter 2010* (Newport: Office for National Statistics).

Office for National Statistics (2011a) *Public Sector Finances: December 2010* (Newport: Office for National Statistics).

Office for National Statistics (2011b) *Consumer Price Indices: January 2011* (Newport: Office for National Statistics).

Office for National Statistics (2011c) *UK Trade: December 2010* (Newport: Office for National Statistics).

Office for National Statistics (2011d) *Labour Market Statistics: February 2011* (Newport: Office for National Statistics).

Osborne, G. (2006) Look and Learn from across the Irish Sea. *The Times*, 23 February.

Osborne, G. (2010a) A New Economic Model. Mais Lecture, London, 24 February.

Osborne, G. (2010b) *Budget Statement*, 22 June.

Osborne, G. (2010c) Financial Assistance (Ireland), *HC Debates*, 22 November, col. 40.

Project Merlin (2011) *Banks' Statement*, 9 February.

Reinhart, C. and Rogoff, K. (2009) *This Time is Different: Eight Centuries of Financial Folly* (Princeton, NJ: Princeton University Press).

Thatcher, M. (1993) *The Downing Street Years* (London: HarperCollins).

Wallop, H. (2011) Top 1% of Workers Pay Quarter of All Income Tax. *Daily Telegraph*, 13 February.

5
The Con–Lib Agenda in Education: Learning the Hard Way?

Simon Griffiths

In December 2010, breaking with the Coalition Agreement, 21 Liberal Democrat MPs voted against the Government's proposals to raise tuition fees in higher education. A further 28 Liberal Democrats voted in favour of the proposals, despite having signed a pre-election pledge to 'vote against any increase in fees in the next parliament' – a promise repeated in the party's 2010 manifesto. The vote marked the biggest challenge the Coalition had faced. It contributed to a new low in the polls for the Liberal Democrats and raised questions about the electoral future of the party, its ideological direction, leadership and the survival of the Coalition. Education policy, more than any other issue, has revealed underlying tensions surrounding what seemed, upon its agreement in the Rose Garden at 10 Downing Street in May 2010, to be an unexpected but happy marriage.

In this chapter, I focus on the Coalition's education policies in two areas: schools and higher education. I set out the principal developments and, where appropriate, the effects of the 2010 spending review; the degree to which there is continuity with the policies of the previous administration; and the extent to which schools and higher education have proved to be a contentious area within the Coalition. There is much else that could have been written about: early years intervention, apprenticeships, the scrapping of the Educational Maintenance Allowance or the 'bonfire' of quangos, such as the General Teaching Council for England and the Qualifications and Curriculum Development Agency. However, I have focused on the two areas that have generated most debate since the 2010 General Election. I argue that in some cases the radical marketization of public services is likely to have a deeply damaging effect, and conclude that higher education (at the time of writing) has been the issue that has most destabilized the Coalition, and which has most obviously split the Liberal Democrat Party between its economically and socially liberal sides.

Schools Policy

One of the flagship policies of the Coalition has been the introduction of a 'Pupil Premium'. The policy was put forward by both Coalition partners in their manifestos, although details varied. The Premium was described as a 'priority policy' by the Liberal Democrats (Liberal Democrat Party, 2010: 7, 34, 101); while the Conservatives argued that 'we can't go on giving the poorest children the worst education' and saw the Pupil Premium ('extra funding for children from disadvantaged backgrounds') as the solution (Conservative Party, 2010: 53). Given the agreement over a policy of this kind, plans for a Pupil Premium were set out in the Conservative and Liberal Democrat Coalition Agreement, reached on 11 May 2010. The Agreement stated that the Coalition would 'fund a significant premium for disadvantaged pupils from outside the schools budget by reductions in spending elsewhere' (Conservative Party and Liberal Democrat Party, 2010: 1).

The Comprehensive Spending Review (CSR) of 22 November 2010 confirmed the introduction of 'a substantial new premium worth £2.5 billion targeted on the educational development of disadvantaged pupils' (HM Treasury, 2010: 7). This was expanded upon in the Schools' White Paper, *The Importance of Teaching*, published two days later, which argued that reforms to the way in which schools are funded were needed, both to 'help the most disadvantaged and encourage new providers into the state school system' (Department for Education, 2010a: 80). The White Paper confirmed that the new Pupil Premium would provide 'additional money for each deprived pupil in the country' (Department for Education, 2010a: 81) and that '£2.5 billion a year on top of existing schools spending will be spent on the Pupil Premium by 2014–15' (Department for Education, 2010a: 81). The Government argued that the policy would mean:

> head teachers [would] have more money to spend on offering an excellent education to [poorer] children: it will also make it more likely that schools will want to admit less affluent children; and it will make it more attractive to open new Free Schools in the most deprived parts of the country. (Department for Education, 2010a: 81)

However, the White Paper also noted that 'This money will not be ring-fenced at school level as we believe that schools are in the best position to decide how the premium should be used to support their pupils' (Department for Education, 2010a: 81).

Support for the policy was stronger in theory than in practice. At the time of writing it is unclear how the Government will target the Premium, with options including the number of children entitled to free school meals or the use of 'pupil level annual school census data'. Several other details are also yet to be confirmed. The left-of-centre think tank the Institute for Public Policy Research (IPPR) supported the Premium, but questioned the devolution of power over how the money is spent down to school level, arguing that it was 'concerned that schools will not spend these funds on the children for whom they are intended' (Clifton and Muir, 2010: 2). An earlier response from the independent economic research centre the Institute for Fiscal Studies (IFS) was similarly cautious, arguing that while

> in principle, a Pupil Premium could narrow the achievement gap between advantaged and disadvantaged pupils . . . Schools are unlikely to actively recruit more disadvantaged pupils as a result of the Pupil Premium: the premium would need to be very high to sufficiently reduce the disincentive for schools to attract such pupils, and schools' ability to select pupils is also limited to some extent by the School Admissions Code. The Pupil Premium may lead to a small reduction in covert selection by schools but is unlikely to significantly reduce social segregation. (Chowdry, Greaves et al., 2010: 2)

Much of the specific criticism for the Premium came over its funding. The Chancellor announced in the CSR that there would be 'a real increase in the money for schools, not just next year or the year after, as the previous Government once promised, but for each of the next four years. The schools budget will rise from £35 billion to £39 billion. Even as pupil numbers greatly increase, we will ensure that the cash funding per pupil does not fall'. However, he continued: 'We will *also* introduce a new £2.5 billion Pupil Premium, which supports the education of disadvantaged children and will provide a real incentive for good schools to take pupils from poorer backgrounds' (Parliamentary Debates, 2010, emphasis added). The Coalition Agreement had explicitly stated that the Premium would be funded from 'outside' the schools budget (as implied by the Chancellor's use of the word 'also') by making reductions elsewhere – a statement repeated in the *The Importance of Teaching*, which promised 'additional money', and the CSR, which promised 'new' money (all cited above).

The Coalition was left making two seemingly contradictory claims: either the schools budget was being cut in real terms and the Pupil Premium was additional money; or the school budget was not being cut, but the Pupil Premium was included in – not additional to – the total budget. Opponents of the Coalition made much mileage out of this difficulty (for example, Katwala, 2010).

The redistributive nature of the Pupil Premium also means that some schools with pupils from better-off backgrounds will have to make significant cuts. This was made explicit by the Secretary of State for Education, Michael Gove, when he admitted that 'there will be some schools that will have less' (Prince, 2010). Indeed, the IFS has estimated that 87 per cent of secondary pupils and 60 per cent of primary pupils are in schools where funding will fall (Harrison, 2010). A leaked Treasury report suggested that as many as 40,000 teaching jobs could be lost (Stratton, 2010). The extent of the changes in the schools budget led to a backlash against the Pupil Premium, particularly in the right-wing press, which strongly associated the scheme with the Liberal Democrats, despite its existence in both Coalition partners' manifestos. *The Daily Mail*, for example, argued that schools in 'middle-class' areas were being hit twice, from cuts to the building programme (the news of which was mismanaged by the Department and caused Gove early difficulties in his role) and from the redistribution of money as a result of the Pupil Premium (Shipman, 2010). One could argue that if, as it has been historically understood, equality is associated with the left, then the Pupil Premium is a left-wing policy introduced in the context of a right-wing attempt to reduce the size and scope of the state – the traditional vehicle for a more equal society.

A second important development in schools policy is over devolution of power to Academies and Free Schools. The Academies Act 2010 was one of the first pieces of legislation to be passed by the Coalition. It aims to make it possible for all state schools in England to gain Academy status. Academies are publicly funded independent schools, free from local authority and national government control. Other freedoms include setting the pay and conditions for staff, freedoms concerning the delivery of the curriculum and the ability to change the length of their terms and school days (Department for Education, 2010b). Most Academies are at secondary level, though there are some at primary. In May 2010, Gove wrote to every head teacher in England to encourage them to apply for Academy status (Shepherd, 2010). The idea is an extension of Grant Maintained Schools introduced by former Conservative Secretary of State for Education Kenneth Baker in 1988 (Baker, 2010) as well as the early

Academies brought in by New Labour from 2000. However, the Coalition has pushed forward the idea with more strength than the previous Labour administration and seems more relaxed about the lack of central control over Academies than many in the Labour Party (Griffiths, 2009: 107).

The Academies Act also made possible the introduction of 'additional schools', more commonly known as 'Free Schools'. This was a part of the Coalition Agreement, which agreed to 'promote the reform of schools in order to ensure that new providers can enter the state school system in response to parental demand' (HM Government, 2010: 28). Derived from Charter Schools in the USA and Free Schools in Sweden, English Free Schools are all-ability state-funded schools, free of local authority control. Under the new plans it will become much easier for charities, universities, businesses, educational groups, teachers and groups of parents to set up new schools (Department for Education, 2010c). Critics of the model have attacked, among other things, the freedoms these new schools have – described by one critic as their ability to teach 'creationism instead of literacy' (Sellgren, 2010); the effect that these schools could have in increasing segregation (Wiborg, 2010: 14–15); and the lack of demand for them among parents (BBC, 2011).

There is some degree of policy continuity between the Coalition and New Labour on schools' policy. The introduction of a Pupil Premium and of Academies and Free Schools is part of the increasing use of market mechanisms in the school system. Academies and Free Schools mark a long-term move from a (theoretically) universal service to one in which the school system is shaped by parental choice, with the quasi-market subsidized by a premium for poor pupils to increase social justice. (A more radical application came from the comedian Paul Merton, who once joked that it would sometimes be easier if parents were given choice of children, rather than just schools.) The idea for the Pupil Premium is said to have originated from Julian Le Grand in the 1980s, writing at the time as a 'market socialist', who originally described a 'positively discriminating voucher' (Freedman and Horner, 2008: 4). From 2003 to 2005 Le Grand became a senior policy adviser to Tony Blair, focusing on introducing choice and competition into education and health care and there are obvious overlaps between Blair's public service agenda and that of the Coalition. The Gove reforms mark a continuation of the 'marketization' of the school system by allowing a greater diversity of provision of schools to increase parental choice and the use of market incentives to persuade schools to compete for poorer pupils.

The Schools' White Paper *The Importance of Teaching*, in which the Pupil Premium was set out, also introduced a plethora of further areas for change. In particular, as the name of the White Paper implies, there was a focus on teacher quality and leadership. The White Paper set out measures to raise the quality of new entrants to the profession and provide better training and development for existing teachers (including the development of a national network of new Teaching Schools). It also set out stricter measures to encourage good behaviour, such as strengthening the authority and disciplinary powers of teachers and the provision of more information on behaviour and safety in schools' Ofsted reports. In addition, the White Paper introduced greater freedom over teaching the National Curriculum, reforms to qualifications, better information on school performance – in particular through sharper performance tables (an important component of a more market-driven schools system in which informed parental choice of school drives up standards) – and it encourages schools to work together to improve quality (Department for Education, 2010a).

Higher Education Policy

The Coalition Agreement committed the Government to waiting for Lord Browne's final report on higher education funding. It was recognized at the time that the future funding of higher education was a divisive issue, which split parties as well as dividing them from one another. As such, the Coalition Agreement noted that 'If the response of the Government to Lord Browne's report is one that Liberal Democrats cannot accept, then arrangements will be made to enable Liberal Democrat MPs to abstain in any vote' (Conservative Party and Liberal Democrat Party, 2010: 5).

In November 2009, John Browne, the former Group Chief Executive of BP and a cross-bench peer, agreed to lead a report making 'recommendations to Government on the future of fees policy and financial support for full and part-time undergraduate and postgraduate students' (The Independent Review of Higher Education Funding and Student Finance website, 2010). Browne had been approached by Lord Mandelson, then Labour Secretary of State for Business, Innovation and Skills. Mandelson discussed the Review's membership with David Willetts, at the time the Conservative Shadow Universities Secretary, to ensure Conservative 'buy-in' and to make sure that both parties were 'committed to ensuring its independent nature' (Gill, 2009).

At the time the Liberal Democrats criticized both Labour and the Conservatives for agreeing on an inquiry that would report after the 2010 election, effectively taking much of the electoral heat out of the debate (*The Independent*, 2009). The party went into the 2010 General Election on a manifesto pledge to 'scrap unfair university tuition fees' (Liberal Democrat Party, 2010: 33) with every Liberal Democrat MP elected in 2010 – much to their subsequent discomfort – signing a pledge stating that they would 'vote against any increase in fees' (NUS, 2010). Reacting to the appointment of Lord Browne in November 2009, Stephen Williams, then Liberal Democrat spokesperson for Innovation, Universities and Skills, said: 'This review is nothing but a conspiracy between Labour and the Tories designed to keep plans to hike up tuition fees off the agenda until after the General Election. Mandelson has shown he will do whatever it takes to shut out any debate on the future of tuition fees, either in Parliament or the country' (Garner, 2009).

The Browne Review, *Securing a Sustainable Future for Higher Education: an independent review of Higher Education Funding and Student Finance*, published its findings on 12 October 2010. Among other things it argued:

- There should be no limit on fees charged by universities.
- The Government will fully underwrite fees charged up to £6,000.
- Universities would be subject to a levy on all fees charged above that level. The university would keep a diminishing proportion of fees over this level, but there would be no upper limit to fees a university could charge.
- Public investment should continue at a level similar to the current one for certain courses, which are largely in the sciences.

The Browne Review also proposed radical changes to the university system:

- A new body, the Higher Education Council, would be responsible for, among other things, investing in priority courses, setting and enforcing quality levels and improving access. It should have the power to bail out struggling institutions and would be able to explore options, such as mergers and takeovers, if institutions face financial failure.
- All new academics with teaching responsibilities should undertake a teaching qualification.
- New providers would be allowed to offer higher education teaching.
- An Access and Success fund should be set up to help universities recruit and retain students from disadvantaged backgrounds. Universities charging more than £7,000 a year would be subject to increased scrutiny over student access.

Browne argued that the funding system would allow a 10 per cent increase in university places over three years. The report modelled an 80 per cent cut in the teaching grant to universities, showing a slight drop in their overall income if all universities charged fees of £6,000, and a slight rise if they all charged £7,000.

Finally, in terms of student funding Browne proposed that:

- Students should not have to pay any tuition fees up front.
- When their earnings reach £21,000, graduates would begin to repay loans back and interest would be charged at the cost of borrowing to the Government, plus inflation.
- All students would be entitled to flat-rate maintenance loans.
- Unpaid student debt would be written off after 30 years.
- Part-time students would be eligible for loans for their fees. (BBC, 2010a; Independent Review of Higher Education Funding and Student Finance, 2010)

The Browne Report rejected the main alternative option, that of a graduate tax. It argued that a graduate tax would lead to a large, short-term funding gap – estimating it would take until around 2041–42 until the gap was met through a tax after graduation. The report also argued that a graduate tax would not provide a mechanism to improve student experience, whereas a loans system empowers the student as consumer.

David Willetts, the Minister of State for Universities and Science (a job title which implies a prioritization of sciences over arts and humanities), announced the Government's response to the Browne Review on 3 November 2010. Although the thrust of the Review was accepted, there were some differences. In particular, the Government put forward an absolute cap on fees of £9,000 per year. This was in the face of opposition from some elite universities which were threatening that any cap would lead to their withdrawal from the state system entirely (Garner, 2010: 22). In an effort to mitigate criticisms that the Review would discourage poorer students from applying, the Government also proposed that universities charging fees of over £6,000 per year would have to contribute to a National Scholarships programme and that there would be a stricter regime of sanctions encouraging high-charging universities to increase participation. It was announced that the Government intends to implement changes in time for the 2012–13 academic year.

The vote on the proposals in December 2010 caused enormous problems for the Coalition. It was held against the background of large-scale protests and some rioting which generated considerable media attention. Vince

Cable, the Liberal Democrat Secretary of State for Business, Innovation and Skills, was charged with guiding the proposals through Parliament. Cable, with other Liberal Democrat MPs, had signed the election pledge to vote against any increase in fees and was clearly uncomfortable in this role. In summer 2010, he floated the idea of a graduate tax – the proposal later explicitly rejected by Browne. This became the Labour Party's preferred solution to higher education funding under its new leader, Ed Miliband. A week before the vote Cable suggested that he might abstain from voting for his own proposals, citing party unity as a prime reason (BBC, 2010b). In the event, Cable did vote in favour. However, of 57 Liberal Democrat MPs, 21 voted against the proposals (contravening the Coalition agreement) and eight abstained (including two who were at a Climate Summit in Mexico).

The reputation of the Liberal Democrats suffered enormously. One poll in early January 2011 gave them just 7 per cent of the vote (Parker, 2011). The same organization had polled the party at 34 per cent shortly before the 2010 General Election – above both the Conservatives and Labour. (Their actual election result gave them 23 per cent of the vote.) As *The Economist* noted, the irony is that the 'unprincipled behaviour' of those Liberal Democrats who voted for the fees was actually before the election, when the party's polling was at its peak. Indeed, 'Neither [Clegg] nor many other senior Lib Dems believed the Party's line on university funding was sustainable in an era of fiscal austerity, but he stuck to it to avoid offending his tribe (and the many student voters it counts on at election time)' (*The Economist*, 2010). The response to the higher education funding debate reflects the splits in the party between social and economic liberals, in particular their differing views on fairness and equality and the respective role of state and market in providing public services, and could be a sign of a much deeper fissure in years to come.

The Browne Review is part of a longer move away from a 'free' higher education system. This shift had been in train since at least the mid-1990s, when Lord Dearing chaired a committee to examine ways to prevent the downward trajectory of funding per student caused by rising student numbers and a limited budget through general taxation. Dearing recommended that graduates make a direct financial contribution to the cost of their courses, suggesting that this should be done through a system of deferred repayments of an initial loan, determined income after university. However, David Blunkett, Secretary of State for Education and Employment in New Labour's first term, decided that it should be an upfront charge, initially set at £1,000 per year. The Higher Education Act 2004 continued the move away from a 'free' system. It scrapped the upfront payment and instituted a system of deferred repayment (which started when the graduate's income exceeded £15,000). It also introduced a system of variable fees, set by individual universities up to a maximum of £3,000 and indexed to inflation. In theory, this would allow universities to compete on price. In fact, all universities soon set their fees at the maximum amount.

Whilst the Browne Review must be seen as part of a longer-term move to a more market-based system, the radicalism of its proposals was much commented upon. The literary critic and intellectual historian Stefan Collini noted that:

> Essentially, Browne is contending that we should no longer think of higher education as the provision of a public good, articulated through educational judgment and largely financed by public funds (in recent years supplemented by a relatively small fee element). Instead, we should think of it as a lightly regulated market in which consumer demand, in the form of student choice, is sovereign in determining what is offered by service providers (i.e. universities). (Collini, 2010)

In particular, Collini highlights the almost complete withdrawal of the present annual block grant that the Government makes to universities to underwrite their teaching. This, he argues, 'signals a redefinition of higher education and the retreat of the state from financial responsibility for it' (Collini, 2010).

One of the sharpest and most intellectually damaging critiques of the Browne Review's marketization of higher education came from the Higher Education Policy Institute (HEPI). John Thompson and Bahram Bekhradnia's analysis for HEPI describes how assumptions about the market shape the Review, noting that

> some fundamental points are asserted by the Committee and taken as a given – that it is right that the contribution from government should reduce relative to the student contribution (and in many cases that it should disappear completely); and that the market is a sufficient mechanism for determining where students go to university and for making judgments about standards and quality. These are highly contested points, and their assertion as a given colours the entire report. (Thompson and Bekhradnia, 2010: §11)

Thompson and Bekhradnia's analysis set out several areas of concern created by this marketization. Two specific points are particularly worth highlighting. The first surrounds those institutions that fail under market conditions. Thompson and Bekhradnia note that

> It is too simplistic to argue, as the report does, that those universities that are not as popular as others will "raise their game" if they see their numbers falling, or will be allowed to fail. Those universities may be doing a perfectly good job, but be less well endowed, have less appeal, may be geographically disadvantaged . . . But nevertheless the national interest would be ill served if they were to fail. (Thompson and Bekhradnia, 2010: §56)

A second concern surrounds the effect on participation levels for potential students from poorer backgrounds. Browne assumes that 'if fees can be deferred, then participation can be protected' (Independent Review of Higher Education Funding and Student Finance, 2010: 26). However, Thompson and Bekhradnia argue that:

> We cannot be so confident in future that the financing arrangements will have no impact on participation. Indeed, to the extent that the decision to participate in higher education is an economic one, it will be entirely reasonable to assume that the much higher costs will put some people off higher education. (Thompson and Bekhradnia 2010: §46)

For Collini, Browne's Review and its near-adoption by the Government is a dangerous gamble. He concludes:

> It is difficult to estimate – though some reports suggest it may be difficult to exaggerate – the damage that may be done to British universities in the short term by the abolition of the block grant and the wild hope that its functions will be taken over by some kind of market mechanism run by university applicants. At present, the block grant is the tangible expression of the public interest in the provision of good quality education across the system, and the means for universities to make informed intellectual choices about the subjects they teach . . . What is at stake is whether universities in the future are to be thought of as having a public cultural role partly sustained by public support, or whether we move further towards redefining them in terms of a purely economistic calculation of value and a wholly individualist conception of 'consumer satisfaction'. (Collini, 2010)

Conclusion

2010 saw the election of a radical coalition, many of the members of which are ideologically committed to reducing the size and role of the state. This belief tended to go hand in hand with an assumption that the level of national debt was unsustainable and needed to be brought quickly under control. This has had a radical effect on education policy. As HEPI's analysis of the Browne Review notes: 'it is unfortunate that the review appears at a time of economic crisis leading to public expenditure cuts, and that the review and its timing offers the Government the opportunity to cut more than would otherwise have been the case' (Thompson and Bekhradnia, 2010: §11).

For its proponents, reducing the size and role of the state includes further marketization of public services. In this respect, the Coalition is continuing a job which previous administrations had started. In some cases reform along these lines has made public services more efficient and responsive to the needs of citizens. Various administrations have used market incentives to promote social justice. The Pupil Premium, if implemented successfully, could provide an example of this. However, recent reforms – particularly in higher education – have turned some public services into commodities, and little regard has been shown for the argument that the market will not necessarily defend some lines of research and institutions that it would be in the broader public interest to protect.

Some in the Liberal Democrats have found these policies hard to accept. Underlying fissures in the party between social and economic liberals are being forced open. Nowhere was this more the case than in the party's divided response to the Browne Review. While some on the right of the party are happy to work with the Conservatives (indeed Clegg and Cameron seem to have more in common with one another than either seem to have with elements in their own parties), others are increasingly feeling that the Coalition has forced them to make compromises that are difficult to reconcile with their deeper beliefs.

References

Baker, M. (2010) Gove's Academies: 1980s Idea Rebranded? *BBC News*, 1 August. www.bbc.co.uk/news/education-10824069 (accessed 1 January 2011).

BBC (2010a). At a Glance: Browne Report. *BBC News*, 12 October. www.bbc.co.uk/news/education-11519147 (accessed 1 January 2011).

BBC (2010b) Vince Cable May Abstain from Vote on Tuition Fees. *BBC News*, 1 December. www.bbc.co.uk/news/uk-politics-11874406 (accessed 1 January 2011).

BBC (2011) Free Schools 'Not Wanted' Say Teachers. *BBC News*, 3 January. www.bbc.co.uk/news/education-12099245.

Chowdry, H. et al. (2010) *The Pupil Premium: Assessing the Options* (London: Institute for Fiscal Studies).

Clifton, J. and Muir, R. (2010) *Room for Improvement: IPPR's Response to the Schools White Paper* (London: Institute for Public Policy Research).

Collini, S. (2010) Browne's Gamble. *LRB* 32(21): 23–5. www.lrb.co.uk/v32/n21/stefan-collini/brownes-gamble (accessed 1 January 2011).

Conservative Party (2010) *Invitation to Join the Government of Britain: The Conservative Manifesto 2010*. media.conservatives.s3.amazonaws.com/manifesto/cpmanifesto2010_lowres.pdf (accessed 1 January 2011).

Conservative Party and Liberal Democrat Party (2010) *Conservative Liberal Democrat Coalition negotiations – Agreements reached – 11 May 2010*. www.conservatives.com/News/News_stories/2010/05/Coalition_Agreement_published.aspx (accessed 1 January 2011).

Department for Education (2010a) *The Importance of Teaching: The Schools White Paper 2010* (Department for Education: The Stationery Office). www.education.gov.uk/publications/eOrderingDownload/CM-7980.pdf (accessed 1 January 2011).

Department for Education (2010b) *Academies*. www.education.gov.uk/schools/leadership/typesofschools/academies (accessed 1 January 2011)

Department for Education (2010c) *Free Schools*. www.education.gov.uk/schools/leadership/typesofschools/freeschools (accessed 1 January 2011).

The Economist (2010) Agreeing to Disagree: Collective Cabinet Responsibility Bumps up Against Coalition Politics. *The Economist*, 9 December. www.economist.com/node/17680864 (1 January 2011).

Freedman, S. and Horner, S. (2008) *School Funding and Social Justice: A Guide to the Pupil Premium*, with a Foreword by Julian Le Grand (London: Policy Exchange).

Garner, R. (2009) Lord Browne Returns to Public Life to Chair Student Fees Review. *The Independent*, 9 November. www.independent.co.uk/news/education/education-news/lord-browne-returns-to-public-life-to-chair-student-fees-review-1817673.html (accessed 1 January 2011).

Garner, R. (2010) LSE Raises Spectre of Private Universities. *The Independent*, 27 October.

Gill, J. (2009) Lord Browne to Lead Fees Review. *Times Higher Education*, 9 November.

Griffiths. S. (2009) Cameron's Conservatives and the Public Services. In M. Beech and S. Lee, *The Conservatives under David Cameron: Built to Last?* (London: Palgrave Macmillan).

Harrison, A. (2010) Most Pupils in Schools Which Will Face Cuts, Claims IFS. *BBC News*, 22 October. www.bbc.co.uk/news/education-11607269 (accessed 1 January 2011).

HM Government (2010) *The Coalition: Our Programme for Government – Freedom, Fairness, Responsibility* (London: The Cabinet Office).

HM Treasury (2010) *Spending Review 2010*. Cm 7942. cdn.hm-Treasury.gov.uk/sr2010_completereport.pdf (accessed 1 January 2011).

Independent (2009) Leading article: Good Start for Fees Review. *The Independent.* www.independent.co.uk/news/education/higher/leading-article-good-start-for-fees-review-1818631.html (accessed 1 January 2011).

The Independent Review of Higher Education Funding and Student Finance (2010, 12 October) hereview.independent.gov.uk/hereview (accessed 1 January 2011).

The Independent Review of Higher Education Funding and Student Finance (2010, 12 October) *Securing a Sustainable Future for Higher Education.*

Katwala, S. (2010) For Now, the Pupil Premium is Another Broken Coalition Promise. *Next Left*, 13 December. www.nextleft.org/2010/12/for-now-pupil-premium-is-another-broken.html (accessed 1 January 2011).

Liberal Democrat Party (2010) *Liberal Democrat Manifesto 2010: Change that Works for You – Building a Fairer Britain.* network.libdems.org.uk/manifesto2010/libdem_manifesto_2010.pdf (accessed 1 January 2011).

NUS (2010) *Lib Dem MPs Sign the Pledge.* www.nus.org.uk/Campaigns/Funding-Our-Future/Lib-Dem-MPs-sign-the-pledge (accessed 1 January 2011).

Parker, G. (2011) Clegg Prepares for Control Orders Compromise. *The Financial Times*, 7 January. www.ft.com/cms/s/0/d50c5df0-1a92-11e0-b100-00144feab49a.html#axzz1AaNCOUMu (accessed 1 January 2011).

Parliamentary Debates (2010) House of Commons, 20 October: col. 964.

Prince, R. (2010) Schools in Better-Off Areas Will Lose Cash to Aid Poor. *The Telegraph.* 24 October. www.telegraph.co.uk/education/8084535/Schools-in-better-off-areas-will-lose-cash-to-aid-poor.html (accessed 1 January 2011).

Sellgren, K. (2010) Tory Free Schools 'Barking Mad' Says Teachers' Leader: BBC News Education Reporter at the ATL Conference. *BBC News*, 31 March. news.bbc.co.uk/1/hi/education/8597572.stm (accessed 1 January 2011).

Shepherd, J. (2010) English Primary and Secondary Schools Offered Chance to Become Academies. *The Guardian*, 26 May. www.guardian.co.uk/education/2010/may/26/primary-secondary-schools-academies (accessed 1 January 2011).

Shipman, T. (2010) School Cash Cuts Hit Middle Classes Twice as Government Reveals Funding and Building Programmes Will Be Slashed. *Daily Mail*, 25 October. www.dailymail.co.uk/news/article-1323438/School-cash-cuts-hit-middle-classes-twice-government-reveals-funding-slashed.htm (accessed 1 January 2011).

Stratton, A. (2010) Spending Review Will Lead to Loss of 40,000 Teaching Jobs. *The Guardian*, 20 October. www.guardian.co.uk/politics/2010/oct/20/spending-review-loss-teaching-jobs (accessed 1 January 2011).

Thompson, J. and Bekhradnia, B. (2010) *The Independent Review of Higher Education Funding: An Analysis*, 19 October. www.hepi.ac.uk/files/49 per cent20Browne per cent20Review per cent20full.pdf (accessed 1 January 2011).

Wiborg, S. (2010) Swedish Free Schools: Do They Work? *LLAKES Research Paper 18.* Centre for Learning and Life Chances in Knowledge Economies and Societies.

6
The Emerging Blue (and Orange) Health Strategy: Continuity or Change?

Robert M. Page

Following a brief overview of underlying Conservative and Liberal Democratic approaches to the NHS, this chapter will examine the health strategies outlined in each party's General Election manifesto for 2010, the subsequent Coalition Agreement on health, the spending review of October 2010, plans for the structural reform of the NHS in England (Department of Health, 2010a) and the direction of public health policy in England (Department of Health, 2010b). In the final section, consideration will be given to the question of whether the Coalition Government is pursuing a new direction in health policy.

Conservative and Liberal Democratic Approaches to the National Health Service

Throughout the postwar period Labour has come to be regarded as the party which has been most supportive of the National Health Service. This is not surprising given the Herculean endeavours of Aneurin Bevan to establish the NHS in July 1948 despite concerted opposition from both the Conservative Party and the British Medical Association, and the subsequent efforts of Labour to ensure that the service became a defining feature of British society. Although the Conservatives eventually came to recognize the political necessity of making a positive accommodation with the NHS, they experienced periodic difficulties in persuading the British public that they were reliable stewards of this respected institution.

Although the Conservatives have never sought to undertake a root-and-branch reform of the NHS when in government, their inclination to curb public spending and their willingness to consider alternative funding arrangements (including social insurance), administrative reform and charging (mainly for non-medical services), coupled with their support for private health care, has resulted in long-running public scepticism about the depth of the party's commitment to the NHS (see Raison, 1990).

Since his election as party leader in 2005, David Cameron has made strenuous efforts to demonstrate that the modern Conservative Party is now fully supportive of the NHS. Although this commitment has a pragmatic basis (it was recognized, for example, that the NHS has what Americans would term 'third rail' – i.e. untouchable – status and that positive overtures towards the NHS would help to persuade the public that the Conservative's 'nasty', 'neoliberal', period was a thing of the past), the *ideological* aspects of this realignment should not be overlooked. As Cameron stated in a speech in August 2009:

> I know perfectly well that some of the changes we have made to this Party over the past few years have not been easy for the Party to accept. But there is one change we've made where frankly, it has felt like pushing on an open door – and that is making crystal clear our wholehearted commitment to the NHS. Conservatives rely on the NHS, work in the NHS, volunteer to help the NHS. This Party wants to improve the NHS for everyone.

Following the formal merger of the Liberal and Social Democratic Parties in 1989, the Lib-Dems have consistently reiterated their support for the NHS. In their first post-merger General Election manifesto of 1992, for example, the party gave its unequivocal support to the NHS: 'Liberal Democrats remain steadfastly committed to the original aims of the NHS: to enable everyone to live free of the fear of illness, injury and disability; to provide health care free at the point of delivery and regardless of ability to pay' (Liberal Democrats, 1992).

The 2010 General Election Manifestos

These positive attitudes towards the NHS were reflected in the parties' respective manifestos for the 2010 General Election. In the Conservative manifesto, *Invitation to Join the Government of Britain* (Conservative Party, 2010), voters were reminded that

More than three years ago, David Cameron spelled out his priorities in three letters – NHS. Since then, we have consistently fought to protect the values the NHS stands for and have campaigned to defend the NHS from Labour's cuts and reorganizations. As the party of the NHS, we will never change the idea at its heart that health care in this country is free at the point of use and available to everyone based on need, not ability to pay. (Conservative Party, 2010: 45)

In order to demonstrate support for the NHS, the Conservatives promised to increase spending in real terms in each year of the next Parliament. It was argued, however, that further structural reforms would be necessary if the NHS was to function effectively. The Conservatives promised to move away from what they regarded as Labour's remote, over- centralized control of the NHS. In an effort to ensure that the needs of patients were prioritized, GPs were to be given budgetary responsibilities to commission health services. Labour's target culture was to be abandoned, administrative costs were to be reduced by one third and Independent Health Boards were to be created. In terms of specific pledges, the Conservatives responded to public anxieties about the unavailability of life-saving drugs (by announcing the establishment of a special cancer drug fund), and the uncertain future of highly valued local health facilities (by promising to end the forced closure of Accident and Emergency and Maternity Services). The growing problem of funding and providing social care for elderly people was to be resolved by the introduction of a special insurance premium and by increased joint health and local authority commissioning.

The Liberal Democrats also reaffirmed their commitment to the NHS in their General Election manifesto. 'We are proud of the NHS – it's built on the basic British principle of fairness' (Liberal Democrats, 2010: 40). Although the Liberal Democrats did not guarantee to protect the NHS from prospective spending cuts, they did share Conservative concerns about the need for reform: 'Liberal Democrats believe that we can improve the NHS; in fact, we believe that it's our duty to do so at a time like this when budgets are tight. We all know that too much precious NHS money is wasted on bureaucracy, and doctors and nurses spend too much time trying to meet government targets' (Liberal Democrats, 2010: 40). More localized forms of health provision were also deemed essential if the NHS was to become more responsive to patients' needs. This would involve, for example, the abolition of Strategic Health Authorities and the establishment of Local Health Boards, which would take over the role of the Primary Care Trusts in commissioning services for local people, working in cooperation with local councils. These Boards would be encouraged to commission services from a more diverse range of providers.

Although there were differences of emphasis in the respective manifestos, such as the strong commitment to localism in the Liberal Democratic manifesto, there were broad areas of agreement that would eventually form the basis of the Coalition Government's health policy.

The Coalition Agreement

Following the inconclusive General Election result of 2010, a joint health strategy was mapped out by the Conservatives and the Liberal Democrats as part of the formal Coalition Agreement. The Agreement underlined the strength of each party's commitment to the NHS. 'The Government believes that the NHS is an important expression of our national values. We are committed to an NHS that is free at the point of use and available to everyone based on need not the ability to pay' (Cabinet Office, 2010: 24). Although the health accord promised to 'stop the top-down reorganizations of the NHS' (Cabinet Office, 2010: 24), there were indications that major reform of the service was imminent.

The Agreement contained a promise to 'cut the cost of NHS administration by a third'; 'strengthen' the role of GPs by giving them the power to 'commission care' for their patients; establish a new 'independent NHS board'; 'develop Monitor (the independent regulator of NHS foundation trusts) into an economic regulator that will oversee aspects of access, competition and price-setting in the NHS' (Cabinet Office, 2010: 25); and put in train reforms which would enable patients to 'choose any health care provider that meets NHS standards, within NHS prices' (Cabinet Office, 2010: 26). In addition, the Coalition document included a number of commitments that were distinctively Conservative (the ring-fencing of health spending and the introduction of a Cancer Drug Fund) and distinctively Liberal Democrat (prioritizing dementia research and robust language and competency tests for overseas health care professionals).

Although the health budget was protected in the Coalition Government's spending review in October 2010, the minuscule nature of the real terms increase (just 0.1 per cent over four years) represented 'a prolonged and sustained spending squeeze' that has not been witnessed since the 1950s (Timmins, 2010a). It is important to recognize that inflation within the NHS has tended to rise faster than prices in general because of the rapidly increasing cost of pharmaceuticals and medical equipment, demographic pressures (the higher costs associated with an ageing population) and ever-increasing patient expectations. Of course, it may prove possible to hold down NHS costs more effectively in the future because of the decision to impose a two-year pay freeze on all NHS staff earning over £21,000 a year (though there will still be cost pressures arising from staff movements up existing pay scales). The diversion of part of the NHS budget (£1 billion) to social care may also save NHS costs by preventing costly and repetitive forms of unplanned hospital admissions by frail elderly patients. In addition, the introduction of a pre-election QIPP (Quality, Innovation, Productivity and Prevention) programme by David Nicholson, Chief Executive of the NHS, which is 'designed' to deliver £15–20 billion of savings over four years by reducing management costs, reconfiguring services and bearing down on the cost of hospital procedures by means of stringent tariffs, may also help to ensure that existing service levels can be delivered for less.

Unlike the cautious approach adopted by the New Labour administration of 1997, the Coalition Government has pressed ahead with its reform agenda in areas such as education, housing and social security (welfare) at breakneck speed. In the case of health care, two significant White Papers – *Equity and Excellence: Liberating the NHS* (Department of Health, 2010a) and *Healthy Lives, Healthy People: Our Strategy for Public Health in England* (Department of Health, 2010b) – were published within four months of the formation of the Coalition Government.

Equity and Excellence: Liberating the NHS

The first White Paper in July 2010, based on what was termed a 'blend of Conservative and Liberal Democrat ideas' (Department of Health, 2010a: 1), built on the earlier Coalition Agreement relating to health policy in England. It focused on four main themes – a patient-centred service, improved health care outcomes, increased autonomy and accountability, a reduction in bureaucracy and improved efficiency. It is useful to look at each of these themes in turn.

A Patient-Centred Service

In order to promote a more consumer-oriented NHS, patients will be encouraged to see themselves as 'partners' in their own health care. They will be able to exercise greater choice in terms of selecting their GP (without geographical restriction), the type of treatment they require and their preferred provider. Some patients will be provided with a personal health budget to buy services of their choice. Patients will also be given better health information about the quality of care and its effectiveness (e.g. waiting times/opening hours and survival rates) and be given greater access to, and control over, their health records. They will be encouraged to evaluate the care they receive, which will then be compiled into so-called Patient-Reported Outcome Measures (PROMS). Those patients who need expert guidance in order to make appropriate choices, or who wish to register concerns about service quality, will be able to get support from two new consumer agencies operating at both local (Local HealthWatch) and national (Health Watch England) level.

Improving Health Care Outcomes

One of the main aims of the Coalition's health reforms in England is to reduce mortality and morbidity rates, increase patient safety and improve the 'patient experience'. To this end, a new NHS Outcomes Framework will be drawn up in consultation with clinicians, patients and the public, which will detail the precise 'clinically credible and evidence-based' objectives. Quality standards, devised by NICE, will be introduced for particular conditions such as strokes and dementia in an effort to ensure best practice. Payment systems will be designed to reward the quality, rather than the volume, of work performed. Doctors will be given greater autonomy in prescribing and will be able to access a new Cancer Drug Fund.

Autonomy, Accountability and Democratic Legitimacy

A major and contentious feature of the White Paper is the decision to give local GP consortia the prime responsibility for commissioning patient services. This is intended to allow professionals, rather than politicians, to 'shape their services around the needs and choices of patients' (Department of Health, 2010a: 27). It is hoped that this initiative will lead to the decommissioning of services that 'do not have appreciable benefits for patients' health or health care' (Department of Health, 2010a: 27). Local authorities will be given an enhanced public health role and will be expected to ensure that effective joint working practices are put in place. An independent NHS Commissioning Board will support the development of GP consortia, provide guidance on best commissioning practice, tackle inequalities, promote patient involvement and choice, commission specialized services, and allocate and account for NHS resources. While the Health Secretary will continue to be politically accountable for the NHS, this role will be strategic rather than operational. In an attempt to bolster localism, local authorities will be expected to promote integrated working arrangements and to take the lead role in strategic needs assessments and on public health issues. In addition, local Directors of Public Health (DPHs), who will be jointly appointed by local authorities and the Public Health Service, will be expected to take a strategic lead in tackling health inequalities at the local level. All current NHS Trusts will be expected to become Foundation Trusts (or part of such a Trust). Staff within these Trusts will be encouraged, where appropriate, to form themselves into non-profit-making social enterprises (Department of Health, 2010a: 36). The Care Quality Commission will act as a quality inspector for health and social care for both public and private providers while, in keeping with the Coalition Agreement, Monitor is to be transformed into an economic regulator.

Cutting Bureaucracy and Improving Efficiency

Although health spending will increase in real terms, it is recognized that the rising demographic pressures and the higher costs of technological advance in an era of financial restraint will require significant efficiency savings. The savings derived from QIPP will be 'reinvested' to secure improvements in service quality and patient outcomes. Management costs will also be reduced by 45 per cent over four years – 'the largest reduction in administrative costs in NHS history' (p. 43). The functions of the Department of Health will be pared back. PCTs and Strategic Health Authorities will be abolished while other NHS bodies and services such as NHS Direct will be 'streamlined'.

Healthy Lives, Healthy People: Our Strategy for Public Health in England

The second White Paper, published in November 2010 (Department of Health, 2010b), sets out the Coalition Government's plans for public health in England. The document suggests that centrally directed public health policy has failed and that it is now time to devolve responsibility to localities:

> We will end this top-down government. It is time to free up local government and local communities to decide how best to improve the health and wellbeing of their citizens, deciding what actions to take locally with the NHS and other key partners, without undue emphasis from the centre. (Department of Health, 2010b: 25)

Subject to parliamentary approval for a Health and Social Care Bill in 2011, a new integrated body – Public Health England – will be established within the Department of Health to oversee a 'radical new approach'

(Department of Health, 2010b: 6) in this sphere with effect from 2012. This new body will be responsible for allocating a ring-fenced budget to upper-tier and unitary local authorities for the purpose of promoting health and wellbeing. Statutory Health and Wellbeing Boards will also be established in upper-tier authorities so that key NHS, public health and social care personnel can secure agreements about community needs and the joint commissioning of services. Although central government will continue to 'protect people from serious health threats and emergencies' (such as a 'flu pandemic) and oversee immunization programmes, local authorities will be granted considerable freedom to devise their own schemes for improving the health status of the local community. Those authorities that can demonstrate that they have secured measurable improvements in the health of the local population will be provided with additional funds. As noted previously, the strategic role to be played by DPHs was confirmed.

In a similar vein, although the Coalition Government acknowledges that central government initiatives, such as the Clean Air Act 1957 and seat belt legislation in 1983, have brought about positive health improvements in the past, it believes that it is no longer 'possible to promote healthier lifestyles through Whitehall diktat and nannying about the way people should live' (Department of Health, 2010b: 2). While accepting that individuals do 'not have total control' over their lives 'or the circumstances' in which they live (Department of Health, 2010b: 29), it is contended that the vast majority of individuals are capable of exercising choice and that the role of government should, accordingly, be to strengthen 'self-esteem, confidence and personal responsibility', promote 'healthier behaviours and lifestyles' and adapt the environment 'to make healthy choices easier' (Department of Health, 2010b: 29). In terms of the 'intervention ladder' developed by the Nuffield Council on Bioethics (2007, Figure 2:1: 42), the Coalition has identified its 'default' position as 'enabling and guiding' rather than 'restricting' or 'eliminating' choice. In particular, it is believed that there is 'significant scope' (Department of Health, 2010b: 30) to encourage or 'nudge' (see Thaler and Sunstein, 2008: John et al., 2009) citizens to make more appropriate health choices. Soft paternalism, rather than stricter regulation of the food and drink industry or legislative intervention, is seen as the best way of improving public health.

Trouble Ahead?

Given that NHS reform has proved so problematic in the past (Edwards, 2010), it seems likely that the Coalition Government will also experience difficulties in implementing their blueprint for change. Although some of their initiatives, most notably the move away from PCT commissioning, have received a cautious welcome in some quarters, reservations have been voiced about other aspects of the Coalition's health reforms from, among others, the new chair of the Royal College of General Practitioners, the British Medical Association, the NHS Confederation, the Nuffield Trust, trades unions (Unite and Unison) and Civitas (a right-of-centre think tank). Seven main concerns have been identified.

First, the need for further reform of the NHS has been questioned (Hunter, 2010). According to Walshe:

> [s]tructural reorganizations don't work. Although NHS performance may be problematic, there is often little evidence to show that the causes of poor performance are structural or that the proposed structural changes will improve performance. (Walshe, 2010: 160)

From this perspective, then, these changes – which have been estimated to cost anything up to £3 billion to implement – are likely to be destabilizing and detrimental to service quality.

The *second* criticism relates to the *pace* of change rather than to the *need* for reform *per se*. For example, the leading health research organization, the King's Fund, has welcomed the move to GP commissioning, the greater degree of patient choice and the granting of an enhanced role to local authorities. However, it has called on ministers to think again about the rapidity of the timetable for change, believing that pilot studies and 'a more measured approach to implementation could ensure the reforms deliver real benefits' (King's Fund, 2010; see also Ham, 2010).

Third, the proposed reforms have reopened debate about whether the NHS will be able to retain its distinctive ethos as a public, tax-funded service provided by dedicated public servants on the basis of clinical need rather than ability to pay. According to one trade union leader, there is a danger that the reforms will result in the NHS becoming 'nothing more than a brand, a logo to be displayed outside increasingly privately run and owned hospitals, wrestled from the health service' (Prentis, 2010: 34). While tax funding of the NHS has been guaranteed, the Coalition's reforms are designed to lead to an increased level of 'non-public' provision (Milne, 2010: Pollack and Price, 2010). For example, the proposal for all hospitals to become non-profit-making Trusts will result in all institutions operating as completive rather than cooperative providers. These Trusts will seek to attract both public and private patients (the cap for the latter is to be lifted; Department of Health, 2010a) and will be free to set their own pay rates and conditions of service.

The Coalition's desire to increase the number of both private and social enterprise providers also represents a challenge to the notion of a 'publicly' provided health service. Private health companies are likely to take an active commissioning role for some of the new GP consortia given the lack of in-house expertise. This will require increased regulatory activity as there is a potential for conflicts of interest. For example, private commissioners employed by GP consortia will have an interest in purchasing services from those hospitals and other providers with which they already have commercial relationships. Similarly, GPs, of whom around one quarter are currently undertaking work for private health providers, could in their new contracting role be effectively commissioning services from themselves (Knight, 2010). Moreover, the commissioning decisions of the GP consortia may, in practice, fail to meet the often complex, costly and not well understood needs of neglected patient groups such as those experiencing mental ill health (Pollack, 2010).

The Coalition Government's decision to establish so-called 'responsibility networks', in which leading food and drink manufacturers will work with the Department of Health in a voluntary capacity to help formulate new public health policies designed to tackle problems such as obesity and alcohol abuse, may also prove problematic (see Lawrence, 2010). According to Lang and Rayner, the Coalition Government's decision to allow those with commercial interests in manufacturing high-calorie products to play a major role in the network 'oriented at culture change' is akin to putting 'the fox in the hen coop' (Lang and Rayner, 2010: 111). One possible outcome of partnerships of this kind is that there will be less emphasis on reducing the number of products containing 'harmful' ingredients or on 'shrinking' the portion sizes of ready-made meals so that consumers can control their daily calorie intake more easily (Hickman, 2010). Instead, the emphasis is likely to switch to the promotion of time-consuming exercise regimes which many of those who are overweight may find difficult to maintain.

Fourth, the emphasis on localism in the White Paper is likely to give rise to questions about who is accountable for the NHS and for the promotion of public health. While the Secretary of State will still be held to parliamentary account for the strategic direction of health policy and expenditure, the establishment of a National Commissioning Board, as well as the decision to make local authorities responsible for public health, is intended to limit government responsibility for operational decision-making. This is likely to lead to a democratic deficit. Who will deal with patient complaints and who will be held accountable for service delivery? If citizens are dissatisfied with the service they receive, should they complain to their MP, their service commissioner (the GP consortia), their service provider (their GP or Foundation Trust) or the local council (which will have enhanced responsibility for improvements in local health services though not for their funding), or should they contact their local Health Watch Group?

Fifth, the prospective dual role of the GP as both service provider and commissioner may undermine the level of trust between patient and doctor. How can patients be reassured that their GP's advice and recommendations will be based solely on clinical criteria? Given that GPs will have greater freedom to prescribe expensive drugs of 'questionable' efficacy (because NICE will no longer have the right to prevent NHS prescribing of this kind; see Duerden, 2010), patients with life-threatening conditions who are denied costly treatments might draw the conclusion that commercial factors are the driving force behind clinical decision-making.

Sixth, given that throughout its 60-year history the NHS has never been able to secure the level of efficiency savings envisaged by the Coalition Government, it is questionable whether either the quality or quantity of current services levels will be maintained, particularly in a period of spending constraint and the disruption caused by commissioning reforms (see House of Commons Select Committee, 2010). Indeed, the revised inflation forecast put forward by the Office of Budget Responsibility (2010) suggests that it might not be possible for the Coalition to guarantee a modest real terms increase in health spending.

Seventh, although the Coalition has taken some steps to tackle problems in social care provision by means of a 'higher' Personal Social Services Grant to local authorities (though this is not ring-fenced and forms part of a lower overall formula grant) and by transferring some NHS funds to local authorities, it is questionable whether this will prove effective in defusing this demographic time-bomb. For example, in a recent report, the House of Commons Health Committee (2010) has pointed out that 'there is a risk' that the £1 billion allocation from the NHS budget to social care 'will be focused on funding certain limited services, rather than being directed towards providing a better overall interface' between the health and social care sectors to 'bring about longer-term improvements in efficiency, preventive care and reablement' (HCHC, 2010: 3). Although a Commission chaired by Andrew Dilnot has been appointed to examine long-term funding issues in social care, this falls short of the holistic planning that is needed in this area. Consideration needs to be given to the introduction of a national care service as well as an accompanying workforce plan which will ensure that there is a reliable supply of well-trained care workers able to deal with the physical and mental needs of an ageing population.

Continuity or Change?

To what extent is it possible to argue that a distinctive blue (and orange) health policy is emerging? Are we seeing the emergence of an ideological shift away from New Labour's modernized 'social democratic' approach (Giddens, 2010) or merely a shift in the parameters of what has been, to all intents and purposes, an underlying cross-party consensus involving all of the three major parties?

During the New Labour era there was a concerted attempt to move the party away from its democratic socialist roots in both theory and practice (Page, 2007). In the case of health policy, this was reflected in dwindling support for the notion that the NHS had a continuing role to play in maintaining social solidarity among citizens and a rejection of the assumption that service providers were necessarily guided by a sense of altruism or public duty (see Le Grand, 2003: 2007). In addition, New Labour was keen to disassociate itself from the perception that they were ideologically wedded to what Hunter (2008) has termed a *bureaucratic* approach to health policy, which holds that a responsive, state-run health service provides the best means of ensuring that health care is provided on the basis of need rather than ability to pay, that services are distributed equitably and that costs are kept under control. While New Labour remained committed to a tax-funded, needs-based service, it was prepared to countenance the increased use of choice and competition within the NHS and the greater involvement of non-state providers, if this could be shown to improve the quality of the service. Support for a plurality of means was not seen as a betrayal of social democratic principles (see the contrasting views of Finlayson, 2010 and Driver, 2005 on this issue) but rather a pragmatic adaptation to changing economic and social circumstances. For New Labour, a flexible combination of both bureaucratic and market methods was judged to be more likely to deliver the best health outcomes (see Ruane, 2010). There are some indications that this 'modernized' approach produced some positive outcomes, such as improvements in waiting times (see Toynbee and Walker, 2010) and high recorded levels of public satisfaction with the NHS (see Park et al., 2010).

New Labour's self-declared determination to pursue a modernized 'social democratic' approach to health policy while in office appears to have cut little ice with their political opponents. Since the formation of the Coalition Government, the new Health Secretary, Andrew Lansley, has continued to characterize the former government's health policy as highly centralized, bureaucratic and wasteful. In a speech made in June 2010, Lansley stated that one of the key tasks of the new government would be to overturn New Labour's statist approach by disempowering 'the hierarchy, the bureaucracy, the Primary Care Trusts and the Strategic Health Authorities' (Lansley, 2010).

The key question is whether such rhetoric is merely representative of a desire on the part of the Coalition Government to oversee a pragmatic shift in the *management and organization* of the NHS or whether prospective health reforms should be seen as part of a broader attempt to secure a fundamental, *ideologically driven* change in British society (see Rutherford, 2010).

If health policy is currently being driven by ideological considerations, there is the added complication of identifying which variant is being pursued. For example, might we be witnessing a reversion to an unashamedly neoliberal approach that seeks a sizeable reduction in state welfare provision (see Greening, 2001; Vaizey, 2002; Laws, 2004)? Alternatively, might we be observing a 'new' ideological approach based on a fusion of modern/liberal Conservatism (see Beech, 2009; Page, 2010) and 'social/orange' Liberalism (see Brack, 2010), which seeks to reduce the state's provider role (though not its funding obligations) while simultaneously bolstering localism (Davey, 2004; Boles, 2010). It is acknowledged, in the case of the latter, that the development of tailored services to reflect the diverse and distinctive needs of a local community may give rise to greater diversity of NHS provision. However, such an outcome is seen as preferable to the imposition of inflexible, centrally determined, uniform levels of service provision.

Although developments in social policy are always likely to reflect different political ideas and beliefs, it is important, as Griffiths (2009) and Prabhaker (2010) remind us, not to overstate their importance. Indeed, some might go as far as to suggest that the Coalition's market-style health reforms are *not* 'ideological' at all, but rather a pragmatic response to the realization that non-state providers are now better placed to deliver the high quality, cost-effective health services that are demanded by an increasingly consumerist and discerning public in a 'post-bureaucratic' age (Knight, 2010). Certainly, the general public might have a limited interest in the question of whether contemporary health policy conforms to social democratic or neoliberal 'doctrine'. They are likely, though, to be interested in how quickly they can see their GP, how long they have to wait for an ambulance or whether they obtain hospital treatment within weeks or months (see Klein, 2005). Crucially, if there is a perceivable deterioration in patient access to health services after what has been a period of steady improvement, there is likely to be growing pressure on the Coalition Government to act quickly to improve the NHS. This scenario, which may confront the Coalition Government more quickly than they have anticipated owing to the cumulative effect of rapid structural changes, efficiency targets and funding constraints, will then provide us with a clearer indication of whether they are pursuing an ideological agenda, which they will persist with despite its short-term unpopularity, or whether they will be prepared to duck and weave in a more pragmatic way in an effort to retain political support.

References

Beech, M. (2009) Cameron and Conservative Ideology. In S. Lee and M. Beech (eds.), *The Conservatives under David Cameron* (Basingstoke: Palgrave Macmillan), pp. 18–30.

Boles, N. (2010) *Which Way's Up?* (London: Biteback).

Brack, D. (2010) The Liberal Democrats and the Role of the State. In S. Griffiths and K. Hickson (eds.), *British Party Politics and Ideology after New Labour* (Basingstoke: Palgrave Macmillan), pp. 173–88.

Cabinet Office (2010) *The Coalition: Our Programme for Government.* (London: The Stationery Office).

Cameron, D. (2009) How the NHS Can Deliver Rising Standards of Health Care. Speech, 20 August.

Conservative Party (2010) *Invitation to Join the Government of Britain.* (London: Conservative Party).

Davey, E. (2004) Liberalism and Localism. In P. Marshall and D. Laws, (eds.), *The Orange Book* (London: Profile Books), pp. 43–68.

Department of Health (2010a) *Equity and Excellence: Liberating the NHS.* Cm 7881 (London: The Stationery Office).

Department of Health (2010b) *Healthy Lives, Healthy People: Our Strategy for Public Health in England,* Cm 7985 (London: The Stationery Office).

Driver, S. (2005) Welfare after Thatcherism: New Labour and Social Democratic Politics. In M. Powell, L. Bauld and K. Clarke (eds.), *Social Policy Review 17* (Bristol: Policy Press), pp. 255–72.

Duerden, M. (2010) From a Cancer Drug Fund to Value Based Pricing of Drugs. *British Medical Journal,* 341, 28 August: 412–13.

Edwards, N. (2010) *The Triumph of Hope over Experience: Lessons From the History of Reorganization* (London: NHS Confederation).

Finlayson, A. (2010) Alan Finlayson. In S. Griffiths and K. Hickson (eds.), *British Party Politics and Ideology after New Labour* (Basingstoke: Palgrave Macmillan), pp. 11–17.

Giddens, A. (2010) Response to Atkins and Leggett. In S. Griffiths and K. Hickson (eds.), *British Party Politics and Ideology after New Labour* (Basingstoke: Palgrave Macmillan), pp. 67–9.

Greening, J. (2001) A Wholly Healthy Britain? Why the NHS is the Sick Man of Europe. In E. Vaizey, N. Boles and M. Gove (eds.), *A Blue Tomorrow* (London: Politico's), pp. 192–9.

Griffiths, S. (2009) Cameron's Conservatives and the Public Services. In S. Lee and M. Beech (eds.), *The Conservatives under David Cameron* (Basingstoke: Palgrave Macmillan), pp. 97–108.

Ham, C. (2010) The Coalition Government's Plans for the NHS in England. *British Medical Journal*, 341, 17 July: 111–12.

Hickman, M. (2010) Public Health Fears as Langley Retreats from Regulation. *The Independent*, 4 December: 5.

House of Commons Health Committee (2010) *Public Expenditure*, Second Report of Session 2010–11, Vol. 1, HC512 (London: The Stationery Office).

Hunter, D. (2008) *The Health Debate* (Bristol: Policy Press).

Hunter, D. (2010) The Impact of the Spending Review on Health and Social Care. *British Medical Journal*, 30 October: 901.

John, P., Smith, G. and Stoker, G. (2009) Nudge Nudge, Think Think: Two Strategies for Changing Behaviour. *The Political Quarterly*, 80(3): 361–70.

Kings Fund (2010) *Too Far, Too Fast: The King's Fund Verdict on Coalition Health Reforms*. www.kings fund.org.uk/ptess/press_releases/too_far_too_fast.html (accessed 20 December 2010).

Klein, R. (2005) Transforming the NHS: The Story in 2004. In M. Powell, L. Bauld and K. Clarke (eds.), *Social Policy Review 17* (Bristol: Policy Press), pp. 51–68.

Knight, S. (2010) This Might Hurt. *Prospect*, December: 29–33.

Lang, T. and Rayner, G. (2010) Corporate Responsibility in Public Health. *British Medical Journal*, 341, 17 July: 110–11.

Lansley, A. (2010) My Ambition for Patient-centred Care. Speech, 8 June.

Lawrence, F. (2010) Good for the Nation's Health – or for Big Business? *Guardian*, 13 November: 6–7.

Laws, D. (2004) UK Health Services: A Liberal Agenda for Reform and Renewal. In P. Marshall and D. Laws (eds.), *The Orange Book* (London: Profile Books), pp. 191–210.

Le Grand, J. (2003) *Motivation, Agency and Public Policy* (Oxford: Oxford University Press).

Le Grand, J. (2007) *The Other Invisible Hand* (Princeton, NJ: Princeton University Press).

Liberal Democrats (1992) *Changing Britain for Good. Liberal Democrat General Election Manifesto, 1992* (London: Liberal Democrat Party).

Liberal Democrats (2010) *Liberal Democrat Manifesto 2010* (London: Liberal Democrat Party).

Milne, S. (2010) The Corporate Grip on Public Life is a Threat to Democracy. *Guardian*, 18 November: 39.

Nuffield Council on Bioethics (2007) *Public Health: Ethical Issues* (London: Nuffield Council on Bioethics).

Office of Budget Responsibility (2010) *Economic and Fiscal Outlook*. Cm 7979 (London: The Stationery Office).

Page, R.M. (2007) Without a Song in Their Heart: New Labour, the Welfare State and the Retreat from Democratic Socialism. *Journal of Social Policy,* 36(1): 19–38.

Page, R.M. (2010) David Cameron's Modern Conservative Approach to Poverty and Social Justice: Towards One Nation or Two? *Journal of Poverty and Social Justice,* 18(2): 147–60.

Park, A., Curtice, J., Clery, E. and Bryson, C. (eds.) (2010) *British Social Attitudes: the 27th Report* (London: Sage).

Pollock, A. (2010) Should NHS Mental Health Services Fear the Private Sector? *British Medical Journal,* 341, 9 October: 760–1.

Pollock, A. and Price, D. (2010) Another Step Towards Private Health Care. *Guardian,* 10 July: 6.

Prabhakar, R. (2010) Reforming Public Services: The Views of the Main Parties. In S. Griffiths and K. Hickson (eds.), *British Party Politics and Ideology after New Labour* (Basingstoke: Palgrave Macmillan), pp. 195–207.

Prentis, D. (2010) The Case for the NHS. *Guardian,* 14 October: 34.

Raison, T. (1990) *Tories and the Welfare State* (London: Macmillan).

Ruane, S. (2010) Health Policy under New Labour: Not What it Seems? In I. Greener, C. Holden and M. Kilkey (eds.), *Social Policy Review 22* (Bristol: Policy Press), pp. 51–70.

Rutherford, J. (2010) Labour's Good Society. *Soundings,* 46, Winter: 6–17.

Thaler, R.H. and Sunstein. C.R. (2008) *Nudge: Improving Decisions about Health and Happiness* (New Haven, CT: Yale University Press).

Timmins, N. (2010a) Where Do the Cuts Leave the NHS? *British Medical Journal,* 341, 30 October: 916–17.

Toynbee, P. and Walker, D. (2010) *The Verdict. Did Labour Change Britain?* (London: Granta).

Vaizey, E. (ed.) (2002) *The Blue Book on Health* (London: Politico's).

Walshe, K. (2010) Reorganization of the NHS in England, *British Medical Journal,* 341, 24 July: 341–2.

7
Welfare Reform and Coalition Politics in the Age of Austerity

Stephen Driver

Welfare reform was at the heart of New Labour politics in the 1990s. It was also a significant aspect of David Cameron's bid for electoral success after 2005. The Liberal Democrats too made reform of the tax and benefit system, in particular for those on low incomes, part of their political pitch on the liberal left. Welfare reform was – and still is – unfinished business for British politics and policy-making. Despite a strong economic performance under the Labour Government after 1997, which saw near full employment, underlying rates of economic inactivity remained stuck at around one fifth of the working-age population. The recession that hit Britain in 2008 heaped unemployment on these already high levels of 'welfare dependency'. If welfare reform proved tough-going in an era of 'non-inflationary consistent expansion', it will be even harder in the 'age of austerity'. So, where is the Conservative–Liberal Democrat Coalition taking welfare reform? Are we seeing a break with previous Labour policies or more of the same? Where do the Coalition's policies stand from a more international and comparative perspective? And does the Coalition Government offer the chance to establish the long-term settlement that welfare in the UK so desperately needs?

Welfare Reform and Building a Coalition

On the face of it, the Conservative Party and the Liberal Democrats looked unlikely bedfellows on welfare reform. The Lib Dems had spent the best part of two decades on the liberal left of Britain's party system with policies on civil liberties and a host of economic and social issues. Indeed, behind the patter of partisan politics at Westminster, it was Labour and the Conservatives who found common cause on welfare to work, not least when former banker David Freud reported on welfare reform to the Labour Government in 2007 (Freud, 2007) and then, after a brief spell advising the Work and Pensions Minster, James Purnell, joined the Tory opposition benches in the House of Lords. But with Nick Clegg and the *Orange Book* economic liberals (see Marshall and Laws, 2004) shifting the ideological axis of the Liberal Democrats to the right, the dividing lines between all three parties blurred.

It is perhaps not surprising, then, that the issue of welfare took a back seat during the 2010 campaign. All three parties shared a broad policy consensus around work-oriented welfare reform. This consensus, as we shall see, focused on 'making work pay', providing support for those out of work to find jobs and insisting that rights to welfare should be balanced with responsibilities to seek and take work. This consensus spanned not just welfare reform in the UK but across Europe, North America and Australasia. Indeed, any understanding of current Coalition welfare policies needs to be put in this international and comparative perspective. The support for active labour market policies and a 'social investment state' cut across political and ideological lines, national boundaries and regimes of welfare capitalism.

Agreeing policy on welfare reform did not prove a stumbling block to coalition-building in the days after the General Election. The degree of accommodation required between the Conservatives and the Liberal Democrats was fairly limited. The Coalition Agreement itself pledged the new government would 'encourage responsibility and fairness in the welfare system [by] providing help for those who cannot work, training and targeted support for those looking for work, but sanctions for those who turn down reasonable offers of work or training' (HM Government, 2010: 23). This was hardly a statement of intent to divide mainstream politicians or policy-makers.

On the details, the Coalition document supported a single welfare-to-work programme to replace the alphabet soup of New Deals; cutting the period between claims for Jobseeker's Allowance and referrals to a welfare-to-work programme; payment-by-results contracts for welfare-to-work providers; greater conditionality on those on welfare to take work; retaining the national minimum wage; the reassessment of incapacity claimants for their 'readiness' to work; measures to support self-employment and business start-ups; and pre-employment training and work placements and local 'work clubs'. The Coalition Agreement also stated the government would 'investigate how to simplify the benefit system in order to improve incentives to work' and, significantly, to 'maintain the goal of ending child poverty in the UK by 2020' (HM Government, 2010: 23 and 19).

Once the terms of the Coalition document had been agreed, the new Prime Minister appointed former Tory leader Iain Duncan Smith as Secretary of State for Work and Pensions. Chris Grayling, who had shadowed the post in opposition for the Conservatives, was made Minister for Employment; Maria Miller became Minister for Disabled People; and Lord Freud given the job once held by Frank Field in the early years of the Labour Government of Minister for Welfare Reform. For the Liberal Democrats, former Institute for Fiscal Studies researcher and social policy academic Steve Webb was given the pension brief. Webb was a leading figure on the social liberal wing of his party. Field himself – much to his obvious delight – was asked by Cameron to carry out a review of 'poverty and life chances' for the government.

The Coalition Government hit the ground running on welfare reform. A bill was one of the centrepieces of its legislative programme outlined in the 2010 Queen's Speech: 'We must be here to help people improve their lives, not just park them on long-term benefits', Duncan Smith told an audience of welfare experts within weeks of taking office (BBC, 2010a). The Coalition, he announced, would create a new integrated work programme, provide support for older workers to find jobs as soon as they became unemployed and rigorously enforce the penalties introduced by Labour on those refusing jobs.

The central role played by Duncan Smith in the new government's welfare reform plans came as little surprise. Since being sacked as Conservative leader in 2003, he had undergone something of a political makeover. Duncan Smith was a leading opponent of the Maastricht Treaty on European Union in the 1990s and had made John Major's time as Prime Minister hell (something many Conservatives MPs never forgave him for). On the right wing of the party, he was, in Philip Norton's terms, a 'pure Thatcherite' committed to free markets, national sovereignty and traditional institutions. As leader, Duncan Smith had, to a certain extent, attempted to reposition the Conservatives on social issues, in particular poverty. With time on his hands as a backbencher, he set up the Centre for Social Justice in 2004.

The Centre was given the welfare brief by David Cameron as he allocated his policy review to specialist groups. In December 2006 and July 2007, the Social Justice Policy Group chaired by Duncan Smith published two reports: *Breakdown Britain* and *Breakthrough Britain* (Social Justice Policy Group, 2006, 2007). These reports put the idea of the 'broken society' centre-stage of Cameron's attack on the Brown Government by pinning the blame on continuing levels of social deprivation on Labour and its 'statist' policies (Cameron, 2008). In reality, as we shall see, there was little to divide government and opposition in the run-up to the 2010 General Election and beyond on welfare reform.

Reforming the Tax and Benefit System

The focus of the Coalition's welfare reforms in its first year in power has been reform of the benefits systems – in particular, the mix of carrots and sticks to 'make work pay'. The problem is widely acknowledged. Despite a buoyant economy under Labour that drove up employment rates and made the UK the destination of choice for economic migrants for the EU accession states in Eastern Europe, levels of economic inactivity remained high: around 20 per cent of the working-age population. Recession made the situation worse. By 2010, over five million people were not just out of work but outside the labour market on long-term social security payments that would never lift them out of poverty. Nearly 1.5 million claimants in 2010 had been on a work-related benefit for nine out of the last ten years, according to figures from the Department for Work and Pensions (2010a: 4).

The Coalition Government's proposals to 'make work pay' shared the same goal as Labour's plans in 1997 – something Duncan Smith acknowledged. The aim was to make taking a job financially worthwhile. Published just a couple of months after the election, the Coalition's White Paper *21st Century Welfare* focused on 'structural reform' of the benefits system to 'maximize work incentives while continuing to protect those most in need' (Department for Work and Pensions, 2010a: 2). Labour's reforms, the White Paper argued, had created a hugely complex system of welfare payments and fiscal transfers (tax credits). This made claiming difficult, undermined what financial incentives there were in the system for individuals to take paid employment and led to a great number of cases of under- and overpayment: 'working legitimately is not a rational choice for many poor people to make' (Department for Work and Pensions, 2010a: 13).

At the heart of the White Paper were plans to simplify the tax and benefit system by creating a 'universal credit'. This would merge out-of-work benefits and tax credits and operate under a single set of entitlements. To 'make work pay', the universal credit would withdraw income support at a 'single, reasonable, rate' as a person found work and started to earn more. The new credit would also disregard earnings up to a certain level to encourage individuals to take work.

Alongside these incentives, the White Paper also proposed making the conditions applying to claiming social security tougher, in particular in relation to accepting the offer of employment. Such a unified system, the White Paper suggested, could be delivered using 'smart automation' and a single public agency; and might also, perhaps most controversially of all, be 'consistent with possible steps to make aspects of the welfare system more localized'(Department for Work and Pensions, 2010a: 3).

The White Paper set out the Coalition's stall on welfare reform. But Duncan Smith had a battle on his hands to persuade George Osborne at the Treasury to agree. The issue was one of cost. Under the proposed universal credit, incentives to work would be generated by allowing individuals to keep more of their earnings. This, Duncan Smith insisted, would cut high marginal tax rates for those taking jobs or extending their hours. The new system, Duncan Smith also argued, would save money in the longer term by reducing fraud and administrative costs. But these measures to 'make work pay' would in the short term be expensive for the Treasury. Osborne feared they were unaffordable at a time when large cuts in public spending were needed.

The deal between Osborne and Duncan Smith paved the way for a second White Paper in November 2010 setting out the details of the universal credit (Department for Work and Pensions, 2010b). As expected, the credit would bring together the main work-related benefits including jobseeker's allowance, child tax credit, working tax credit, income support and employment support allowance. Claimants would receive a basic allowance and additional payments would be made for disability, child care and housing. Whether this removes all the complexity from the system is a moot point. There would be different rates for single people and couples and the under-25s. Households would make just one claim and the whole system would, it was suggested, operate closer to 'real time' via an integrated, internet-based system (though there is considerable scepticism over whether this will work). Under the proposed reforms, certain benefits would remain, including child benefit, disability living allowance and the NI-based contributory jobseeker's allowance. The new rules would come into force in 2011, with a plan to get all claimants on the new system in the early part of the next Parliament after 2015. The White Paper also proposed significantly tougher rules for claiming social security. The conditionality of the benefits system would increase, with sanctions for those refusing work three times losing their benefit for three months (and those found to have committed benefit fraud on a repeated basis losing their support for three years). Indeed, ahead of the new universal credit, there are plans for a much tougher benefits regime across the board.

Benefits and the Budget

The price for the deal struck between the Treasury and Work and Pensions was cuts to the real value of benefits over time. Already, in Osborne's first budget in June, reductions in social security spending were announced amounting to £11 billion by the end of parliamentary term. These would be driven by linking all benefits bar the state pension to the consumer prices index (CPI) rather than the retail price index (RPI). The CPI is typically lower than the RPI, resulting in cuts to living standards for those on social security. By contrast to this austerity politics on welfare, Osborne announced the state pension would in future increase in line with earnings, prices or 2.5 per cent, whichever was the greatest. Other measures in the budget included a reduction of tax credit payments to those families earning more than £40,000 and a three-year freeze on child benefit payments.

Cuts to social security were also at the heart of the Government's autumn comprehensive spending review. These would come principally from changes to health and disability payments and the removal of child benefit from families with a higher rate taxpayer. Politics, however, trumped consistency and other universal payments such as the winter fuel allowance remained. While the child benefit changes grabbed all the headlines, the new rules for incapacity benefit and its successor, the employment support allowance, were the more important. These would see insurance-based social security paid for just one year before means-testing commenced. Those claimants with severe disabilities and health conditions, the Government insisted, would be protected under the new system. But all others would be expected to go onto lower-value, work-related benefits or find paid employment.

The outcome of the comprehensive spending review made clear that while Duncan Smith might have got his universal credit, the Treasury had got its cuts. Certainly, the stringent settlement for social security was apparent in some of the details of Duncan Smith's November White Paper which forms the basis for the Welfare Reform Bill in 2011. Indeed, the compromises raise a number of important concerns about the Coalition's welfare reform plans. The first is the rate at which benefits are withdrawn. It was expected that claimants finding work or extending their hours would keep up to half of the new earnings. The figure is likely to be nearer a quarter. This may save money for the Treasury, but do little for high marginal tax rates on lower income households. Smaller pay packets for those lucky enough to find work are also likely to exacerbate the impact on low-income households. While the Coalition was keen to emphasize that 'we're all in it together', the reality is that the combination of welfare reform and the spending review will fall hardest on those that have least. The inconvenient truth may be that this is necessary to sharpen the incentives to take work. But how the state continues to support those 'most in need' is another matter.

There is a broader point here about the costs and benefits of welfare reform. Cutting social security rates is relatively easy and shifts the pain of reform onto poorer households. Making work pay has a cost and the Government has already had to revise upward the financial estimates of its benefit reforms. Welfare to work is a much harder nut to crack, as all parties agree. The provision of services to the long-term unemployed is an expensive business – and always has been. For many stuck on welfare, changes to marginal tax and benefit rates will not in themselves prove the incentive to make the 'rational choice' into employment. While tougher rules on entitlements should help to shift expectations, publicly funded services, whoever delivers them, are needed to support claimants get ready for work. So, the savings from welfare reform are some way down the line as people find jobs, stop claiming and start paying taxes. Poor employment prospects post-recession and as a result of the budget cuts will put this time-line back further.

Politicians and policy-makers, then, have to be prepared for the long haul on welfare reform. Indeed, if Frank Field is right in his review of poverty published in December 2010 (Field, 2010), then seriously tackling the underlying social divisions that shape life chances will take a generation or more. The consensus that has emerged around welfare reform, as we see in the final section, may help in this respect, as may the necessities of sharing power in a Coalition Government.

The New Politics of Welfare

Shadow Chancellor Alan Johnson, responding to the comprehensive spending review (CSR) in the House of Commons, echoed the views of many on the left. The CSR was little more than an ideologically motivated attack on the state by an ideologically driven Conservative Party, whatever formal Coalition might be in power (Stratton, 2010). The 'age of austerity' was a cloak for a return to Thatcherism and its neoliberal policies. Talk of a 'big society' masked a desire for a small state and a safety-net welfare regime. The Coalition was dismantling what was left of social democratic social policy (Bale, 2010). Labour's response to the Coalition Government's proposals to reform the tax and benefit system was, by contrast, muted. In government, Labour leader Ed Miliband admitted, his party had not done enough to reform welfare and he was broadly supportive of the Coalition plans (BBC Online, 2010b).

These apparently contradictory positions point to the difficulties of assessing the new politics of welfare under the Coalition. Certainly the period of high Thatcherism in the 1980s was marked by a belief that the problem with welfare – and 'welfare dependency' – was that the state did too much and should do less. The unemployed, as Norman Tebbit memorably put, should, like his father in the 1930s, get on their bikes and find work somewhere else. This perspective on welfare inspired by American libertarians such as Charles Murray focused on the disincentives government put in place by providing too much welfare to individuals looking for jobs. Remove the welfare – or at least significant elements of it – and claimants would have all the incentives they needed to find work and get out of poverty (Murray, 1984).

Conservative critics of this neoliberal view, notably Laurence Mead, challenged the assumption that getting rid of welfare solved the problem of welfare dependency (Mead, 1992, 1997). It assumed, Mead argued, that those on welfare were capable of responding to these new market signals and going out, finding work and holding down a job. Mead's criticism of Murray was that most claimants weren't, as we might put it, 'work-ready'. Therefore, Conservatives had to support 'big government' to provide the 'help and hassle' to make welfare to work, work. A residual welfare state was not enough.

This policy debate within the New Right camp in the 1980s and 1990s reminds us that conservative politics on both sides of the Atlantic has never been clear-cut on welfare reform – and any labelling of the Coalition's welfare reforms as 'Thatcherite' problematic. It is also worth remembering that the reform of the provision of social security to those out of work was not simply a right-wing policy agenda. Indeed, in the US, advocacy of policies to support claimants back into work ('welfare to work') and measures to deal with high marginal tax rates for those looking for work ('making work pay') was as much led by New Democrats (in particular, David Ellwood, 1998) as by neoconservatives such as Murray and Mead. In the UK, the Conservatives in government experimented with both welfare to work (Project Work) and in-work benefits to boost the incomes of those finding low paid jobs (Family Credit). The Commission on Social Justice set up by Labour in 1994 was instrumental in establishing welfare reform as a core feature of New Labour. In government after 1997, Labour moved quickly to establish the New Deal welfare-to-work programme, as well as the national minimum wage and the system of tax credits to increase work incentives.

To be sure, the political devil has always been in the detail of welfare policies, in particular, what services the state should supply as part of a welfare-to-work programme, the timing and provision of these services, the balance of skills training and job-related activities (the human capital and labour force attachment debate), the elements of conditionality and compulsion in any reform programme, the placing of time limits on the receipt of benefits and the reforms to the tax and benefit system to remove disincentives to take paid employment. Broadly speaking, the left have generally taken an approach to welfare reform that highlights human capital and the demand for labour; the goals of ending poverty and promoting equality; and the non-conditional universal provision of social security. By contrast, the right has put greater emphasis on the individual rather than collective responsibility for social security; the adverse behavioural consequences of 'welfare dependency'; the need to get claimants into work over training (so-called 'work first'); and the placing of significant conditions and time limits on entitlements to welfare.

But what political differences there have been to welfare reform over the past two decades have blurred – and in the UK, Frank Field was at the forefront of this political convergence. Certainly, in government Labour's welfare reforms became more work-focused, with increasing elements of conditionality and compulsion (Finn, 2005). But Labour's approach to welfare reform was not out of step with what was happening across Europe, including social democratic Scandinavia. Indeed, while it was all too easy to see how New Labour was learning policy lessons from North America, not least because of its connections with Bill Clinton's New Democrats, the process of social policy exchange was more complex (Annesley, 2003; Driver, 2003).

Certainly, the welfare reforms of successive governments in the 1980s, 1990s and 2000s, not least the erosion of universal and insurance-based social security, shifted the UK further towards the liberal model of welfare capitalism. But Labour's broader social policies, in particular the investments in early years provision and income transfers to poor families as part of an explicit anti-poverty strategy, ensured the British welfare state continued to be something of a hybrid, combining elements of the Scandinavian social democratic model and the Continental European conservative model, as well as the Anglo-Saxon liberal model exemplified by the US, Canada and Australia (Lewis and Giullari, 2004; see also McKay and Rowlingson, 2008). The 'social investment state' (Lister, 2003), which puts the responsibility on 'citizen workers' (or 'adult workers') to adapt to a changing labour market supported by government investments in human and social capital, should be viewed as part of a wider readjustment to public policy by states across all regimes of welfare capitalism as they struggled to promote employment in open market economies (Scharpf and Schmidt, 2000). The Conservative–Liberal Coalition's welfare reforms need to be understood not just in the context of UK social policy under successive governments, but also in this international and comparative perspective.

The final phase of New Labour in government after 2005 was marked by market-driven reforms to the delivery of welfare to work following the publication of the Freud Report. Tony Blair may have left office, but his successor, Gordon Brown, was in important respects continuing his public service reform agenda (Driver 2009; see also Greener, 2008). With the Blairite James Purnell at the Department for Work and Pensions there was greater use of contracts with the private and voluntary sectors to deliver welfare to work; tighter conditions on eligibility for those claiming health-related benefits; and some streamlining of these benefits to reduce complexity, in particular, creating a new employment support allowance to replace incapacity benefits (though overall the benefits system remained fearsomely complicated, as the Conservatives and others pointed out).

Freud's move to Cameron's Conservative camp and his later appointment as Minister for Welfare Reform made what would have been a relatively smooth transition from one government to another on welfare reform almost seamless. Freud's job is to get right the market for welfare to work provision that he inspired under Labour. The reshaping of Labour's New Deals into a single work programme is planned for 2011. There are tricky issues for the Coalition to tackle, not least ensuring the market for welfare to work has the right incentives in place for providers to deliver the support to those who really need it. This targeting of provision and ensuring that economic inactivity, not just unemployment, is tackled will not be easy when economic growth is slow and jobs harder to come by.

Managing Welfare Reform in the Coalition

The Coalition, for the time being at least, is likely to find the political management of welfare reform relatively straightforward. Indeed,

Coalition Government and a broad policy consensus may offer an opportunity for one of the most intractable areas of domestic public policy. Labour in government on its own struggled on welfare reform, not least because of opposition from its own backbenches as it faced down a series of revolts on changes to social security (all of which it won). Labour too faced considerable resistance from its supporters in the trade unions hostile to the Government's wider public service reform agenda. Welfare reform may have been at the heart of New Labour as it sought to balance 'economic efficiency and social justice', but it was outside the party's ideological and policy comfort zone.

The junior partners in the Coalition may also find certain aspects of welfare reform difficult to live with. Many Liberal Democrats, especially those on the social liberal wing of the party, are, like Labour members, not just ideologically but also morally and emotionally opposed to a welfare reform agenda that is seeing cuts to benefit rates and tougher conditions and time limits on entitlements to social security. Having said this, Steve Webb, junior minster and leading figure on the left of the party, came out quickly in support of his Government's benefit reforms (Webb, 2010). The Coalition, as we saw earlier, remains committed to early years provision, a national minimum wage and the goal of ending child poverty by 2020 – all core features of New Labour's post-Thatcherite social policy supported by the Liberal Democrats. The deal struck between Osborne and Duncan Smith over welfare payments is likely to make achieving the Coalition's anti-poverty targets all the harder. While work may be the only assured way to address poverty, there remain a great many families in work still in poverty – 2.1 million children according to the latest Monitoring Poverty report from the Joseph Rowntree Foundation (Parekh, MacInnes and Kenway, 2010). In the short run, this is unlikely to change. But the Government will have to make progress on addressing poverty as it reforms welfare if it is to avoid another potential fault-line between the Coalition partners.

Cameron is unlikely to face much opposition from his own parliamentary party on welfare reform. Indeed, one problem he may face is managing the expectations of some on his backbenches (and among Conservative voters and the media), not least the hardened Thatcherites, who would like nothing better than to slash and burn the welfare state. While this is pressure the Coalition can afford to resist, there remains a political tipping point on welfare reform, as the Democrats in the US found to their cost when welfare reform turned radically right after President Clinton lost support in Congress following the 1996 mid-term elections (Weaver, 2000).

References

Annesley, C. (2003) Americanised and Europeanised: UK Social Policy since 1997. *British Journal of Politics & International Relations*, 5(2): 143–65.

Bale, T. (2010) Thatcher's Ideology is behind this Spending Review. *The Guardian*, 22 October. www.guardian.co.uk/commentisfree/2010/oct/22/thatcher-and-cultural-hegemony.

BBC Online (2010) *Welfare Reform Proposals Revealed*. news.bbc.co.uk/1/hi/uk_politics/8707652.stm.

BBC Online (2010b) *Labour Failed on Welfare – Ed Miliband*. www.bbc.co.uk/news/uk-politics-11842711.

Cameron, D. (2008) Fixing Our Broken Society. Speech. Glasgow, 7 July. www.conservatives.com/News/Speeches/2008/07/David_Cameron_Fixing_our_Broken_Society.aspx.

Department for Work and Pensions (2010a) *21st Century Welfare*, Cm 7913 (Norwich: The Stationery Office).

Department for Work and Pensions (2010b) *Universal Credit: Welfare that Works*, Cm 7957 (Norwich: The Stationery Office).

Driver, S. (2003) North Atlantic Drift: Welfare Reform and the Third Way Politics of New Labour and the New Democrats. In W. Leggett, S. Hale and L. Martell, *The Third Way and Beyond: Criticisms, Futures and Alternatives* (Manchester: Manchester University Press).

Driver, S. (2009) Work to be Done? Welfare Reform from Blair to Brown. *Policy Studies*, 30(1): 69–84.

Ellwood, D. (1998) *Poor Support: Poverty in the American Family* (New York: Basic Books).

Field, F. (2010) *The Foundation Years: Preventing Poor Children Becoming Poor Adults* (London: Cabinet Office). povertyreview.independent.gov.uk/media/20254/poverty-report.pdf.

Finn, D. (2005) Welfare to Work: New Labour's Employment First Welfare State. *Benefits*, 13(2): 93–7.

Freud, D. (2007) *Reducing Dependency, Increasing Opportunity: Options for the Future of Welfare to Work* (Leeds: Department for Work and Pensions/Corporate Document Services). www.dwp.gov.uk/welfarereform/freud_report.asp.

Greener, I. (2008) The Stages of Labour. In M. Powell (ed.), *Modernising the Welfare State: The Blair Legacy* (Bristol: Policy Press).

HM Government (2010) *The Coalition: Our Programme for Government* (London: Cabinet Office). www.cabinetoffice.gov.uk/media/409088/pfg_Coalition.pdf.

Lewis, J. and Giullari, S. (2004) The Adult Worker Model: Family, Gender Equality and Care. *Economy and Society*, 34(1): 76–104.

Lister, R. (2003) Investing in the Citizen-Workers of the Future: Transformations in Citizenship and the State under New Labour. *Social Policy and Administration*, 37(5): 427–43.

Marshall, P. and Laws, D. (eds.) (2004) *The Orange Book: Reclaiming Liberalism* (London: Profile Books).

McKay, S. and Rowlingson, K. (2008) Social Security and Welfare Reform. In M. Powell (ed.), *Modernising the Welfare State: The Blair Legacy* (Bristol: Policy Press).

Mead, L. (1992) *The New Politics of Poverty: The Nonworking Poor in America* (New York: Basic Books).

Mead, L. (1997) From Welfare to Work: Lessons from America. In A. Deacon, *From Welfare to Work: Lessons from America* (London: Institute of Economic Affairs).

Murray, C. (1984) *Losing Ground: American Social Policy, 1950–1980* (New York: Basic Books).

Parekh, A., MacInnes, T. and Kenway, P. (2010) *Monitoring Poverty and Social Exclusion* (York: Joseph Rowntree Trust). www.jrf.org.uk/sites/files/jrf/poverty-social-exclusion-2010-full.pdf.

Scharpf, F.W. and Schmidt, V.A. (eds.) (2000) *Welfare and Work in the Open Economy: From Vulnerability to Competitiveness* (Oxford: Oxford University Press).

Social Justice Report Group (2006) *Breakdown Britain* (London: Social Justice Report Group).

Social Justice Report Group (2007) *Breakthrough Britain: Ending the Costs of Social Breakdown*, Volumes I–VI (London: Social Justice Report Group).

Stratton, A. (2010) Spending Review 2010: Alan Johnson Says Coalition Cuts 'Ideological'. *The Guardian*, 20 October. www.guardian.co.uk/politics/2010/oct/20/alan-johnson-says-spending-cuts-ideological.

Weaver, K. (2000) *Ending Welfare as We Know It* (Washington, DC: Brookings Institute).

Webb, S. (2010) Why Liberal Democrats Should Welcome the Welfare Reforms. *Liberal Democrat Voice*, 16 November. www.libdemvoice.org/steve-webb-writes-why-liberal-democrats-should-welcome-the-welfare-reforms-22068.html.

8
Vote Blue, Go Green, What's a Bit of Yellow in Between?

James Connelly

Introduction

On 14 May 2010, three days after the formation of the Coalition Government, David Cameron pledged that 'This will be the greenest government ever'. He also announced his commitment to the 10:10 campaign, with all government departments to cut their greenhouse gas emissions by 10 per cent by the end of 2010. So it seemed that the famous slogan 'Vote Blue, Go Green', which defined the Conservative Party's approach in the two or three years leading up to the General Election of May 2010, was alive and well. However, we are no longer dealing with the Conservative Party alone: it is the Coalition we now have to deal with. In this chapter I consider both the shape and direction of Coalition environmental policy and also the tensions and compromises which are an inevitable consequence of Coalition formation and practice.

There are three obvious starting points for a consideration and evaluation of Conservative–Liberal Democrat Coalition policy on the environment. The first is their manifesto commitments; the second is their view on the economy and the deficit; and the third lies in the declaration that 'we share a conviction that the days of big government are over; that centralization and top-down control have proved a failure' (HM Government, 2010: 7).

In its joint programme, the Coalition stated boldly:

this Coalition has the potential for era-changing, convention-challenging, radical reform . . . we both want to build a new economy

118

from the rubble of the old. We will support sustainable growth and enterprise, balanced across all regions and all industries, and promote the green industries that are so essential for our future. This document shows how, with radical plans to reform our broken banking system and new incentives for green growth. (HM Government, 2010: 7)

They added that this was to be done in a way that avoided governmental interference, by seeking to change people's behaviour not through rules and regulations, but in a 'smarter' fashion, 'shunning the bureaucratic levers of the past and finding intelligent ways to encourage, support and enable people to make better choices for themselves' (HM Government, 2010: 7–8). So: we find a commitment to green industries, green growth and smarter government. What does this add up to in practice? Before addressing that question, we need to examine the party policy strands that fed into the Coalition mix.

In their manifestos the Conservatives claimed that 'environmental issues must be at the heart of politics' and the Liberal Democrats that all their policies 'have a green thread running through them'. Both parties agree on the need to move to a low-carbon economy and they have common ground on environmental initiatives. A key commitment in the Conservative manifesto was to the Green Investment Bank. Although the idea had been developed in opposition by George Osborne as Shadow Chancellor, this was a commitment shared by the Labour Government and it featured in their last budget in March 2010. Their proposal was to launch it with £2 billion equity. In the Conservative manifesto it appears without a figure.

On green energy development, the Conservatives want 15 per cent of UK energy to come from renewable sources by 2020 while the Liberal Democrats want 40 per cent of electricity to come from renewable sources. Both parties agree on the need for new rules to limit emissions from fossil fuel power stations and to develop a smart electricity grid. Nuclear power, however, is more contentious. The Liberal Democrats were committed to 'no to nuclear power'; the Conservatives were in favour of nuclear power, although without a public subsidy for new nuclear plants.

The Coalition Programme

Rootes and Carter comment that *The Coalition: Our Programme for Government* is 'remarkable for the range of green measures it contains – more than on any other topic'. However, they point out, on climate change the policy commitments are almost identical to those of the

Labour Government, including the emphasis on renewable energy (Rootes and Carter, 2010: 996). The formation of the Coalition, they suggest, provided the opportunity for Cameron to cement the modernization of the Conservative Party and to enact the green rhetoric with which he had been identified since becoming party leader in 2005.

The document contains a lengthy section on Energy and Climate Change, which commences by stating that climate change is a grave threat and requires urgent action. It continues by asserting the need to use a wide range of levers 'to cut carbon emissions, decarbonize the economy and support the creation of new green jobs and technologies' (HM Government, 2010: 16). It states that the Government will 'push for the EU to demonstrate leadership in tackling international climate change, including by supporting an increase in the EU emission reduction target to 30 per cent by 2020' (HM Government, 2010: 16). Moving to particulars, it announces that 'We will seek to increase the target for energy from renewable sources, subject to the advice of the Climate Change Committee' (HM Government, 2010: 16) and that 'we will continue public sector investment in carbon capture and storage (CCS) technology for four coal-fired power stations' (HM Government, 2010: 16). This is followed by a brisk confirmation that 'We will establish a smart grid and roll out smart meters . . . establish a full system of feed-in tariffs in electricity . . . introduce measures to promote a huge increase in energy from waste through anaerobic digestion' (HM Government, 2010: 16). On the next line we discover the bland statement that the Coalition will 'create a green investment bank' (HM Government, 2010: 16). We return to the saga of the Green Investment Bank below. Among other things they intend to 'establish an emissions performance standard that will prevent coal-fired power stations being built unless they are equipped with sufficient carbon capture and storage to meet the emissions performance standard' (HM Government, 2010: 16) and to cancel the third runway at Heathrow and also refuse permissions for additional runways at Gatwick and Stansted Airports.

In relation to the Emissions Trading Scheme (ETS) there is a commitment to the introduction of a floor price for carbon and to 'make efforts to persuade the EU to move towards full auctioning of ETS permits' (HM Government, 2010: 16). And through the 'Green Deal', they 'will encourage home energy efficiency improvements paid for by savings from energy bills. We will also take measures to improve energy efficiency in businesses and public sector buildings' and 'reform energy markets to deliver security of supply and investment in low carbon energy, and ensure fair competition' (HM Government, 2010: 16). They will deliver an offshore electricity grid to support the development of a new generation of offshore wind power and encourage community-owned renewable energy schemes where local people benefit from the power produced. On the international front they will 'work towards an ambitious global climate deal that will limit emissions and explore the creation of new international sources of funding for the purpose of climate change adaptation and mitigation' (HM Government, 2010: 17).

On environment, food and rural affairs, the document proposes the introduction of measures to make the import or possession of illegally felled timber a criminal offence, to introduce measures to protect wildlife and promote green spaces and wildlife corridors; to launch a national tree planting campaign; to review the governance arrangements of National Parks to increase local accountability; to work towards a 'zero waste' economy by encouraging councils to pay people to recycle; and to create a presumption in favour of sustainable development in the planning system (HM Government, 2010: 18).

On transport, there is a commitment to making the transport sector 'greener and more sustainable, with tougher emission standards and support for new transport technologies' (HM Government, 2010: 31). This includes 'a national recharging network for electric and plug-in hybrid vehicles' and longer rail franchises to give operators 'the incentive to invest in the improvements passengers want – like better services, better stations, longer trains and better rolling stock' (HM Government, 2010: 31). There is also a commitment to reform decision-making on the prioritization of transport projects 'so that the benefits of low carbon proposals (including light rail schemes) are fully recognized' and to the establishment of a high-speed rail network 'as part of our programme of measures to fulfil our joint ambitions for creating a low carbon economy. Our vision is of a truly national high speed rail network for the whole of Britain' (HM Government, 2010: 31).

Nuclear power is perhaps one of the most interesting areas of Coalition environmental policy because it is a locus of overt doctrinal conflict between the parties. The Conservative manifesto commits to securing UK energy supplies by 'clearing the way for new nuclear power stations', provided that they receive no public subsidy (Conservative Party, 2010: 92), whereas the Liberal Democrats' manifesto promised to 'reject a new generation of nuclear power stations', because 'based on the evidence nuclear is a far more expensive way of reducing carbon emissions than promoting energy conservation and renewable energy' (Liberal Democrat Party, 2010: 58). There is acknowledgement of the fact that the Liberal Democrats have for a long time been opposed to new nuclear power stations while the Conservatives are committed to replacing existing nuclear power stations, subject to the normal planning process and without public subsidy. However, it is the Conservatives' position that forms the basis of the Coalition nuclear policy. Liberal Democrat MPs will be able to demonstrate their opposition, but only through abstention; and it has been agreed that it will not be treated as a confidence issue. This labyrinthine squaring of the circle produces a peculiar state of affairs in which the Secretary of State for Energy and Climate Change 'will be entitled to denounce his own government's policy on nuclear power' (Salmon, 2010). It has also been suggested that this explains why 'responsibility at DECC for new nuclear power lies with a Conservative minister' (Salmon, 2010).

The Coalition and the Environment: Promise and Practice

From the environmental point of view the appointment of Chris Huhne as Secretary of State at the Department of Energy and Climate Change (DECC) was a significant development as he had championed green issues in his Liberal Democrat leadership campaign. However, it is important also to look at the balance of the ministries and to consider the curious difficulty prompted by the Coalition's policy on new nuclear power. The other ministers at DECC are both Conservatives; at the Department for Environment, Food and Rural Affairs (Defra), the all-Conservative team is led by Secretary of State Caroline Spelman, who had a career as a lobbyist for the food and biotechnology industry. At the Department for Transport, Secretary of State Philip Hammond is flanked by two Conservative ministers and Norman Baker. Overall, out of the 12 ministers in the relevant departments, two are Liberal Democrats.

One of the key environmental policies of the Coalition is the *Green Deal*. What does this amount to? Essentially, it is an energy policy which encourages individuals, whether home owners or in rented accommodation, to reduce their energy consumption through the smarter approaches identified above. The Coalition's programme stated that 'through our "Green Deal", we will encourage home energy efficiency improvements paid for by savings from energy bills. We will also take measures to improve energy efficiency in businesses and public sector buildings' (HM Government, 2010: 16). The Green Deal was duly announced in the Queen's Speech with the claim that it would deliver energy efficiency to homes and businesses through a framework including incentives to energy suppliers and households to 'transform the provision of energy efficiency in the UK by enabling a "pay as you save" approach'. In September, Huhne linked it directly to the idea of green job creation in his announcement that 'were all 26 million households to take up the Green Deal over the next 20 years, employment in the sector would rise from its current level of 27,000 to something approaching 250,000' (DECC 2010). The Energy Bill was introduced to Parliament in December 2010.

The Liberal Democrats have a longstanding reputation for environmental concern, whereas the Conservatives (whether fairly or unfairly) do not, although Cameron as leader promoted environmental concerns and has maintained a reasonably consistent and committed position on the matter since becoming leader of the party in 2005. One clear point of tension within the Conservative part of the Coalition is that on the environment there are many MPs who are now, through the Coalition, committed to positions which do not sit comfortably with their traditional beliefs, allies and allegiances. As Rootes and Carter note:

> the environment might yet prove to be a source of political discontent within the Conservative Party – and therefore potentially destabilizing for the Coalition. Before the election, there was considerable hostility towards Cameron's green agenda within the Conservative parliamentary party and the wider grassroots membership, often expressed in vitriolic language on the party blogs. Climate change, in particular, could be a divisive issue. One pre-election poll revealed that Conservative candidates in the most winnable seats ranked 'reducing Britain's carbon footprint' bottom of a list of 19 priorities for the new government, and there will be fierce resistance from many Conservatives to any measures, such as the introduction of green taxes or new environmental regulations, that can be perceived as threatening economic recovery or imposing unnecessary costs on business. (Rootes and Carter, 2010: 997)

What has the Coalition done so far? On the minus side it has withdrawn funding for the Sustainable Development Commission (of which more later) and it has announced that it will not carry out its proposal to make it an offence to possess illegally felled timber or to bring it into the country; nor will it extend the subsidy for small-scale solar production under the Feed-In Tariff. On the plus side it has halted the third runway at Heathrow and stated that it would not approve new runways at Gatwick and Stansted. Whether this is primarily a policy motivated by environmental concern or more an attempt to show a clear difference between them and the preceding Labour Government is a moot point –

especially if one factors in other considerations such as Boris Johnson's demands for new airports in London. Again, the Coalition has committed itself to HS2, the high-speed rail system from London to the North along the western route. Whether this is a prime environmental concern is a matter of some debate and dispute. First, there is little evidence that it will take traffic off the roads, second, many argue – among them Friends of the Earth and others – that the best use of the same resources would be to upgrade other parts of the rail system. High-speed rail, although it *sounds* environmentally friendly because trains are assumed to be so, is not in fact *necessarily* so. The use of fuel and corresponding emissions increase rapidly and exponentially with increased speed, so the faster a train goes the less environmentally friendly it is. Or, in a nutshell, competing with air travel tends to generate emissions comparable with air travel.

Friends of the Earth suggest that although investment in faster, better rail travel is urgently needed, 'current high-speed rail plans will do little to cut climate-changing emissions or entice people out of planes and cars'. They go on to argue that 'The Government's priority should be to upgrade our existing overcrowded rail network – so ordinary travellers can benefit from better commuter and longer-distance services' and that 'more must also be done to encourage greener motoring and boost cycling and walking for short distances – which is better for our health and the environment'. Their view of high-speed rail is that it 'could play a part in a low-carbon transport network, but only if it is powered from renewable sources and backed by action to make rail travel cheaper and more attractive than flying or driving' (FOE, 2010).

The focus on high-speed rail has deflected attention away from the fact that the Coalition Agreement says virtually nothing about road transport and motor car use, other than pledging support for a national recharging network for electric and hybrid vehicles (HM Government, 2010: 31). Another largely missing item is buses. In the programme we find the statement: 'We will support sustainable travel initiatives, including the promotion of cycling and walking, and will encourage joint working between bus operators and local authorities' (HM Government, 2010: 31). However, in practice 'joint working' appears to be a victim of expenditure cuts: according to a report by the Campaign for Better Transport, more than two-thirds of local authorities plan cuts to public transport budgets. Norman Baker, the Liberal Democrat Transport Minister, admitted that the cuts could endanger unprofitable services, such as rural routes, which rely on local government subsidy for survival (Milmo, 2010).

Nuclear power, as we have seen, has already proved to be contentious. Admittedly, there is a serious debate about nuclear power in relation to its environmental credentials. There are many who would argue that it is the only way of keeping carbon emissions down, whatever its disadvantages. However, it is not clear that the Conservatives support it because of its green credentials, and besides, once all the other environmental costs associated with nuclear power – mining, transport, processing, long-term storage – are factored in, its carbon emissions rapidly catch up with alternatives: hence it is deceptive to claim that it represents an easy solution to the problem of carbon emissions. Huhne, at DECC, will be responsible for drafting a national planning statement enabling new nuclear power stations and placing it before Parliament, but a Liberal Democrat spokesman will speak against nuclear energy and Liberal Democrats will be allowed to abstain from the parliamentary vote (HM Government, 2010: 17). That the Liberal Democrats are embarrassed by the nuclear issue is apparent from the disappearance of their website 'No to nuclear power' and by having to face sharp questioning from critics such as Adrian Ramsay, deputy leader of the Green Party, who asked why the Liberal Democrat Party 'overcame its opposition to nuclear power in October to approve the construction of eight new nuclear power stations' (Ramsay, 2010).

There is a more general question here concerning claims that the Government will be 'the greenest ever'. How, for instance, do we measure such a claim? If we look at DECC, we can see the difficulties. On the one hand, the department has taken steps to stimulate growth in green energy, for example, allowing councils to sell renewable electricity generated on their land, but on the other, DECC has been subject to budget cuts which have led to the scrapping of funds or the scaling down of operations to support offshore wind, biomass and geothermal energy. Again, some green commitments are relatively costless and perhaps more symbol than substance: for example, the cancelling of the third runway at Heathrow. How is this to be measured against the abolition of the Royal Commission on Environmental Pollution or the Sustainable Development Commission? And how do all the promises of generating green jobs through the development of a green economy square with the damp squib that the proposal to found a Green Investment Bank has so far proved to be?

Taking these issues in turn, the Government is to stop funding the Sustainable Development Commission (SDC), its independent environmental watchdog and advisory body. Jonathon Porritt, the SDC's chairman between 2000 and 2009, responded angrily to this announcement, claiming that the Government's 'justification for getting rid of the SDC is transparently vacuous, if not downright dishonest' and that 'this is an ideological decision . . . a decision driven by dogma not by evidence-based, rational analysis'. More worryingly, he asserted that 'the only conceivable reason for allowing dogma to dominate in this way is that the government doesn't want anyone independently auditing its performance on sustainable development – let alone a properly-resourced, indisputably expert body operating as "a critical friend" on an inside track within government' (Black, 2010). If the Government is to be 'the greenest ever', why would it not want help to audit its performance? The Secretary of State for the Environment, Caroline Spelman, argues that the matter is so important that she wants the department to take control of it themselves, not devolve it to an outside body. This smacks either of megalomania, insincerity or ignorance. The crucial point, though, is that the decision to withdraw funding for the SDC has raised the question of whether the Coalition is prepared to seriously address the large and vital issue of whether the UK economy, with its 'continued commitment to growth, is developing along inherently unsustainable lines' (Black, 2010).

Porritt points out that the Government offered four justifications for axing the SDC. First, it will save money. As Porritt points out, half of the funding came from Defra and half from the devolved administrations and other Whitehall departments, all of which wanted to carry on working with the SDC. Second, the justification was that sustainable development is now mainstreamed across government. Given the claim that sustainable development is now embedded in every department, the inference is that 'no specialist capability at the centre is any longer required, simply because the government "gets it"'. On this claim Porritt is scathing:

> Like hell it does. To hear Caroline Spelman, Secretary of State in Defra, make such a totally fatuous claim after a few weeks in power is irritating beyond belief. She clearly knows nothing of the constant slog required (of the SDC and many other organizations) to achieve the limited traction that is all that can be laid claim to today. (Porritt, 2010)

He then observes that there is a certain irony in that the SDC is a UK-wide body, and that Wales and Scotland, which have done a better job than Whitehall in 'mainstreaming' sustainable development, are not in favour of abolition.

The only justification for abolition to which Porritt gives any credence is to eliminate duplication, but only because the SDC does admittedly do a number of different things and hence is bound to overlap with the work of others, for example, it advises ministers. The point, however, is that it is pretty much the only input regularly doing this from the point of view of integrated sustainable development. In addition, it works with many other public sector bodies in offering advice on sustainable development, work done by no other government body. Further, it provides independent scrutiny of government performance across the *whole* sustainable development agenda (that is, not just climate change) and this work is not done by any other body.

The final justification offered is that sustainable development is too important to delegate to an external body. Here Porritt reminds us of Spelman's precise words, in which she casts this as a matter of high decision and the expression of the utmost in personal responsibility 'Together with Chris Huhne, I am determined to take the lead role in driving the sustainable agenda across the whole of government, and I'm not willing to delegate this responsibility to an external body' (Porritt, 2010). Porritt cannot contain his amazement at the audacity of this claim: 'even after nine years working with dozens of government ministers, I'm astonished at such utterly brazen cynicism.' He points out that the only thing, to that date, that Spelman had done as Secretary of State at Defra was to publish a new departmental strategy which contains no serious reference to sustainable development. His conclusion is that the Government's justification for closing down the SDC is 'transparently vacuous, if not downright dishonest' and that it is an ideological decision, 'driven by dogma not by evidence-based, rational analysis'. From this he claims that it follows that the only reason for allowing dogma to dominate is that the Government does not 'want anyone independently auditing its performance on sustainable development – let alone a properly-resourced, indisputably expert body operating as "a critical friend" on an inside track within government' (Porritt, 2010). Here there is both a substantive and a symbolic claim, and even if the former could be disputed the latter cannot. It is hard to disagree with Porritt's remark that the closure of the SDC sends an anti-environmental signal, thereby jeopardizing Cameron's claim that this will be the 'greenest government ever'. As Porritt says, it is perhaps too early to make a definitive judgement about how green the agenda is under the Coalition, but the prospects are certainly not encouraging: '"Greenest ever" has to mean something substantive. Simply smearing a sickly ideological slime over everything just won't cut it' (Porritt, 2010).

The Comprehensive Spending Review and Environmental Policy

On 20 October 2010 the Comprehensive Spending Review (CSR) was published. Many of its proposed cuts hit hard at environmental spending.

Defra's budget was cut by 30 per cent (compared with a government average of 19 per cent). This equates to efficiency savings of £700 million by the end of the four-year review period. The relatively small DECC is cut by 18 per cent. The Environment Agency will lose 5,000–8,000 of its 30,000 jobs; Natural England's budget is cut by 30 per cent, about 800 full-time jobs; flood defence spending will be cut by 27 per cent. The CSR also included proposals to sell off national nature reserves, privatize parts of the Forestry Commission (since abandoned) and sell off the Meteorological Office. The former proposals proved to be immediately unpopular and have led to widespread campaigning against the idea of 'selling off our woodlands'. Rather less has been heard of the latter, although in many ways it might prove more important. Certainly, concerns have been expressed that privatization might undermine the position of an organization which has contributed a great deal to the public understanding of climate change.

The Green Investment Bank: a War of Attrition

'As part of the creation of a green investment bank, we will create green financial products to provide individuals with opportunities to invest in the infrastructure needed to support the new green economy' (HM Government, 2010: 17). The bald statement that 'we will create a green investment bank' (HM Government, 2010: 16) is interesting not only for its clarity but also for what it omits: the level of funding. The Conservative manifesto likewise omitted to mention a figure; the Liberal Democrats proposed an Infrastructure Bank, but again without a figure attached. Everything, as we shall see, hinges on the figure: in it lies the difference between a marginal contribution to the creation of a green economy and a seriously committed contribution.

In the middle of October 2010 there were reports of fierce fighting between DECC and the Treasury (Stratton, 2010). Interestingly, this was a debate not between the Liberal Democrats and the Conservatives, but between ministers in relation to their ministerial roles rather than their party. A commitment to the Green Investment Bank was included in the CSR, but with a start-up figure of only £1 billion against the originally anticipated £2 billion. It is generally reckoned by campaigners, analysts and green lobbyists to need £4–6 billion to make any significant impact. Huhne and the Climate Change Minister, Greg Barker, took the lead in negotiations with the Treasury and were supported by the Cabinet Minister of State, Oliver Letwin, with assistance from the Business Secretary, Vince Cable. But Cable's support was qualified by the fact that he wanted the bank to support general infrastructure projects, not just low-carbon infrastructure. In this he appears to be harking back to the Liberal Democrat manifesto commitment to an Infrastructure Bank rather than the Green Investment Bank (GIB) proposed by the Conservatives.

The battle for the GIB came to a head in November. The Treasury continued to oppose it, proposing instead a repackaging of existing green pledges in a new fund. The issue is whether the institution be set up as a government-backed bank capable of raising private finance by issuing bonds. A member of the GIB commission was reported as saying that if the GIB did not have the ability to raise money by issuing government-backed bonds, there was no point in its coming into being. On the same day (18 November) the Prime Minister made an intervention in which he promised that the GIB would be a proper bank:

> Appearing before the House of Commons Liaison Committee for the first time, Cameron offered a short but revealing response to a question from Labour chair of the Environmental Audit Committee Joan Walley about whether the Green Investment Bank will be a bank and whether the prime minister will take a 'personal interest' in the debate surrounding its formation. 'Yes, and yes,' he replied. (Murray, 2010)

The next day Huhne openly attacked the Treasury and compared its opposition to the bank with its vetoing of demands for a bank to finance small companies in the 1930s.

The matter was finally resolved in December, with the Treasury victorious: the proposal for the GIB was to be scaled back and it would begin life as a fund – which would jeopardize the provision of billions of pounds of loans to green technology.

Thus there is to be no GIB, at least initially, but only a green fund (Huhne, 2010b). Huhne appeared to concede to the Treasury's concern that the liabilities taken on by a GIB would be added to the Government's budget book and suggested instead that the new institution could develop into a bank as the deficit is reduced. Ballard suggested that Huhne was 'forced humiliatingly into repudiating his principles, saying that sustainability must not take precedence over cutting the deficit' (Ballard, 2010). Certainly, he stated that 'if we were to turn around and have the GIB borrowing vast amounts of money tomorrow I can understand that managers of the national debt would be a little alarmed' and that he was 'at one with the Treasury on the need to make sure our fiscal credibility is completely re-established' (Huhne, 2010b). He then argued that the key issue was what happened once fiscal credibility had been established and indicated that 'There are phasing issues, there are transition issues.

What is the point at which maybe it begins as a fund and later is a bank, whatever. Let there be no doubt that the first overwhelming priority of the government has to be to get the deficit down' (Huhne, 2010b). Finally, the priorities he had been forced to accept became clear: 'Fiscal credibility is key. But we also have to decarbonize the economy. Governments by definition do not have one objective. We are able to walk and chew gum at the same time. Therefore we are able to have low carbon investment and fiscal credibility. That is what we have to combine and that is what we're going to do' (Huhne, 2010b).

It is not known whether this will be merely a delay, an indefinite postponement or a cancellation: certainly, the consequences are serious for meeting carbon targets: Ernst & Young have said that, without a bank, only about a fifth of the £450 billion investment needed for Britain to meet its carbon emissions targets over the next 15 years would be made.

How all this squares with Huhne's promise to make Britain 'greener for less' is an intriguing question. His plan was for electricity bills to be lower and power plants twice as green as under existing energy policies inherited from Labour. When told that this sound-bite sounded like a Tesco promotion, he remarked: 'I am very happy to be the Tesco of the energy industry' (Huhne, 2010b). It is perhaps a better slogan than it is a policy: the tensions in the Coalition are certainly beginning to show in this policy area, with the pull of being the greenest ever tugging against the priority of deficit reduction and with the rhetoric and reality of green growth and green jobs apparently losing out. In general Huhne's approach to the environment is very much in line with his neoliberal credentials, partly derived from his experience: 'As a former businessman and an economist, I have been quite firm in my belief: that we must build a new kind of economy. It must be cleaner, greener and more sustainable. It must secure the economic recovery, promote growth, and meet the challenge of climate change. And it must deliver jobs, investment and profits' (Huhne, 2010a).

Other measures announced by Huhne in December included changes to the electricity market. Thus, despite its decision on the GIB, the Government hopes to find other ways of channelling private sector investment into renewables. However, the plan will also break a Conservative pledge on cleaning up coal plants. In a speech to environmentalists in 2009, Cameron repeated his promise to introduce rules requiring new power stations to be as clean as a modern gas plant. This would have required fitting carbon capture and storage equipment (CCS) to about two-thirds of new coal plants: but it is likely that the final requirement will be that CCS be fitted to only one-third of coal plants (Huhne, 2010a).

Conclusion: Walking and Chewing Gum?

Huhne claimed that 'we are able to walk and chew gum at the same time'. But in the fight over the GIB his gum lost most of its flavour and Huhne appears to have come unstuck. The classic opposition between environmental investment and fiscal credibility reasserted itself and even the proponent of the former was forced to adhere to the rhetoric of the latter.

Thus the big problem for the Government is how to keep the pressure on environment policy in a time of recession and cuts. There are several issues to consider here, however. The first is that although the cuts can be used as an excuse for not taking environmental action or for closing down organizations or reducing funding, this presupposes that the cuts are necessary rather than ideologically desired. If it is the latter, then the cuts are being used as an ideological excuse rather than anything else. The second point is that it can be argued that many environmental policy commitments are themselves to be encouraged in so far as they lead to green growth and green employment. Whether this sector of environmental policy receives the weight that ideologues have previously given it will be an interesting test of the Government's resolve in this area. Overall the issue is whether the Government's structural and fiscal reforms will work against its stated environmental commitments. Certainly, some of the budget cuts to various bodies are hard to justify. For example, Natural England, the statutory conservation agency for England, is likely to lose around a third of its staff. A group of organizations, including the Royal Society for the Protection of Birds, have sent a letter to the Government warning that cuts 'could have profound and perhaps irreversible consequences for wildlife, landscapes and people' (Black, 2010). They have also expressed concern at proposals to sell off some of the UK's wildlife reserves.

Another issue is the Government's stated commitment to localism. Localism may be a very good idea for some things, but not necessarily for everything, including biodiversity, which is why many have argued that the Government's decision to place important wildlife sites under local control effectively preclude the possibility of developing a coherent biodiversity strategy across regions.

Spelman maintained in her speech to the October 2010 Conservative party conference that 'our pledge to be the "Greenest Government Ever" isn't just a campaign slogan. It's a mission statement.' She went on to claim that this was why the Government had commissioned the first Natural Environment White Paper in 20 years and that 'protecting our environment is the very essence of Big Society' (Spelman 2010). There is time yet, but for the moment the balance has tilted away from the Coalition being the greenest ever government and only time will tell how far, if at all, it tilts back.

References

Ballard, E. (2010) Seven Months of Savage Cuts Leave Coalition's Green Hue Fading. *New Statesman*, 16 December. www.newstatesman.com/blogs/the-staggers/2010/12/government-green-bank (accessed 1 February 2011).

Black, R. (2010) A Hundred Days of the 'Greenest-Ever' Government. *BBC News*, 18 August. www.bbc.co.uk/news/science-environment-10981853 (accessed 28 December 2010).

Conservative Party (2010) *Invitation to Join the Government of Britain: The Conservative Manifesto 2010* (London: Conservative Party).

DECC (2010a) Green Deal to Create Green Jobs. DECC press release: 2010/104, 21 September. www.decc.gov.uk/en/content/cms/news/pn10_104/pn10_104.aspx (accessed 31 January 2011).

DECC (2010b) *The Green Deal: A Summary of the Government's Proposals*. www.decc.gov.uk/assets/decc/legislation/energybill/1010-green-deal-summary-proposals.pdf (accessed 30 January 2011).

FOE (2010) High Speed Rail: Upgrading Existing Rail Network Should Be Priority. Press release, 20 December. www.foe.co.uk/resource/press_releases/high_speed_rail_05012011.html (accessed 24 December 2010).

HM Government (2010) *The Coalition: Our Programme for Government* (London: The Cabinet Office).

Huhne, C. (2010a) Chris Huhne on climate change, the CRC and green growth, *Greenwise*. 17 November, http://www.greenwisebusiness.co.uk/news/chris-huhne-on-climate-change-the-crc-and-green-growth-1937.aspx. (accessed 17 December 2010).

Huhne, C. (2010b) Chris Huhne admits green bank may be scaled back, *Greenwise*, 15 December, http://www.greenwisebusiness.co.uk/news/chris-huhne-admits-green-bank-may-be-scaled-back-2004.aspx. (accessed 17 December 2010).

Liberal Democrat Party (2010) *Liberal Democrat Manifesto 2010* (London: Liberal Democrat Party).

Milmo, D. (2011) Bus Services under Threat from Cuts. *Guardian*, 3 February. www.guardian.co.uk/uk/2011/feb/03/bus-services-under-threat (accessed 3 February 2011).

Murray, J. (2010) Cameron Promises Green Investment Bank will be a Bank. *Business Green*. www.businessgreen.com/bg/news/1899130/cameron-promises-green-investment-bank-bank. (accessed 31 January 2011).

Porritt, J. (2010) *Porritt Condemns 'Dogmatic' Decision to Axe Money-Saving SDC*. www.forumforthefuture.org/blog/Porritt-condemns-dogmatic-decision-to-axe-money-saving-SDC Jonathon Porritt (accessed 20 January 2011).

Ramsay, A. (2010) Letter to *The Guardian*, 22 December.

Rootes, C. and Carter, N. (2010) Take Blue, Add Yellow, Get Green? The Environment in the UK General Election of 6 May. *Environmental Politics*, 19(6): 992–9.

Salmon, B (2010) *Coalition Politics: Blue + Yellow = Green?* 9 July. www.inhouselawyer. co.uk/index.php/environment/8082-Coalition-politics-blue-yellow-green (accessed 28 December 2010).

Spelman, C. (2010) Labour has Run Our Rural Areas Down. Speech, Conservative party conference, 4 October.

Stratton, A. (2010) Treasury Locked in Battle over Green Investment Bank. *Guardian* 15 October. www.guardian.co.uk/environment/2010/oct/13/Treasury-battle-green-investment-bank (accessed 30 January 2011).

9
The Con–Lib Agenda for Home Affairs

John Benyon

The principal functions of a government are to maintain national security and to regulate conflict and secure order in society. Consequently, what is often referred to as 'law and order' or 'home affairs' is a key policy arena for any government.

It was clear from the outset of the Coalition that one of the central issues that united the Conservatives and the Liberal Democrats was common opposition to what they perceived to be the Labour Government's illiberal policies, which had changed the relationship between individual citizens and the state. This was described in the Foreword to the Coalition programme as 'the relentless incursion of the state into the lives of individuals' (HM Government, 2010a: 8). Section 3 of the programme asserted that the new government believed that 'the British state has become too authoritarian and over the past decade it has abused and eroded fundamental human freedoms and historic civil liberties. We need to restore the rights of individuals in the face of encroaching state power' (HM Government, 2010a: 11).

These are strong statements about civil liberties in Britain and the extent to which they were undermined by New Labour, and subsequent government statements and policies have reinforced them. For example, on 13 July 2010, announcing a rapid review of counter-terrorism powers, the Home Secretary, Theresa May, said:

National security is the first duty of government but we are also committed to reversing the substantial erosion of civil liberties. I want a counter-terrorism regime that is proportionate, focused and transparent. We must ensure that in protecting public safety, the powers which we need to deal with terrorism are in keeping with Britain's traditions of freedom and fairness. (Home Office, 2010c: 1)

This view of the shifting balance of power between citizens and the state in terms of law and order dovetailed with the Coalition Government's narrative that under New Labour there had been too much 'big government', too much centralization and too much 'top-down control'. The Coalition programme declared that it was time to disperse power and hand it back to people and communities. This theme of a smaller state and greater local involvement and influence is evident in the Coalition's policies and approach to home affairs.

In the United Kingdom 'home affairs' includes a wide assortment of policies and activities, some of which are retained by the national government, while others are devolved to the administrations in Scotland, Wales and Northern Ireland and yet others are the responsibility of local authorities. They range from the regulation of burials and cremation through electoral administration and 'modernization' to the use of surveillance by local authorities and the regulation of the use of animals for research. However, the principal policy areas of home affairs are crime and criminal justice, punishment and imprisonment, policing, security and public order, immigration, and civil liberties and equalities.

The Home Office is the lead department for matters such as immigration and passports, drugs policy, counter-terrorism, crime and its prevention, and the police. Until a few years ago it was also responsible for punishment and prisons, the probation service and youth justice. This changed when the Ministry of Justice was set up on 9 May 2007. This is a large department with some 95,000 staff and as well as punishment its work includes criminal, civil and family justice and responsibility for the courts and a range of tribunals. Its activities also include supporting victims of crime, reducing reoffending and safeguarding human rights. Another department involved in home affairs is the Attorney General's Office, which oversees the work of the Crown Prosecution Service and the Serious Fraud Office.

The Prime Minister and the Deputy Prime Minister play important roles in the home affairs arena, for example in policies and debates on national security and counter-terrorism and also on the civil liberties agenda. The Home Secretary, Conservative Theresa May, is also Minister for Women and Equalities. Minister of State Nick Herbert, who is a joint appointment with the Justice Department, has responsibility for crime and policing, including anti-social behaviour. Fellow Conservative Damian Green is Minister of State leading on immigration and asylum and border controls. The third Minister of State, Baroness Neville-Jones, has responsibility for security and counter-terrorism, security for the Olympic Games and extradition and mutual legal assistance. Parliamentary Under-secretary of State James Brokenshire has responsibility for crime prevention as well as drugs and alcohol, public order, CCTV and DNA. The only Liberal Democrat is a junior minister, Lynne Featherstone MP, who has responsibility for equality issues and for freedom of information.

The Secretary of State for Justice and Lord Chancellor is the Conservative political heavyweight Kenneth Clarke. There are two ministers of state – Lord McNally, the only Liberal Democrat in the department, and Nick Herbert, the joint appointment with the Home Office. Crispin Blunt is the Parliamentary Under-Secretary of State with responsibility for prisons and probation, youth justice, and sentencing, and his fellow Conservative junior minister, Jonathan Djanogly, leads on legal aid, the courts, parole and tribunals. The Attorney General is Dominic Grieve and the Solicitor General is fellow Conservative MP Edward Garnier. All but two of the 12 politicians appointed to the Home Office, Ministry of Justice and Attorney General's Office were Conservatives, with Conservatives in the top positions.

The Coalition Reform Agenda

In the home affairs arena the new government swept into action with much activity and many policy announcements. In keeping with their declarations on civil liberties and the reversal of New Labour's 'authoritarian' policies, the first piece of legislation was the Identity Documents Bill to scrap identity cards and the National Identity Register. The bill was introduced to the House of Commons on 26 May and received the Royal Assent on 21 December 2010.

Crime and Criminal Justice

During the Labour Party's period in office crime fell significantly. Overall crime fell by 43 per cent between 1997 and 2010 while violent crime was down by over 40 per cent. Figures published in July 2010 showed that the fall in crime had persisted despite the recession. The figures were confirmed by the 2010 British Crime Survey but, perversely, that also showed that although a majority of people believed crime had fallen in their own neighbourhood, 66 per cent continued to believe that crime was rising nationally.

The Coalition programme included a raft of commitments on home affairs, a number of them in keeping with its commitment to 'localism'. These included publication of monthly local crime statistics, regular beat meetings with the police and ensuring hospitals shared information about gun and knife crime with local police (HM Government, 2010a: 13). In addition, the Coalition promised to take action on the abuse of alcohol, which is linked to nearly half of all violent crimes. This included banning the sale of alcohol below cost price, reviewing alcohol taxation to tackle binge drinkers and revising the licensing laws to give stronger local powers to revoke licences. Stating 'we take white-collar crime as seriously as other crime' (HM Government, 2010a: 9) the Coalition undertook to create a single agency to tackle serious organized crime, absorbing the work of the Serious Fraud Office and other bodies.

On criminal justice, the Coalition promised a fundamental review of legal aid and a Green Paper was published on 15 November 2010. The proposals were intended to 'reform and rebalance the justice system' and make it quicker and cheaper. The Justice Secretary, Kenneth Clarke, said that the current legal aid system was one of the most expensive in the world and must be reformed. Another paper on civil litigation proposed to tackle the rising costs incurred by people who are sued in 'no win no fee' cases. The Coalition also pledged to give individuals more legal protection to prevent crime and apprehend criminals and powers to defend themselves against intruders (HM Government, 2010a: 13). In addition, the programme said that criminal records bureau checks would be scaled back to sensible levels (HM Government, 2010a: 20).

Punishment and Imprisonment

When Labour came into office in 1997 the prison population in England and Wales was 61,114 and when it left in May 2010 it had increased to 85,009 – a rise of 39 per cent. Even more striking was the rise since 1993, when Kenneth Clarke was Home Secretary. Then the prison population was an average of 44,566, but by November 2010 it had risen by 92 per cent to 85,454 (HM Prison Service, 2010). Clarke, in charge of prisons once more, confessed he was amazed at this increase. He said that if such a prediction had been made in 1993 he would have dismissed it as 'ridiculous'.

One factor raised in the debate about the incarceration rate was the volume of legislation on crime under New Labour and the consequent huge rise in the number of criminal offences on the statute book. In 2003 alone there were six criminal justice statutes, most notably the Criminal Justice Act, which led to longer prison sentences. It was reported that 3,600 new criminal offences were created during Labour's time in office.

In July 2009 Lord Judge, the Lord Chief Justice, pleaded: 'can we possibly have less legislation, particularly in the field of criminal justice'. The Coalition pledged to stop 'the proliferation of new criminal offences' (HM Government, 2010a: 11).

The Coalition announced a 'rehabilitation revolution' involving a comprehensive sentencing policy review aimed at deterring crime, protecting the public, punishing offenders and cutting reoffending (HM Government, 2010a: 23). Initiatives were promised to find new secure treatment for the mentally ill and drug offenders, and to pay independent providers to reduce reoffending. Deductions from prisoners' earnings would be paid into the victims' fund, up to 15 new rape crisis centres would be established, and anonymity would be introduced for defendants in rape cases.

A Green Paper on sentencing, entitled *Breaking the Cycle: Effective Punishment, Rehabilitation and Sentencing of Offenders*, was published on 7 December 2010. The focus of the proposals was to 'punish criminals more effectively and reduce reoffending' (Ministry of Justice, 2010f: 1). The proposals included more emphasis on work in prison, more demanding community punishment, tougher curfew requirements, greater use of restorative justice and increased reparations to victims, improved youth justice and introducing payment-by-results for independent providers.

In addition, and importantly, the Green Paper promised to reform the use of indeterminate sentences of imprisonment for public protection (IPP). This form of sentencing was introduced in the Criminal Justice Act 2003 and came into effect in 2005. It was modified in 2008. The object was to keep the offenders in prison until they could show they were not a threat to the public. Each IPP prisoner received a minimum tariff but the great majority remained in prison long after they had served it. One reason was that IPP prisoners were obliged to complete certain offender behaviour courses before being considered for release by the Parole Board, but many prisons did not have the resources to offer such courses. The IPP was described by Anne Owers, Chief Inspector of Prisons, as 'a worked example of how not to legislate' (Owers, 2010: 28).

In 2010 there were 6,130 people serving IPP sentences of whom 2,850 were being held well beyond their tariff point. Only 94 IPP prisoners had ever been released. The Coalition reforms proposed that IPP sentences should be reserved for the most serious offenders and the onus of the release test should be on the authorities to prove why the prisoner posed a serious risk of harm to the public. The Justice Department estimated that reducing remand time in prison would save 1,300 places a year, while offering foreign offenders the chance to pay a fine and leave the country would save another 500 places annually. Offering defendants a reduction of up to half their sentence if they pleaded guilty was expected to save 3,400 prison places by 2014–15.

The Coalition also promised to bring in 'effective measures' to reduce anti-social behaviour and low-level crime, including restorative justice. The Home Secretary subsequently announced the abolition of ASBOs – anti-social behaviour orders – seen by some as a hallmark of Tony Blair's approach to crime. At their peak, in 2005, 4,122 new ASBOs were issued. They were not just used against young offenders but included a wide variety of people such as an 87-year-old man who was abusive to his neighbours and a woman who was banned from making excessive noise while having sexual relations anywhere in England. Problems with ASBOs were that some young people saw them as a mark of distinction and they were difficult to enforce, with up to 61 per cent not being observed.

Policing, Security and Public Order

The Coalition promised reform of policing with greater freedom from ministerial control and more accountability to local people. 'Time-wasting bureaucracy' would be reduced, better technology would be used and health and safety laws would be changed to enable 'common sense policing' (HM Government, 2010a: 13). A key and controversial proposal was to bring in a directly elected individual to oversee each police force. The policing minister, Nick Herbert, called for 'new thinking', with the police holding regular beat meetings with local residents. Police forces would be relieved of central targets and top-down controls.

The Coalition Government stated that its 'primary responsibility is to ensure national security' and it had already set up a National Security Council (HM Government, 2010a: 24). It would undertake a security review, publish a National Security Strategy and review all counter-terrorism legislation, including the highly controversial control orders. Groups that incited violence and hatred would be proscribed and the use of intercept evidence in the courts would be pursued. On 18 October 2010 the Government's National Security Strategy White Paper was published. One of its themes was that Britain faced 'an age of uncertainty' with often unforeseen threats (HM Government, 2010b: 3).

The review identified four 'tier one' threats to the country – international terrorism, including the use of chemical, biological, radiological or nuclear (CBRN) materials, cyber-attacks, international military crises and major accidents or natural hazards. 'Tier two' threats included an attack by another state involving CBRN weapons, overseas instability or insurgency, a big rise in the level of organized crime and disruption to the transmission of information by satellites. 'Tier three' risks included a conventional military attack, a significant rise in terrorism, organized crime, illegal immigrants, disruption to oil or gas supplies, an accident at a UK civil nuclear site and disruptions to international supplies of resources.

Among the measures under review was the use of stop and search, about which there were accusations of misuse. In June 2010 it was announced that thousands of people had been unlawfully stopped and searched under the Terrorism Act 2000 and 14 police forces were reported to have illegally used the powers since 2001. The Home Office released figures showing that 101,248 people had been stopped and searched under counter-terrorism legislation in 2009 with not a single arrest for a terrorist offence. Following a ruling in the European Court of Human Rights, the Home Secretary decided to scrap the police use of section 44 random stop and search powers, although Alan Johnson, then the shadow Home Secretary, said this would restrict policing.

There was also criticism of the activities of the National Public Order Intelligence Unit (NPOIU) run by the Association of Chief Police Officers (ACPO). It came to the fore in January 2011 when the activities of an undercover police officer led to the collapse of the prosecution of six environmental activists in Nottinghamshire. It became clear that he was only one of several undercover police officers operating within the green movement at an estimated annual cost of £200,000 each. Considerable concern was expressed about whether the undercover officers were acting as *agents provocateurs* and about the accountability and propriety of ACPO itself. The policing minister announced significant changes in early 2011.

The Coalition's planned police reforms were outlined in *Policing in the 21st Century: Reconnecting Police and the People*, published on 26 July 2010 (Home Office, 2010d). It was described by the Home Secretary as the 'most radical change to policing in 50 years' (Home Office, 2010d: 3). It proposed to replace police authorities in England and Wales with elected police and crime commissioners. 'Community crime fighters' would be created – local people who would take part in patrols with police officers (Home Office, 2010d: 36). The Green Paper also proposed the end of the National Policing Improvement Agency and the Serious Organized Crime Agency (SOCA) and the creation of a more wide-ranging National Crime Agency.

The resultant Police Reform and Social Responsibility Bill was introduced to the House of Commons on 30 November 2010. In addition to the elected commissioners, the bill would change the regulation of protest around Parliament Square and also the process for issuing private arrest warrants. It included the promised overhaul of the licensing regime to give more power to local authorities and the police to tackle problematic premises. The Minister for Crime Prevention, James Brokenshire, said: 'It's now time that local communities are put in charge and allowed to reclaim our high streets for sensible law-abiding drinkers' (Home Office, 2010f: 1).

Immigration

The Coalition programme declared that immigration must be controlled and capped to ensure cohesion and protect public services (HM Government, 2010a: 21). Among the promised initiatives were an end to the detention of children, an annual limit on non-EU economic migrants, the reintroduction of exit checks, action to reduce abuse of the system by students and improvements to the asylum system. A key proposal was to set up a dedicated border police force to improve national security and immigration controls, and to prevent trafficking of people, drugs and weapons.

Two cases highlighted the human issues surrounding asylum seekers. On 2 August 2010 a 27-year-old Iraqi Kurd, Osman Rasul, described as 'a destitute asylum-seeker', jumped to his death in Nottingham. He had lost legal aid for his nine-year quest to stay in the UK and had been turned away from the Home Office immigration office in Croydon. In October 2010 an Angolan man, Jimmy Mubenga, died after he became unwell while private security guards attempted to deport him forcibly on a BA flight to Luanda. He had spent 16 years in the UK trying to be allowed to stay. He left a wife and five children.

On 23 November the Home Secretary announced measures to control immigration from outside Europe. The aim was to reduce annual non-EU immigration from 196,000 in 2009 to 'tens of thousands' by 2015. The new rules set an annual limit of 21,700 for tier-one and tier-two migrants. Changes to the points-based system would restrict workers transferred by companies to those earning £40,000 a year, and would limit immigration of skilled workers. A further consultation was announced on students – the largest category of migrants. It was proposed that student visas would largely be limited to degree level with a more onerous regime for students at public and private colleges. It was estimated that this would result in a cut of around 40 per cent to the 300,000 students visas issued each year.

Civil Liberties and Equalities

The new government affirmed 'we will be strong in defence of freedom' (HM Government, 2010a: 11). That would entail 'a full programme of measures to reverse the substantial erosion of civil liberties and roll back state intrusion' (HM Government, 2010a: 11). The Coalition programme promised to bring in a freedom bill, scrap identity cards, halt the next generation of biometric passports and extend the scope of the Freedom of Information (FOI) Act. The Coalition also promised to protect trial by jury, restore rights to non-violent protest, introduce safeguards against the misuse of anti-terrorism laws, further regulate CCTV and stop storage of internet and e-mail records. A commission would look into a British bill of rights which would protect British liberties, although in fact this was designed to defuse a potential row between some Conservatives and Liberal Democrats over whether to retain the Human Rights Act. The programme also promised greater protection for people against aggressive bailiffs, making repossession a last resort (HM Government, 2010a: 12). In the section on equalities the Coalition programme said action was needed to 'tear down' barriers to social mobility and equal opportunities (HM Government, 2010a: 18). Policies included promoting equal pay, ending discrimination at work and improving community relations and opportunities for black, Asian and minority ethnic people.

Another key concern was the assortment of counter-terrorism measures bequeathed by the Labour administration. A controversial issue was control orders on suspected terrorists who had not been charged with any offence. These were introduced by New Labour in 2005 after the internment of suspects in Belmarsh prison was declared unlawful. Control orders imposed significant restrictions on the affected individual, including tagging, curfews and bans on movement. A review of counter-terrorism was set up in July 2010 with the aim of looking at the balance between security and civil liberties and where possible providing 'a correction in favour of liberty'. The review was conducted by the Office for Security and Counter Terrorism, part of the Home Office, under the oversight of Lord Macdonald. It was asked to examine six anti-terrorism measures, including control orders, police stop and search powers, the use of the Regulation of Investigatory Powers Act 2000 by local authorities and access to communications data, the use of 'deportation with assurances', measures to deal with organizations that promote hatred and the detention of suspects without charge.

It became clear that finding agreement within the Coalition was proving difficult and divisive. It was not until January 2011 that a compromise was reached reportedly involving the Prime Minister, Deputy Prime Minister and Home Secretary. The new measures were outlined on 26 January, when the independent report was also published (Macdonald, 2011). Among the changes were the replacement of control orders by 'terrorism prevention and investigation measures' which would stop house arrest, tighten the criteria for approving such restrictions and be limited for two years. A new Protection of Freedom Bill would implement the changes, including an end to indiscriminate use of section 44 stop and search by the police, limiting the use of surveillance under the Regulation of Investigatory Powers Act, and reducing the maximum period a terrorist suspect can be held without charge to 14 days.

Implications of the Comprehensive Spending Review

The budgets for both the Home Office and the Ministry of Justice were cut as expected in the October 2010 Comprehensive Spending Review (CSR), with both departments subject to a reduction of 23 per cent in the period up to 2014–15. The Law Officers' departments were subject to a 24 per cent cut. The CSR reported that Home Office savings would be achieved through reducing overheads, expenditure on consultants, the size of the workforce and 'reprioritising resources to the front line' (HM Treasury, 2010: 54). Funds were provided to support the Coalition's policing changes, including elected police and crime commissioners, but overall there would be a reduction of 14 per cent in police resources – and that assumed that police authorities increased the police precept each year. Savings were expected to result from improved efficiencies and less back office paperwork. Capital investment was earmarked to protect the UK's borders and to tackle crime and terrorism. Central targets would be ended and wasteful bureaucracy and form-filling would be cut. Furthermore, the Government would 'modernize pay and conditions' (HM Treasury, 2010: 54). Money had been earmarked to set up a new National Crime Agency to fight organized crime, protect the UK's borders and provide other national services. The UK Border Agency would be expected to save £500 million. Migration fees would rise to include a contribution towards managing the UK's borders.

The Ministry of Justice's budget would fall from £8.9 million to £7.3 million in 2014–15. This would necessitate delivering better value for money, reforms to legal aid and changes to sentencing to stop the 'unsustainable' rise in the prison population and to cut reoffending. The proposals for reforming the legal aid system were published in a consultative paper in November 2010 and the Justice Secretary said that the annual expenditure of over £2 billion could not continue. If fully implemented, the changes would result in estimated savings of £350 million a year.

The CSR admitted the cuts in legal aid 'will involve taking tough choices' (HM Treasury, 2010: 56). The implications were that some vulnerable groups, such as asylum seekers including victims of torture and violence, would be adversely affected. The Legal Services Commission (LSC) plays a central role and its recent track record had been subject to considerable criticism even before the cuts. For example, in June 2010 the Refugee and Migrant Justice group folded because of delayed payments from the LSC, amounting to nearly £2 million, some of which had reportedly been owed for two years. As a result of the closure, up to 10,000 asylum seekers were left without legal representation.

Reform of sentencing policy is fundamental to the Government's plans. The relentless rise in the prison population under New Labour would be halted and a number of new prisons which Labour had planned were stopped. In December 2010 the decision to cancel a new 600-place prison in Merseyside was announced and on 13 January 2011 the Ministry of Justice said that two prisons – Lancaster Castle and Ashwell – would be closed with the loss of 849 places. It was reported that it cost around £45,000 a year to keep each prisoner in jail. Even more strikingly, it was reported in 2010 that over 2,000 children aged between 10 and 17 were held in prison and each one cost some £100,000 a year – over three times the cost of sending a child to Eton (Knuutila, 2010).

The Coalition's plans included tougher community penalties, restorative justice and paying private and voluntary providers to deliver reductions in reoffending. A significant proposal was to set up mental health liaison services to try to divert mentally ill offenders away from the justice system and into treatment. Alongside the sentencing reforms, the Coalition planned to reform the wider criminal justice system. Many of the reforms were designed to save money, such as the plan to close under-used courts and to try to find alternatives such as mediation. In December 2010 it was announced that 142 magistrates and county courts would be closed to save £37 million. The budget cuts will also necessitate fewer staff at the Justice Ministry's headquarters and a reduction in capital spending of 50 per cent, including prison building.

The budget cuts for the Law Officers' departments will affect funding for bodies such as the Crown Prosecution Service (CPS) and the Serious Fraud Office. The CSR stated that the CPS will 'radically reduce its cost base while maintaining and strengthening its capability' (HM Treasury, 2010: 56). Quite how this will be achieved remains to be seen.

Radical Reform or Continuity?

The Coalition's plans for home affairs represented a radical break with the approach of the previous Labour Government. The Home Office *Draft Structural Reform Plan* set out the Coalition's plans 'to turn government on its head' by putting power in the hands of people and communities (Home Office, 2010b: 1). It highlighted the Government's five departmental priorities:

1. Enable police and local communities to tackle crime and anti-social behaviour.
2. Increase the accountability of the police to citizens.
3. Secure the UK borders and control immigration.
4. Protect people's freedoms and civil liberties.
5. Protect people from terrorism. (Home Office, 2010b: 2)

In each of these policy fields the Coalition's agenda included marked departures from what had gone before. The Coalition's decision to curtail late-night drinking reversed Labour's attempt to stop binge-drinking and create a 'café culture' by relaxing licensing hours. The changes to policing included in the Police Reform and Social Responsibility Bill, such as the introduction of local police and crime commissioners and the reduction of national targets, were also a radical change from Labour's policies. This was the case with tighter immigration controls and the introduction of the new border police force.

The break between the Labour Government and the new administration was clearly illustrated by their different policies on civil liberties and particularly identity cards. The Labour manifesto stated: 'we are proud of our record on civil liberties' (Labour Party, 2010: 5). By contrast, the Coalition parties were highly critical of the 'authoritarianism' of New Labour and the 'abuse and erosion' of civil liberties. The programme of the new government included a commitment to 'roll back state intrusion', but for some this was a huge task. In *The Guardian* on 26 May 2010, Simon Jenkins wrote: 'The Queen's speech and pre-announced cuts will cleanse only the most fouled of Labour's stables. Illiberal registers, databases, inspectorates and regulatory quangos typified the regimes of Tony Blair and Gordon Brown and obsessed such control-freak ministers as David Miliband and Ed Balls' (Jenkins, 2010: 29).

Theresa May said that scrapping the proposed identity cards was the 'first step of many' to 'reduce control of the state over decent, law-abiding people' and Clegg said it was a 'major step in dismantling the surveillance state' (Home Office, 2010a: 1). However, concern was voiced by opponents of 'the database state' when the Deputy Prime Minister said that from 2014 a new form of electoral register would mean that people would have to provide more information about themselves, including signature, national insurance number and date of birth. Some saw this as the introduction of a national identity register by another means and argued that this information would be sold to private companies.

There were also clear differences between the Coalition and the Labour Party on civil liberties and counter-terrorism. In January 2011 Ed Balls, then Shadow Home Secretary, alleged that the Coalition was putting their parties' interests before those of the country. On the issue of control orders, Balls said on BBC Radio Four: 'It increasingly looks as though politics and holding the Coalition together and appeasing backbenchers is becoming more important in the minds of Nick Clegg and the Prime Minister than doing the right thing' (Balls, 2011: 1).

The Ministry of Justice *Draft Structural Reform Plan*, published in July 2010, listed five departmental priorities some of which echoed those of the Home Office:

1. Reform of sentencing and penalties.
2. Rehabilitation revolution.
3. Courts and legal aid.
4. Reform of the prison estate.
5. Civil liberties. (Ministry of Justice, 2010a: 2)

On the first, second and fourth priorities there was a huge contrast between the Coalition's policies and those of the last Labour Government. The Commission on English Prisons Today (2009) pointed out that the prison population rates placed England and Wales among the very highest in Europe with 155 people per 100,000 in prison compared with 96 in France, 88 in Germany and 71 in Denmark. The rise in the prison population over 50 years has been dramatic, from 26,198 in 1960, a rate of some 52 per 100,000 people, to 42,264 in 1980 (83 per 100,000), to 61,114 in 1997 (120 per 100,000) when New Labour came into power, to the level at the end of 2010 of 85,454 (155 per 100,000 people). The outgoing Chief Inspector of Prisons, Anne Owers, reported that the increases in the number of people incarcerated had brought all sorts of pressures and made the system 'brittle'. She welcomed Clarke's wish to reduce the size of the prison population and the promise of a fresh look at sentencing (Owers, 2010: 28).

The former Chief Inspector of Prisons, General Lord Ramsbotham, wrote that New Labour had left the prison and probation service 'dysfunctional' and 'in crisis' (Leech, 2010: 9). In his foreword to the annual *Prisons Handbook* he accused Labour of 'government on the back of a fag packet' and said that 'the prisons are full of people who should not be in there for a variety of reasons' (Leech, 2010: 9). Ramsbotham added that the Labour administration had virtually destroyed the National Probation Service.

The Coalition's Green Paper on sentencing was published on 7 December 2010. The Justice Secretary said it represented a 'radically different approach' (Ministry of Justice, 2010f: 1). He set out three priorities – punishing offenders, protecting the public and reducing reoffending – and said the previous Government's policy had fundamentally failed because of a lack of firm focus on reform and rehabilitation. 'The criminal justice system cannot remain an expensive way of giving the public a break from offenders, before they return to commit more crimes' (Ministry of Justice, 2010e: 1). Clarke stated: 'Our plans represent a fundamental break with the failed and expensive policies of the past' (Ministry of Justice, 2010e: 2).

A significant proportion of people who are sent to prison – some put the figure at over 85 per cent – are suffering from mental health problems. Some judges have said that the prison system is being used as a dustbin for people who need treatment. The Green Paper outlined plans to work with the Department of Health to divert more offenders with mental illness and drug dependency into treatment, marking another break with the Labour administration.

Underlining the differences in the field of home affairs between the Labour governments and the Coalition, in early January 2011 Clegg said that the Government intended to restore civil liberties in Britain with the same 'systematic ruthlessness' that the Labour Government had taken them away. He highlighted the forthcoming reforms to Britain's libel laws which were intended to promote freedom of speech and a free press (Clegg, 2011: 1).

Political Tension and Controversy

Several of the Coalition Government's policies in the home affairs arena are controversial. As well as arguments with the Labour opposition there are also political disagreements within the Coalition itself. There have been some tensions between the Conservatives and the Liberal Democrats, but there are also arguments within both parties themselves.

There is some disaffection within the Conservative Party, both within Parliament and without. A number of MPs have said that they feel that various promises in the 2010 manifesto have been ignored in the Coalition programme. Complaints have surfaced that the party's principles and values have been compromised and that too much ground has been conceded to the Liberal Democrats. One backbench Conservative MP was quoted as saying: 'There is a very strong sense that the tail is wagging the dog.'

One policy field where tension is especially evident is that of punishment and imprisonment. Clarke questioned whether 'prison works', but Lord Howard, who coined this phrase when he succeeded Clarke as Home Secretary in 1993, has criticized the Coalition approach on several occasions and in late 2010 said that Clarke's approach was 'marred by a flawed ideology'. Howard's criticisms appeared to reflect the views of a section of Conservative thinking. Under the headline 'Prison Works', the *Spectator* made its opposition to Clarke's approach clear and said that 'locking people up offers a very good return on the taxpayer's investment' (*Spectator*, 2010: 5). In December 2010 the Home Secretary appeared to disagree with Clarke when she appeared before the Home Affairs Select Committee and said: 'prison works. But it must be made to work better' (House of Commons, 2010: Q. 44). She explained that the rate of reoffending of ex-prisoners must be reduced. Some tabloid newspapers as well as backbenchers have expressed considerable disquiet at the new policy of reducing the prison population and developing other forms of punishment.

Another issue which has caused divisions is the proposal to allow people in prison to vote in elections. This change is needed to comply with a 2005 judgment by the European Court of Human Rights. It is a divisive issue as the Liberal Democrats support votes for prisoners, but many Conservatives are opposed. The Coalition announced a compromise of giving the vote only to prisoners serving up to four years, but Labour argued for just one year. Then a motion was tabled on 10 February 2011 and the Commons voted to maintain the ban on the rights of prisoners to vote with 234 MPs voting to keep the ban against 22 MPs who supported a repeal of the ban in line with the European Convention on Human Rights (BBC, 2011). Other contentious issues included the decision to close 93 magistrates' courts and 49 county courts and the cuts in the number of police officers. Arguments over a British bill of rights to replace the Human Rights Act were somewhat defused by referring the issue to an independent commission, but the disagreements may resurface in the future.

The reductions to legal aid may also lead to disputes between Conservatives and Liberal Democrats. In addition to the effects on vulnerable groups such as asylum seekers, the cuts seem likely to disadvantage women. The Ministry of Justice equality impact statement found that women would be disproportionately affected by the cuts in legal aid for family cases and divorce, immigration, employment, housing and welfare benefits.

Another area of potential disagreement between the Coalition partners is counter-terrorism. Both parties have been united in their criticism of the 'authoritarian' regime that New Labour established, but arguments have persisted about the appropriate balance between civil liberties and counter-terrorism. The use of control orders was one issue on which there was division, and further disagreements may arise.

Conclusion – Turning Old Thinking on its Head

Introducing the Coalition programme, David Cameron and Nick Clegg stated that they believed in 'radical, reforming government, a stronger society, a smaller state, and power and responsibility in the hands of every citizen' (HM Government, 2010a: 8). This is a highly ambitious aspiration, especially in an age of austerity, and in the arena of home affairs the new Government made a brisk and energetic start.

The new government's policies on home affairs contrast markedly with those of the preceding administration. The commitment of both partners to reverse Labour's 'erosion of civil liberties' was evident from the outset. This was given impetus by the requirement to save money, for example on identity cards. The huge cuts in public expenditure and the need for economies have also underpinned other Coalition policies, such as the decision to review legal aid and sentencing and to stop the ever-increasing and costly rise in the prison population.

Cameron and Clegg stated: 'we are both committed to turning old thinking on its head and developing new approaches' (HM Government, 2010a: 7). In terms of home affairs that is what seems to have happened. The policies of New Labour, and now their reversal by the Coalition, have turned old thinking on law and order 'on its head' and have forced a rethink of the conventional view of different political approaches in the law and order arena.

As shown in Figure 9.1, the conservative 'traditionalist' perspective is more authoritarian and tough-minded. It stresses punishment and retribution, deterrence, discipline and the removal of offenders from society. In office New Labour seems to have been increasingly drawn to this conservative approach and this was reflected in its policies and outcomes, such as the growing number of criminal offences, the curtailment of liberties and the ever-rising prison population. By contrast, the Coalition policies seem to fit more within the liberal 'progressive' perspective. This tends to place more emphasis on civil liberties and rehabilitation, education and treatment for addictions and mental health problems. It stresses restorative justice and personal responsibility.

Many people and groups – perhaps the majority – accept views from both the perspectives shown in Figure 9.1. It might be said that these paradigms are over-simplifications of the real world of political argument (Benyon, 1994). Nonetheless, the two contrasting perspectives were evident in much of the political discussion about home affairs in 2010. For example, when the new Coalition abolished ASBOs the Labour frontbench spokesman Alan Johnson said this was 'yet another example of this government going soft on crime' (Johnson, 2010). Home Secretary May's view was that sanctions 'should be rehabilitating and restorative rather than criminalising and coercive' (May, 2010: 5).

Liberal 'Progressive' Perspective	Conservative 'Traditionalist' Perspective
Liberal and humanitarian	Authoritarian and disciplinarian
Tender-minded	Tough-minded
Rehabilitation and rewards	Punishment and retribution
Remove social and economic causes	Deterrence through penalties
Emphasis on civil liberties	Emphasis on police powers
Stresses education and treatment	Stresses removal and restraint
Stresses responsibility	Stresses discipline
Rejects authoritarianism	Rejects 'permissiveness'
Stresses 'social justice'	Stresses 'rule of law'

Figure 9.1   Different Approaches to Law and Order and Home Affairs

On 30 June 2010 Jack Straw, who served as both Home Secretary and Justice Secretary in the Labour administration, used an article in the *Daily Mail* to attack the Coalition's policies on prisons and punishment. Straw accused the Coalition of being soft 'hand-wringers' on crime and seemed to boast about the increase in the prison population under Labour (Straw, 2010: 9). It was an extraordinary indication of how far the Labour Party's policy reflected the traditional conservative perspective on law and order and the extent to which the Coalition Government's approach represented a radical transformation.

Of course, as Harold Macmillan once noted, events can blow a government off course. Whether the Coalition is able to sustain its direction and momentum in home affairs will depend on factors such as public expenditure cuts, political leadership and the quiescence or otherwise of opponents within the Coalition, especially within the Conservative Party. Above all it will depend on how successful the new policies are and whether terrorism, crime and anti-social behaviour or disorder decline – or increase, as many think they will. The Coalition has begun with a convention-challenging reforming approach but it may be difficult to maintain the course it has set.

References

Balls, E. (2011) Interview with the World at One on control orders. www.edballs4labour.org/blog/?p=1343. Reported in *The Guardian*, 7 January: 13; and others newspapers.

BBC (2011) www.bbc.co.uk/news/uk-politics-12409426 (accessed 22 February 2011).

Benyon, J. (1994) *Law and Order Review 1993* (Leicester: CSPO).

Clegg, N. (2011) *Speech by Deputy Prime Minister Nick Clegg on Civil Liberties at the Institute for Government in London on 7 January 2011* (London: The Cabinet Office). www.dpm.cabinetoffice.gov.uk/news/civil-liberties-speech.

Commission on English Prisons Today (2009) *Do Better Do Less – The Report of the Commission on English Prisons Today* (London: Howard League for Penal Reform).

Conservative Party (2010) *Invitation to Join the Government of Britain* (London: Conservative Party).

HM Government (2010a) *The Coalition: Our Programme for Government* (London: The Cabinet Office).

HM Government (2010b) *A Strong Britain in an Age of Uncertainty: The National Security Strategy*, Cm 7953 (Norwich: The Stationery Office).

HM Prison Service (2010) *Population Bulletin – Monthly November 2010* (London: HM Prison Service).

HM Treasury (2010) *Comprehensive Spending Review 2010*, Cm 7942 (Norwich: The Stationery Office).

Home Office (2010a) Identity Cards and National Identity Register to be Scrapped. Press release, 27 May (London: Home Office).

Home Office (2010b) *Draft Structural Reform Plan* (London: Home Office).

Home Office (2010c) Rapid Review of Counter-terrorism Powers. Press release, 13 July (London: Home Office).

Home Office (2010d) *Policing in the 21st Century: Reconnecting Police and the People*. Cm 7925 (Norwich: The Stationery Office).

Home Office (2010e) *Business Plan 2011–15* (London: Home Office).

Home Office (2010f) New Plans to Overhaul Alcohol Licensing Regime. Media Centre News, 1 December (London: Home Office).

House of Commons (2010) *The Work of the Home Secretary: Uncorrected Transcript of Oral Evidence Taken on 14 December 2010 before the Home Affairs Committee*, Session 2010–2011, HC 647-i, London: House of Commons.

Jenkins, S. (2010) Radical? Hardly. But So Much More Than Blair Reincarnated. *The Guardian*, 26 May: 29.

Johnson, A. (2010) Asbos Worked – and Theresa May Knows It. *Guardian online*, 29 July. www.guardian.co.uk/commentisfree/2010/july/29.

Knuutila, A. (2010) *Punishing Costs: How Locking up Children is Making Britain Less Safe* (London: New Economics Foundation).

Labour Party (2010) *A Future Fair for All* (London: Labour Party).

Leech, M. (2010) *The Prisons Handbook 2010* (Manchester: PRISONS.ORG.UK).

Liberal Democrats (2010) *Liberal Democrat Manifesto 2010* (London: Liberal Democrats).

Macdonald, Lord (2011) *Review of Counter-Terrorism and Security Powers: A Report by Lord Macdonald of River Glaven QC*, Cm 8003 (Norwich: The Stationery Office).

May, T. (2010) Moving Beyond the ASBO. Speech by the Home Secretary, Coin Street Community Centre London, 28 July. Media Centre – speeches (London: Home Office).

Ministry of Justice (2010a) *Draft Structural Reform Plan* (London: Ministry of Justice).

Ministry of Justice (2010b) *Business Plan 2011–15* (London: Ministry of Justice).

Ministry of Justice (2010c) *Proposals for the Reform of Civil Litigation Funding and Costs in England and Wales*, Cm 7947 (Norwich: The Stationery Office).

Ministry of Justice (2010d) *Proposals for the Reform of Legal Aid in England and Wales*, Cm 7967 (Norwich: The Stationery Office).

Ministry of Justice (2010e) *Breaking the Cycle: Effective Punishment, Rehabilitation and Sentencing of Offenders*, Cm 7972 (Norwich: The Stationery Office).

Ministry of Justice (2010f) Time to Break the Cycle of Crime and Reoffending. Press release, 7 December (London: Ministry of Justice).

Owers, A. (2010) The Prison System is Too Big to Fail, and Too Big to Succeed. *The Guardian*, 14 July: 28.

Spectator (2010) Prison Works, 19 June: 5.

Straw, J. (2010) Mr Clarke and the Lib Dems Are Wrong. Prison DOES Work – and I Helped Prove it. *Daily Mail*, 30 June: 9.

10
The Con–Lib Agenda for the 'New Politics' and Constitutional Reform

Philip Norton

Principal Features and Developments

The creation of the Coalition Government heralded a new form of politics. It was necessarily a new form given the unique circumstances in which the Government came into being. The UK had not previously witnessed a coalition government formed as a result of post-election bargaining after an indecisive election result (Norton, 2010). The new politics entailed the parties to the Coalition adhering to the terms of a published agreement. This created the potential for a different mode of opposition (see Norton, 2008), as well as exacerbating an existing mode. Tensions within the Coalition (inter-party conflict within government, the different mode) and within each party to it (intra-party conflict, the existing mode) emerged soon after its formation.

The Coalition Government was formed despite the parties' views on constitutional reform and not because of them. Though the ideological divide between the main parties in 1997 was seen as being slight, one area where there was a clear divide was that of constitutional reform. The Liberal Democrats in 1997 advocated, as they had in previous General Elections, a radical overhaul of the nation's constitution, in effect a new constitutional settlement for the United Kingdom (Liberal Democrat Party, 1997). They adhered to the liberal view of the constitution (see Norton, 1982: 275–9). The Conservatives wished to preserve the essential features of the extant constitution, adhering to the traditional, or Westminster, view (Norton, 1982: 279–87), and were therefore against the changes – proportional representation, home rule, a predominantly elected second chamber, regional assemblies, a bill of rights – advocated by the Liberal Democrats. What changes they did advocate were within the existing constitutional framework.

Labour entered office with Tony Blair having inherited the commitment to a reform programme generated by his predecessor, John Smith (Seldon, 2004: 204–5; Norton, 2007b: 270–1). Under the Labour Government, a Cabinet Consultative Committee was formed of ministers and leading Liberal Democrats to discuss constitutional change. The Government achieved passage of several major pieces of constitutional reform. Foremost among these were the devolution of power to elected bodies in Scotland, Wales and Northern Ireland, the incorporation of the European Convention of Human Rights into UK law and the removal of most hereditary peers from the House of Lords (see e.g. Bogdanor, 2009; King, 2009). The Government's approach to constitutional change as such lacked coherence (Norton, 2007a: 119–20; 2007b) and did not deliver all that the Liberal Democrats would have wished (Seldon, 2004: 275–7). Nonetheless, there was a closer relationship between Labour and the Liberal Democrats on the issue of constitutional reform than there was between the Liberal Democrats and the Conservatives. Both Blair and the then Liberal Democrat leader, Paddy Ashdown, had toyed with achieving a closer alliance between the two parties (see Ashdown, 2002; Seldon, 2004: 266–77), Ashdown pushing Blair to concede proportional representation for parliamentary elections in a way that would have been inconceivable with a Conservative leader. After a committee had been set up to consider an alternative electoral system and reported (Jenkins Commission, 1998), it was the Conservatives who led the opposition to any change (see Norton, 1998). For the Liberal Democrats, Labour was seen as a potential ally in achieving a new constitutional settlement; the Conservative Party was not.

The divide that existed in 1997 was maintained through subsequent General Elections, including that of 2010. The Liberal Democrats pursued a reform agenda, including electoral reform (with a preference for the single transferable vote), a fully elected second chamber and fixed-term parliaments. Labour promised referendums on introducing the Alternative Vote for parliamentary elections and on reform of the House of Lords, as well as proposing fixed-term parliaments and a commission to chart a course for a written constitution. The Conservative manifesto concentrated on legislative change to give power back to people at the local level. It proposed to replace the Human Rights Act with a UK bill of rights and to have English MPs alone vote on English legislation. It also included a commitment (reflecting a shift undertaken by William Hague and maintained by his successors) to 'work to build a consensus for a mainly-elected second chamber to replace the current House of Lords'. However, despite these radical tinges, the Conservative approach overall was not to do damage to the existing constitutional arrangements. Cameron conceded that reform of the second chamber was 'a third-term issue' and it was clear that addressing economic issues would take priority. As I have written elsewhere, 'Though the party's stance had not been thought through from the perspective of first principles, it was nonetheless not expected to do violence to the Conservative view of democracy' (Norton, 2011).

The relative distance between the parties in 2010 was therefore not very different from that of 1997. Though the Liberal Democrats and Conservatives had made common cause on a number of issues relating to civil liberties, in the field of constitutional change they remained committed to different, indeed incompatible, approaches. The preference of Liberal Democrat parliamentarians in the wake of the 2010 election results for a 'progressive alliance' of Labour and the Liberal Democrats (Norton, 2010: 252) would encompass their views on constitutional reform. However, the problem for the Liberal Democrats was that the election results militated against such an alliance. Labour and the Liberals could not command a majority in the House of Commons and a coalition of the two parties, each having lost seats in the election, would have been seen as a coalition of the losers. As Paddy Ashdown neatly encapsulated the dilemma, 'our instincts go one way but the mathematics go the other' (quoted in Fox, 2010: 27). The mathematics dictated going with the party that did not share their reforming zeal.

Compromising Positions

On Friday, 7 May, after the election results were known, Cameron made a statement, not demanding that Gordon Brown quit Downing Street but rather making a 'big, open and comprehensive offer' to the Liberal Democrats, an offer that enticed the latter into negotiations. It is instructive that in those negotiations 'Electoral reform was the sticking point' (Wilson, 2010: 162; see also Laws, 2010: 104). Cameron in his public statement on 7 May offered an all-party committee of inquiry into political and electoral reform. The Liberal Democrats wanted a referendum on a system of proportional representation. In the initial negotiations, the Conservatives indicated they were prepared to support a free vote in the House of Commons on the Alternative Vote (AV). However:

> The Liberal Democrats rejected the plan and no deal was possible on the issue of AV. They made it clear that this was a red line issue for them and 'without the ability to move forward on electoral reform we'd feel it was much more difficult to go into a Coalition'. George Osborne and William Hague said that it was a similar red line issue for the Conservative Party and they could not move. (Wilson, 2010: 163)

The negotiating teams had made good progress on other matters. Electoral reform was now the principal issue that stood between them and a Coalition agreement. It was agreed that it be referred to the two party leaders. In the interim the talks continued, if necessary for the parties to pursue a 'confidence and supply' option. That option entailed the Liberal Democrats supporting the Government on votes of confidence and supply in return for the introduction of certain measures, but falling short of the two going into government together (see Laws, 2010: 293–7 for a draft agreement). The problem was frustrating for the two sides, but, as Boulton and Jones observed, wholly unsurprising:

> Any well-informed commentator would have predicted the problem. On one side, you had a Conservative Party fundamentally wedded to the system of first past the post; on the other the Lib Dems for whom proportional representation is the holy grail. (Boulton and Jones, 2010: 183)

The issue was to be resolved by the two party leaders. Cameron was not certain how far he could go and still carry his parliamentary party. An initial survey by the whips suggested they might be willing to accept a referendum on AV (Wilson, 2010: 179) and he decided to pursue that option. As Mark Stuart has shown in his contribution to this volume, Cameron was influenced by the fact that he understood Brown had offered to implement AV without a referendum. It is not clear that this had been offered, but Cameron believed that it had (Norton, 2010: 256; Wilson, 2010: 206). When the two leaders spoke, Cameron offered a referendum on AV. As *The Sunday Times* observed: 'It was a huge risk on the Tory leader's part, threatening uproar in his own party' (Oakeshott, Woolf and Oliver, 2010). In making the offer public, Hague said the party was willing to go 'the extra mile'. The offer helped clinch the deal.

The agreement on a referendum constituted a compromise – each side having to concede its preferred position – but it was only one of several issues of constitutional change that was agreed and to some degree it masked a more fundamental concession by the Conservatives.

The constitutional measures embodied in the agreement fell into two categories: those that constituted a compromise between competing positions (as on electoral reform) and those that entailed conceding a policy (as on fixed-term parliaments). Indeed, in large measure it involved conceding a basic approach. The prologue to the section on political reform reveals the extent to which it is inspired by the Liberal Democrat rather than the Conservative approach. It stated: 'The Government believes that our political system is broken'. That may be the Government's view; it is not a Conservative view (Norton 2011). That is the first point to note relative to our later discussion.

The Coalition Agreement in respect of constitutional reform is worth quoting, at least the first four components. 'Political reform' constitutes the 24th section of the Agreement. It states:

- We will establish five-year fixed-term Parliaments. We will put a binding motion before the House of Commons stating that the next General Election will be held on the first Thursday of May 2015. Following this motion, we will legislate to make provision for fixed-term Parliaments of five years. This legislation will also provide for dissolution if 55 per cent or more of the House votes in favour.
- We will bring forward a Referendum Bill on electoral reform, which includes provision for the introduction of an Alternative Vote in the event of a positive result in the referendum, as well as for the creation of fewer and more equal sized constituencies. We will whip both Parliamentary parties in both Houses to support a simple majority referendum on the Alternative Vote, without prejudice to the positions parties will take during such a referendum.
- We will bring forward early legislation to introduce a power of recall, allowing voters to force a by-election where an MP is found to have engaged in serious wrongdoing and having had a petition calling for a by-election signed by 10 per cent of his or her constituents.
- We will establish a committee to bring forward proposals for a wholly or mainly elected upper chamber on the basis of proportional representation. The committee will come forward with a draft motion by December 2010. It is likely that this will advocate single long terms of office. It is also likely that there will

be a grandfathering system for current Peers. In the interim, Lords appointments will be made with the objective of creating a second chamber that is reflective of the share of the votes secured by the political parties in the last General Election. (HM Government, 2010: 26–7)

There are then 23 other proposals, including a commission to consider the 'West Lothian question', but mostly proposals that fall under the rubric of political rather than major constitutional reform.

A Liberal Democrat Agenda

The proposals I have outlined reinforce the point that they follow primarily a Liberal Democrat agenda. As Ruth Fox noted of the Coalition Agreement, 'Overall the Conservatives got the better of the deal in the economic arena, and the Liberal Democrats the political and constitutional reform agenda' (Fox, 2010: 34). Had a Conservative minority government been formed, hardly any of these proposals for constitutional change would have been pursued: no referendum on the electoral system, no fixed-term Parliaments and probably no moves initially on reform of the House of Lords. The nod in the direction of the Conservative stance is a commission on the West Lothian question. Elsewhere, the document concedes the case for a commission to examine the possibility of a British bill of rights (HM Government, 2010: 11), as well as examining 'the case for a United Kingdom Sovereignty Bill' (HM Government, 2010: 19). At the core of the legislative agenda, though, stands the referendum on AV and fixed-term Parliaments.

Reinforcing the extent to which constitutional change is skewed towards the Liberal Democrat agenda is the appointment of Deputy Prime Minister Nick Clegg to be responsible for delivering the programme. Most of the legislation for constitutional reform comes under the aegis of the Cabinet Office, with Clegg as the lead minister. Various changes were made within Government to reinforce the support for the Deputy PM. What doesn't come under the Cabinet Office comes under the Justice Ministry, headed by Kenneth Clarke, a Conservative proponent of reform, assisted by a Liberal Democrat, Lord McNally, as Minister of State.

A Rushed Programme

The second feature of the constitutional reform programme is the extent to which it is rushed. There are two elements to this. One is in respect of drawing up the Coalition Agreement. The other is the speed with which legislation was introduced.

The pressure to reach agreement resulted in a document promising changes that could not be delivered. There were notable differences between what was in the Coalition Agreement and what was in the legislation designed to give effect to the Agreement. This was notably the case in respect of fixed-term Parliaments.

The proposal for a 'binding motion' was dropped. The formal explanation was that the Government wished to avoid placing the monarch in a difficult situation if a request for an early dissolution was made (Constitution Committee, 2010d: 8). This derived from the realization that there was no one who could formally be 'bound' by such a resolution. The proposal for a 55 per cent vote of MPs for a dissolution resolution was replaced with one for a two-thirds majority. The original proposal was unique in that no other parliament adopted a 55 per cent threshold and was criticized for being a political fix. The Conservative and Liberal Democrat negotiators knew that Scotland utilized a two-thirds majority, but one member of the Conservative team, George Osborne, thought this was rather a high threshold:

After some work on Ed Llewellyn's calculator, and consideration of by-election risks, it was decided that a 55 per cent vote of MPs would be required to provide a dissolution. This was just greater than the combined opposition and Lib Dem parliamentary parties, thereby safeguarding the Conservative position. No one could pretend it was a scientific process, but it would seek to deliver the stability and responsibility which both sides considered so important, and from which the country itself should gain. (Laws, 2010: 184)

The haste which attached to the negotiations was also reflected in the section dealing with the House of Lords. A committee was to be appointed to produce a 'draft motion' by December 2010, but this was ambiguous as motions are not laid in draft and do not usually take months to prepare. It soon became clear that what was intended was a draft bill. The declared intention to appoint peers reflecting the share of the votes secured by parties at the election caused difficulties as the only new peers created after the election were drawn from the three main parties. There was no move to appoint peers from other parties, such as the United Kingdom Independence Party (UKIP) or the British National Party (BNP), in proportion to their vote share at the election.

The agreement, in short, was drawn up quickly and by negotiators who were not themselves expert in the nature and provisions of the constitution. The rushed nature of what was agreed was also reflected in the mismatch between rhetoric and reality. The avowed aim of the 'new politics' was to restore trust in politics and to strengthen Parliament and limit the power of the executive. People, Clegg said, 'expect to be given clear and transparent choices' (Hansard Society annual lecture, 16 November 2010). However, it was not clear why a constricted choice of electoral systems – denying electors the opportunity to express a preference for other options – delivered on this goal. Clegg said there were no empirical data to support the claims as to what the reforms would achieve; the evidence base, he said, was 'as much one of judgment as it is of empirical data' (Constitution Committee, 2010a: 21, Q. 55). Similarly, with the provision for a fixed-term of five years rather than of four for Parliament: electors were not to be consulted. When the question was put to the Deputy PM that electors might wish to express a view, he side-stepped it (Constitution Committee, 2010a: 24, Q. 66). The judgement left out what electors might prefer. The Constitution Committee of the Lords, in its report on the Fixed-term Parliaments Bill, noted that a five-year term may make the legislature less accountable, not more (Constitution Committee, 2010d: 8). 'The policy behind the Bill', it declared, 'shows little sign of being developed with constitutional principles in mind' (Constitution Committee, 2010d: 8).

The second element was the speed with which the legislation was introduced. The creation of a coalition created something of an initial void in the legislative schedule for Parliament. The civil service had prepared for the eventuality of a Conservative Government – senior civil servants had been meeting with Conservative Shadow Cabinet ministers since early in 2009 (see Riddell and Haddon, 2009) – but had no idea what a coalition would agree. Indeed, their initial gaming had suggested there was unlikely to be a stable government (Robinson, 2010). Legislation had to be produced quickly by parliamentary counsel and the void was filled by the Government's measures of constitutional reform. The Parliamentary Voting System and Constituencies Bill was introduced, followed by the Fixed-Term Parliaments Bill. In the Lords, the Public Bodies Bill to reduce the number of non-departmental public bodies was introduced. The Parliamentary Voting System and Constituencies Bill, after it was introduced into the Commons, was subject to extensive amendment at the behest of the Government. The Public Bodies Bill encountered difficulties in the House of Lords, not least on constitutional grounds: it was an enabling, or 'Henry VIII', Bill, allowing ministers to alter primary legislation by order (secondary legislation). Ministers had decided what they wanted to do with some public bodies, but a number they had yet to review were put in a holding category in the bill (Schedule 7, referred to by some peers as 'death row') until they decided what to do with them.

The speed with which the measures were introduced, with no time for consultation or pre-legislative scrutiny, encountered objections, not least from the Political and Constitutional Reform Committee in the House of Commons (2010) and the Constitution Committee in the House of Lords (2010b, 2010c, 2010d). The Constitution Committee's report on the Public Bodies Bill provided a focus for objections when the bill had its Second Reading in the Lords, a debate in which the bill appeared largely friendless. The Constitution Committee pursued the issue of process. In its report on the Fixed-term Parliaments Bill, it declared:

> The speed with which the policy was introduced, with no significant consultation, no Green Paper and no detailed assessment of the pros and cons of a five year term over a four year term, suggests that short-term considerations were the drivers behind the Bill's introduction. (Constitution Committee, 2010d: 9)

It quoted the Hansard Society and Democratic Audit making similar points, before concluding:

> We take the view that the origins and content of this Bill owe more to short-term considerations than to a mature assessment of enduring constitutional principles or sustained public demand. We acknowledge the political imperative behind the Coalition Government's wish to state in advance its intent to govern for the full five year term, but this could have been achieved under the current constitutional conventions. (Constitution Committee, 2010d: 9)

The Government appeared prepared to face such criticism for the sake of getting the measures enacted. The need to maintain the Coalition was given precedence over legislative scrutiny – and over the proposal in the Coalition Agreement (HM Government, 2010: 27) to introduce a new 'public reading' stage for bills and a dedicated 'public reading day' during a Bill's committee stage for public comments to be debated.

Implications of the Spending Review

In one respect the spending review had no particular relevance for the Coalition's proposals for constitutional reform. In another respect, it was crucial.

The constitutional measures brought forward by the Coalition had no significant financial implications. Questions were raised about the cost of holding a referendum and of replacing the House of Lords with an elected chamber, but overall the measures created no major problem for the Treasury. This, as with the constitutional reforms of the Labour Government, was a particular attraction. In monetary terms, they were largely cost-free. They could therefore be introduced quickly.

There was also an imperative for their speedy introduction. The economic crisis was a necessary but not sufficient condition for the formation of a Conservative–Liberal Democrat Coalition. The Conservatives required Liberal Democrat support to deliver a stringent economic programme. The imperative was embodied in the final page of the Coalition Agreement:

> The deficit reduction programme takes precedence over any of the other measures in this agreement, and the speed of implementations of any measures that have a cost to the public finances will depend on decisions to be made in the Comprehensive Spending Review. (HM Government, 2010: 35)

The early bills made no significant claim on the public finances and were seen as necessary to lock the Liberal Democrats into supporting the Conservative's position on the economy. The constitutional measures – not least the referendum on AV – were essential to ensure that the Liberal Democrats got out of the arrangement what they had always regarded as a prerequisite for power sharing. Now there was the prospect of a new electoral system. There were concerns that if they lost the referendum, the Liberal Democrats might contemplate pulling out of the Coalition, but the fixed-term Parliament was designed to bind them to the Coalition. The logic of this line of reasoning was unclear. The Liberal Democrats did not have the money to fight an early election and their low support in the opinion polls suggested that it was not to their political advantage to have an early election. If they knew they could leave the Coalition without triggering an early General Election and spend the remainder of the Parliament rebuilding political support, then it was not clear why a fixed term, especially one of five rather than four years, would lock them into the Coalition. It is possible that recognition of this on the part of leading Conservatives was responsible for the Fixed-Term Parliament Bill, having been introduced, then making slow progress through the House of Commons. Another possible explanation is that it was not popular with Conservative backbenchers. Whatever the explanation, the Coalition remained formally committed to ensuring fixed-term Parliaments became a feature of the UK Constitution.

Priority, however, was given to the referendum on AV. This was the real key to cementing the Liberal Democrats to the Coalition. As one Cabinet minister said in a private meeting in rallying support for the bill, 'without it, there would be no Coalition'. In terms of legislative scheduling, it took precedence. When it made slow progress in the Lords, additional days were allocated.

Political Tension

With the return of a new government, it is relatively rare for dissent by government backbenchers to be pronounced in the first session of the Parliament. As Cowley and Stuart note (2010: 3): 'The first session . . . is usually the calm before the storm.' Under the Coalition there was to be no period of calm – dissent by government MPs was to reach unprecedented levels within the first few months of the Coalition being formed (Cowley and Stuart, 2010). Of the 110 votes held in the House of Commons between 18 May and 5 November 2010, there were rebellions by government MPs in no fewer than 59.

The Coalition Agreement on constitutional measures in particular generated the potential for tension, but not so much tension between the parties as within the parties, primarily the Conservative Party. As we have seen, in the sphere of constitutional reform, the Conservatives in the negotiations largely conceded the Liberal Democrat case. The Conservatives were able to protect their own 'red lines' outside the context of constitutional issues, but on the constitution their red line had to give way.

The potential for division was thus on the Conservative benches, with a number of backbenchers objecting to the concessions made. Conservatives were reluctant to concede that the political system was broken. Some, such as the former Chancellor, Lord Lamont, in the Lords, explicitly disavowed the claim that it was. It was not surprising, then, that opposition to some of the bills introduced by the Government encountered opposition from within, more so in some cases than from the Opposition. The Labour Party had manifesto commitments in support of a referendum on AV and fixed-term Parliaments. The commitments blunted any attempt to oppose the measures to give effect to such provisions. On the Second Reading of the Fixed-Term Parliaments Bill, for example, the Opposition criticized the measure but abstained from voting. The 25 MPs (23 + 2 tellers) to vote against included 11 Conservatives. On some amendments, though, the Opposition was able to join with the dissident Conservatives. It thus voted, for example, for the amendment to the Parliamentary Voting System and Constituencies Bill, moved by Conservative MP Charles Walker, to ensure than any reduction in the number of MPs was matched by a proportionate reduction in the number of ministers.

Given the stance taken on constitutional issues, it is not surprising that Cowley and Stuart were to record that 'The issue to have caused the most frequent dissent so far this session has been the Coalition's plans for constitutional reform' (Cowley and Stuart, 2010: 4). Of the 59 votes to witness backbench dissent in the first months of the Parliament, 26 of them took place on the Parliamentary Voting System and Constituencies Bill.

The tensions were not confined to MPs. The Public Bodies Bill encountered criticisms from all parts of the House of Lords, including the government benches (on this occasion, Liberal Democrats as well as Conservatives). The criticism was notable in both qualitative and quantitative terms (former Cabinet ministers being among the large body of critics), and the Government was soon signalling that amendments would be made. It suffered an early defeat on the bill. The referendum on AV also attracted opposition, not least from some Conservatives who favoured a threshold requirement for the referendum. Given that there is no provision for programme motions or guillotines in the House of Lords, the debates on the Bills proved protracted.

However, the potential for inter-party conflict also began to emerge. So long as the Coalition stuck to the constitutional reform agenda, the principal objectors were to be found among Conservative backbenchers in the two chambers. However, if it deviated from or failed to deliver on the reform agenda, the likelihood was that there would be tensions between the parties. There were some signs of increasing Conservative unease, not confined to backbenchers, as the Fixed-Term Parliaments Bill made its way through Parliament. Some Conservatives gained the impression that enthusiasm for it among party leaders was waning and that what they wanted was a five-year term for the current Parliament but not necessarily for subsequent ones. They were, though, stuck with the bill. Where slow progress was made was in respect of reform of the

House of Lords. The draft bill promised by the end of 2010 failed to materialize. A working group of frontbenchers (from all three parties) was delayed in agreeing a draft bill in part because of the election of a new leader of the Labour Party and also because of failure to reach agreement on a number of points. The Government announced that the bill would appear in the New Year. But there was increasing scepticism as to when. When a minister in the Lords repeated that it would be in the New Year, some peers shouted 'Which year?' The Government conceded that when it was published, it would be subject to pre-legislative scrutiny by a joint committee of both Houses. This it was accepted would not necessarily be a quick process.

Though all three parties had a manifesto commitment to a wholly or partly elected second chamber, they were not in the same terms, and the only enthusiasm for moving ahead quickly on the issue appeared to be in Liberal Democrat ranks. Though Conservative ministers continued to express support for the process of reform, they did little to hasten the process. A lack of enthusiasm was likely reinforced by knowledge that any bill would run into substantial opposition in the House of Lords. Peers on all sides variously made clear their opposition in a number of short debates in the House. Among opponents was former Speaker of the House of Commons Betty Boothroyd. She spoke in one of the short debates, with her speech being described privately by one member as 'gently fertilizing the long grass'.

So long as the process was continuing, the Coalition held together. The initial focus was in any event on the referendum on AV. Only if that failed to materialize or resulted in a 'no' vote was attention expected to shift significantly to reform of the Lords (Chapman, 2010). However, if the referendum did not produce what the Liberal Democrats wanted and the proposed reform of the second chamber failed to materialize, then there was the prospect of a conflict between the parties to the Coalition. Some Conservatives in both Houses admitted that they were voting reluctantly – 'holding my nose' as one put it – for the referendum on AV, because that was crucial to maintaining the Coalition. Supporting the Coalition on Lords reform did not come into the same category.

For the Coalition whips, there was a fine balancing act to be undertaken, trying to ensure that Conservative MPs and peers did not derail the constitutional reform programme while delivering on that programme. Backbench dissent in the Commons was not sufficient to prevent the Government getting its measures – the number of dissenters being too small or not being joined by the Opposition (Cowley and Stuart, 2010) – but support in the Lords was less assured. For the Government, it was a case of holding together the parties to the Coalition and holding together the members within each party. According to one Conservative MP, Nick Boles:

> As the missiles rain down, Conservatives and Liberal Democrats will stick together only if each party's MPs believe that they are being true to their most fundamental values and are making steady progress on the issues that matter most to them. (Boles, 2010: 130)

This was possible, though, only if the MPs were placing the emphasis on different policy sectors, the Conservatives on economic issues and the Liberal Democrats on constitutional issues. If both focused on constitutional issues, then there was the potential for fissures to occur. On constitutional measures, the Conservatives had made concessions to achieve a majority government. Though that enabled them to take tough economic measures, it also – in the eyes of some Conservatives – jeopardized the long-term constitutional health of the nation for short-term political advantage. For the Liberal Democrats, it offered the possibility of moving forward towards their ultimate goal of achieving proportional representation for parliamentary elections. A 'no' vote in the referendum would largely destroy the prospect of achieving that goal in the foreseeable future. As I have noted elsewhere, durability should not be confused with harmony (Norton, 2010: 260). As comparative studies show, a coalition can absorb tensions between the parties that form it (Andeweg and Timmermans, 2008: 269–300) and the most enduring governments – after single-party majority governments – are those that constitute minimal winning coalitions (Laver and Schofield, 1998: 150–5). The Conservative–Liberal Democrat Government constitutes such a minimal winning coalition. The Coalition may endure, but at its heart is an uncertain tension over what constitutes the best for the constitution of the United Kingdom.

References

Andeweg, R. and Timmermans, A. (2008) Conflict Management in Coalition Government. In K. Strøm, W.C. Müller and T. Bergmann (eds.), *Cabinets and Coalition Bargaining: The Democratic Life Cycle in Western Europe* (Oxford: Oxford University Press).

Ashdown, P. (2002) *The Ashdown Diaries, Volume Two 1997–1999* (London: Penguin Books).

Bogdanor, V. (2009), *The New British Constitution* (Oxford: Hart Publishing).

Boles, N. (2010) *Which Way's Up?* (London: Biteback).

Boulton, A. and Jones, J. (2010) *Hung Together* (London: Simon & Schuster).

Chapman, J. (2010), House of Lords to be Abolished and Replaced by Elected Senate. *Daily Mail*, 4 December.

Constitution Committee, House of Lords (2010a) *The Government's Constitutional Reform Programme*, 5th Report, Session 2010–11, HL Paper 43 (London: The Stationery Office).

Constitution Committee, House of Lords (2010b) *Public Bodies Bill [HL]*, 6th Report, Session 2010–11, HL Paper 51 (London: The Stationery Office).

Constitution Committee, House of Lords (2010c) *Parliamentary Voting System and Constituencies Bill*, 7th Report, Session 2010–11, HL Paper 58 (London: The Stationery Office).

Constitution Committee, House of Lords (2010d) *Fixed-term Parliaments Bill*, 8th Report, Session 2010–11, HL Paper 69 (London: The Stationery Office).

Cowley, P. and Stuart, M. (2010) *A Coalition with Wobbly Wings: Backbench Dissent Since May 2010*. www.revolts.co.uk (accessed 20 December 2010).

Fox, R. (2010) Five Days in May: A New Political Order Emerges. In A. Geddes and J. Tonge (eds.), *Britain Votes 2010* (Oxford: Oxford University Press).

HM Government (2010) *The Coalition: Our Programme for Government* (London: Cabinet Office).

Jenkins Commission (1998) *Report of the Independent Commission on the Voting System*, Cm 4090-I (London: The Stationery Office).

King, A. (2009) *The British Constitution* (Oxford: Oxford University Press).

Laver, M. and Schofield, N. (1998) *Multiparty Government: The Politics of Coalition in Europe* (Ann Arbor, MI: University of Michigan Press).

Laws, D. (2010) *22 Days in May* (London: Biteback).

Liberal Democrat Party (1997) *Make the Difference: The Liberal Democrat Manifesto* (London: Liberal Democrat Party).

Norton, P. (1982) *The Constitution in Flux* (Oxford: Basil Blackwell).

Norton, P. (1998) *Power to the People* (London: Conservative Policy Forum).

Norton, P. (2007a) The Constitution. In A. Seldon (ed.), *Blair's Britain 1997–2007* (Cambridge: Cambridge University Press).

Norton, P. (2007b) Tony Blair and the Constitution. *British Politics*, 2(2): 269–81.

Norton, P. (2008) Making Sense of Opposition. *The Journal of Legislative Studies*, 14(1/2): 236–50.

Norton, P. (2010) The Politics of Coalition. In N. Allen and J. Bartle (eds.), *Britain at the Polls 2010* (London: Sage).

Norton, P. (2011 forthcoming) Speaking for the People: A Conservative Narrative of Democracy. *Policy Studies*.

Oakeshott, I., Woolf, M. and Oliver, J. (2010) Against the Wall. *The Sunday Times, New Review*, 16 May.

Political and Constitutional Reform Committee, House of Commons (2010) *Parliamentary Voting System and Constituencies Bill*, 3rd Report, Session 2010–11, HC 437 (London: The Stationery Office).

Riddell, P. and Haddon, C. (2009) *Transitions: Preparing for Changes of Government* (London: Institute for Government).

Robinson, N. (2010) Sir Humphrey Praises Politicians Shock. *Nick Robinson's Newsblog*, 14 July. www.bbc.co.uk/blogs/nickrobinson (accessed 20 December 2010).

Seldon, A. (2004) *Blair* (London: The Free Press).

Wilson, R. (2010) *5 Days to Power* (London: Biteback).

11
The Con–Lib Coalition Agenda for Scotland, Wales and Northern Ireland

Arthur Aughey

This chapter is divided into three sections. The first considers the Coalition's inheritance in devolved matters in terms of the legacy of Labour's period in office and of the strategy of the main Coalition partner – if only because the Conservative Party was expected to win the General Election of 2010 and had most to do to establish its devolutionary bona fides. The second examines the formation of Coalition policy and the third looks at Scotland, Wales and Northern Ireland, respectively. A very brief conclusion reflects on the prospects for this agenda.

Territorial Legacy and Cameron's Strategy

There have been some longstanding criticisms of the Labour Government's approach to devolution relevant to the Coalition Government's inheritance. In 1998, Professor Robert Hazell outlined the logic of the new devolutionary dispensation:

> To come to terms with the new political culture the centre will have to relax and be willing to let go. It will have to treat the devolved governments as equal partners, not subordinates. The centre needs to understand and respect the political forces which have been unleashed, and to channel and direct them by working with the flow. (Hazell, 1998)

For Hazell, this required a strategic conception of relationships between the devolved institutions and Westminster, obliging the centre 'to give a lead, in its actions and its words, to bind the Union together in order to counter-balance the centrifugal political forces of devolution'. That conclusion, however, was at odds with his interpretation of Labour Government practice, which thought of devolution as 'been there and done that' such that central government could now move on with little effect on traditional behaviour (Hazell, 1998). A decade later similar criticisms of Labour's approach were being made, especially that devolutionary practices were 'based on gentlemen's agreements and Blair's sofa-style approach to politics'. With the emergence of 'a new territorial politics, characterized more by conflict and confrontation than in the past', central government was ill-equipped to deal with its challenges (Lodge and Schmuecker, 2007: 93). When Labour former junior ministers reflected on their period in office there was little mention of territorial politics. As Trench has noted: 'Given that many consider Labour's constitutional agenda to have been one of its most successful areas of policy, it's telling that middle-ranking ministers simply never even noticed this particular part of Labour's record' (Trench, 2010a).

What connected institutional practice and constitutional justification in Labour's approach was another aspect of devolution: the electoral factor. Labour (and Liberal Democrat) commitment to devolution in Scotland had been in part to provide electoral insurance against any future Conservative majority at Westminster, a legacy of Margaret Thatcher's terms of office. That consideration was also a factor in Wales and not entirely absent in Northern Ireland either. Devolution, then, was intended to counterbalance Conservative electoral strength in England. This represented a 'nationalization' of electoral mandates, raising implicit questions about the UK mandate. For most of Labour's period of office this was not an issue because Labour was continuously in office in Wales (either alone or in coalition with first the Liberal Democrats and later Plaid Cymru); and until 2007 in Scotland (in coalition with the Liberal Democrats). In Northern Ireland until 2006, Labour Secretaries of State had mainly governed by direct rule. This meant that Labour could rely on informality of party relations to secure goodwill with Edinburgh and Cardiff and on executive authority in Belfast. Devolution made potentially much more difficult cooperative relationships between a Conservative, or Conservative-dominated, Government at Westminster and non-Conservative administrations in Scotland, Wales and Northern Ireland.

A non-Labour administration would inherit a very different UK from the one Conservatives last governed. Devolution confirmed that the UK was a diverse state rather than a unitary state – a 'state of unions'

(Mitchell, 2009: 15). However, if devolution addressed *particular* problems of sub-state legitimacy, then one consequence was the problem of general *state* function. Trench pointed out that, from a UK point of view, Labour's legacy was debates on devolution which rarely joined up. There had been 'the opportunity to widen the debate and seek to show what the UK offers people from all parts of it that makes living in one state worthwhile'. But this opportunity had been missed under Labour because, 'in keeping with the piecemeal way devolution has developed so far, it has ducked that opportunity whenever it has been presented' (Trench, 2008: 17). This critique expressed a desire for a coherent narrative of governance though the task facing a new government would be daunting. In Hazell's terms, it would need to treat devolved governments more like equal partners; it should respect the political forces to which devolution had given institutional expression; and it would need to bind together the UK, counterbalancing the centrifugal tendencies of territorial mandates. Moreover, it would have to do all this in an age of austerity, making party differences susceptible to populist opportunism.

These concerns animated David Cameron's leadership and what emerged after 2005 was a three-fold strategy. Cameron was intent on recommitting the party to its Unionist vocation. He made it clear that he shared the broad party consensus – that the Union contributed to the security of all its component parts; gave its citizens a more powerful voice in the world; best secured economic prosperity; promoted fairness through commonly financed health and social services; and had a common cultural inheritance which all could share (Cameron, 2007a). The first part of his strategy, addressing what bound the UK together, restated an older, One Nation tradition. This informed Cameron's call (2006) to his party conference that 'we are all in this together'. The 'we' was everyone in the UK, whose interests a future Conservative government was pledged to protect.

The second strand was to signal that Cameron's Conservatives did understand the new political forces and wished to work with, rather than against, differing institutional mandates. His proposed contract of governance intimated a willingness to treat the devolved governments as respected, if not equal, partners. The message of this 'respect agenda' was that a Conservative government would deal seriously with those having a different mandate, that to attain the common objectives of the UK, differences of approach should be acknowledged. Whether a respectful relaxation at the centre and letting go – up to a point, that point being the integrity of the Union – would be conducive to inter-governmental harmony was moot, but it was important for Conservatives to show willing. 'If we win the next election at Westminster,' Cameron wrote:

> we would govern with a maturity and a respect for the Scottish people. I would be a Prime Minister who would work constructively with any administration at Holyrood for the good of Scotland, and I would be in regular contact with the First Minister no matter what party he or she came from. (Cameron, 2009a)

Addressing the Scottish Conservative conference, he marked the tenth anniversary of devolution by announcing: 'I stand here, the leader of the Conservative Party, and say loudly and proudly, we support devolution, we back it heart and soul, and we will make it work for everyone' (Cameron, 2009b). Speaking in Wales, Cameron also confirmed that his would be 'the party that supports devolution and makes it work', establishing a relationship between Cardiff and Westminster that would be 'one of co-operation, not confrontation' (Cameron, 2009c).

The third strand addressed the question of the Conservative mandate outside England. The objective was to secure a majority at Westminster with representation from all parts of the UK. Cameron devoted organizational resources to promote his party's prospects not only in Scotland and Wales but also in Northern Ireland, where the party campaigned under the title Ulster Conservatives and Unionists – New Force (UCUNF), a rather fractious alliance between the Ulster Unionist Party (UUP) and local Conservatives. The purpose in each case was to stress how Conservative values, local identity and UK purpose nested comfortably together. Cameron could proudly claim that 'we are now the only major party to field candidates in all four parts of the UK' (Cameron, 2009c). If the larger objective was to 'detoxify' the Conservative brand inside England, this strategy was designed for the same purpose outside it (Snowden, 2010). In the event, it failed to deliver electorally in Scotland where 'the much vaunted "Cameron effect" had no impact' (Mitchell and van der Zwet, 2010: 709). The Conservative vote increased only marginally to 16.9 per cent, there was a failure to win its 11 target seats and the party retained just one MP. There was some success in Wales where the number of seats increased from three to eight, qualified by the fact that the expectation had been 12 (Bradbury, 2010: 730). Polling 15.2 per cent of the vote in Northern Ireland, none of the UCUNF candidates was successful. Conservatives also failed to make crucial gains in the North of England, so that their territorial base remained much as before and fell short of an overall majority (Denver, 2010).

Coalition Formation

When it came to negotiating a programme of government, the Conservatives and Liberal Democrats easily found common ground on devolution matters. This would have been unlikely before 1997 since the Conservative Party had opposed devolution while the Liberal Democrats were advocates of federalism. Until recently, Vince Cable had expressed continued suspicions about Cameron's ability to change traditional Conservative belief in a strong, centralized state. Cable asserted: 'Although there is, now, more willingness to use the language of localism, nothing concrete has emerged. Devolution to Scotland and Wales is still regarded with great suspicion and regionalism in England is treated with ridicule' (Cable, 2007). By 2010, clear distinctions could be made no longer since localism had become a Conservative campaign issue. Indeed, there was little differentiation of substance on devolution in the manifestos of the three major parties. On Scotland, they all promised to implement the main proposals of the Calman Commission, a consensual unionist project to review the Scotland Act 1998 as an alternative to the SNP Government's canvassing of independence. On Wales, they agreed to support a referendum on primary legislative powers for the National Assembly under the terms of the Government of Wales Act 2006. On Northern Ireland, there was consensus on supporting the power-sharing institutions established by the Belfast Agreement of 1998. Rhetorically, Liberal Democrats continued to locate devolved relations within a narrative of a federal UK, an aspiration which found no resonance with Conservatives. However, as Anthony Barnett (2010) argued (and which private sources have confirmed), 'the desire to preserve the Union and prevent a boost for the SNP in Scotland was an important motive for Cameron's offer of a Coalition'.

Cameron's devotion to the Union must never be discounted. 'If it should ever come to a choice between constitutional perfection and the preservation of our nation,' he told an Edinburgh audience, 'I choose our United Kingdom. Better an imperfect union than a broken one' (2007b). In 2010 it was better an imperfect coalition than a threat to the UK. And he was sincere when he said that walking into Downing Street as Prime Minister, he was deeply conscious of being responsible for the 'future of our United Kingdom', making clear that: 'When I say I am prime minister of the United Kingdom, I really mean it. England, Scotland, Wales, Northern Ireland – we're weaker apart, stronger together, so together is the way we must always stay' (Cameron, 2010). This is not to neglect, of course, the utility of the Coalition with the Liberal

Democrats, which helped to address the vexed issue of the mandate. As David Mundell (2010), the only Scottish Conservative MP, could now claim: 'we are working with the Liberal Democrats in a broad-based government that enjoys a bigger electoral mandate in Scotland than the SNP Government at Holyrood'. Liberal Democrats offered 'the Conservatives cover in governing Scotland' as well as consolidating the Coalition's mandate in Wales (Mitchell and van der Zwet, 2010: 722). The Coalition Government represented 59 per cent of the UK vote, 64 per cent of the English vote, 46 per cent of the Welsh vote and slightly less than 36 per cent of the Scottish vote. Only in Northern Ireland was there no explicit mandate. If this did not dispel the tensions of territorial policy it did put to rest immediate problems of legitimacy. Here was a potential dual-benefit dividend. If the first addressed the territorial limits of the Conservative vote, the second was the possibility of convincing electors that the Liberal Democrats were a credible party of government (Cutts, Fieldhouse and Russell, 2010: 705–6).

The respect agenda found a comfortable home in the Coalition since it corresponded with Liberal Democrat policy. Cameron fulfilled his promise to visit both the Scottish Parliament and the Welsh Assembly as the first official acts of his premiership. In Edinburgh (BBC, 2010a) he tied together the personal, the political and the constitutional, announcing that the agenda 'is about parliaments working together, of governing with respect, both because I believe Scotland deserves that respect and because I want to try and win Scotland's respect as the prime minister of the United Kingdom', a message repeated by Michael Moore, the Liberal Democrat Secretary of State for Scotland, when he addressed Holyrood. Speaking to the National Assembly in Cardiff, the new Conservative Secretary of State for Wales, Cheryl Gillan (2010), put institutional flesh on the words of the 'agenda of co-operation and optimism'. She argued that the 'solid proof of the Government's commitment to work in collaboration with the devolved institutions, and to integrate devolution into our policy making' would be the more frequent meeting of the Joint Ministerial Committee 'to consider matters of common mutual interest'. This change – contrasting the new approach with the informality of Blair and the authoritarianism of Brown – 'indicates the way in which we wish to approach devolved priorities' (Gillan, 2010).

Confirmation of this came from an unusual source. When the First Ministers of Scotland, Wales and Northern Ireland issued a joint declaration expressing reservations about the Coalition's spending plans, they also 'welcomed the general spirit in which the new Coalition Government has approached inter-governmental relations' (BBC, 2010b). Moreover, the new draft Cabinet manual incorporated the respect agenda into its code in paragraph 289: 'The foundation of the relationship between the Government and the Devolved Administrations is mutual respect and recognition of the responsibilities set out in the devolution settlements' (Cabinet Office, 2010). Nevertheless, the Coalition already has been criticized for lack of consultation on the date of the Alternative Vote referendum, to be held on the same day as elections to Scottish Parliament and the Welsh and Northern Ireland Assemblies (Kirkup, 2010a). This suggests that the mantra of 'taking devolution seriously' may not have been entirely absorbed in Westminster.

The programme for government was expressed in a manner which seemed to satisfy Hazell's requirement for a compelling narrative. In the foreword (HM Government, 2010: 7), Cameron and Clegg argued that top-down control had been a failure and the time had come to 'disperse power more widely in Britain today'. They claimed that 'hoarding authority within government' was counterproductive and the ambition of the Coalition was nothing less than 'a radical distribution of power away from Westminster and Whitehall to councils, communities and homes across the nation'. Here was a grand narrative of localism which Conservative and Liberal Democrat discourses now shared and into which devolution could be said to fit. Nonetheless, the proposals for Scotland, Wales and Northern Ireland represented continuity with Labour policy rather than radical change. For Northern Ireland, the Coalition supported the devolved institutions but inserted the language of the Conservative manifesto on working 'to bring Northern Ireland back into the mainstream of UK politics'. It also repeated the Conservative commitment to produce a paper examining corporation tax. On Scotland, the commitment to implementing Calman was reaffirmed, to which was added a Liberal Democrat promise to review the fossil fuel levy. On Wales, the promise was restated of a referendum to increase the powers of the Welsh Assembly. The programme also acknowledged that Wales had a legitimate grievance about its level of funding but that addressing it should be deferred until 'the stabilization of the public finances'. If the referendum approved further Welsh devolution, a 'process similar to the Calman Commission' (HM Government, 2010: 7) was proposed.

There were mixed signals about the management of devolution. On the one hand, acceptance that inter-governmental relations would be conducted more regularly through the Joint Ministerial Committee (JMC) and its two sub-committees, JMC (Domestic), chaired by the Deputy Prime Minister, and JMC (Europe), chaired by the Foreign Secretary, intimated a different approach by the Coalition (Cabinet Office, 2010: 103). On the other hand, the three territorial departments, the Scotland, Wales and Northern Ireland Offices, were maintained. The Coalition did not follow the long-standing recommendation of the Constitution Unit and, later, of the House of Lords Committee on the Constitution that there should be one department for the nations and regions. Some have argued that such a department would deliver a more coherent approach, helping to reconcile UK-wide and devolved policy (Hazell, 1998). Moreover, the civil servant post of Director-General, Devolution Strategy, responsible for an overview of territorial policy, was lost in the official restructuring attending coalition formation. This represented modification within continuity and 'it is likely that different agreements will be reached between different parts of the UK', an approach which seemed to chime well with the respect agenda and with the pragmatic traditions of UK governance. If there was a strategy it was this: 'the very fact that electoral and parliamentary arithmetics [the mandate issue] will force the Coalition to adopt a negotiated approach to governing the UK [the respect agenda] – working with the nations on a case by case basis – might help ensure that it succeeds in working with the devolved nations in an effective way [securing the Union]' (Jeffery, Lodge and Schmuecker, 2010: 24–6).

Scotland

The Scotland Bill, published on St Andrew's Day 2010, reflected general pro-Union opinion, but its intention was captured in a remark by Cameron about what was required of the Scottish Conservative Party: 'more Scottish and more pro-Union' (Settle, 2010). According to Jim Gallagher (2010), who had been Secretary to the Calman Commission (almost echoing Cameron's words), the bill is 'obviously in Scotland's interest, but it will be good for the entire UK too'. What links the Scottish and Union sides is the principle of accountability. Cameron argued that the Scottish Parliament has the power to spend money but little responsibility to raise money, but 'This doesn't make sense. If you believe in people power and accountable government, the two should be joined up' (Cameron, 2010b). Under the Coalition's proposals taxation and expenditure would be joined up, with the Scottish Parliament granted tax and borrowing facilities of about £12 billion. From 2015, the Treasury will deduct 10 pence from rates of income tax in Scotland, reducing the UK block grant commensurately (currently the Scottish block grant is £30 billion). The Scottish Parliament becomes responsible for raising about 35 per cent of its revenue from designated 'Scottish taxpayers'. Scottish ministers will also be empowered to borrow in order to fund both current

(£500 million) and capital (£2.2 billion) expenditure. Stamp duty, land and landfill taxes will also be devolved and the Scottish Parliament may, subject to the approval of Westminster, propose new taxes. According to Moore, this 'is the biggest transfer of fiscal power to Scotland since the creation of the United Kingdom' (Scott, 2010a). One aspect of the respect agenda included in the bill is the statutory recognition of the term 'Scottish Government' which replaces 'Scottish Executive'. The Bill is intended to fulfil a double purpose for the Coalition. It allows the Conservatives to show serious commitment to devolution and to the respect agenda. It also allows the Liberal Democrats to claim that the bill is Calman-plus, both fulfilling a party pledge and providing an example of the positive value of their role in the Coalition. There have been, of course, dissenting voices.

On the one hand, there are Conservative critics who argue that the bill concedes too much to nationalists and that 'respect' should not be a cover for constitutional surrender. It is doubly perverse, they argue, to advance such radical change when the SNP ideal of independence within Europe, with Ireland as its model, has been dealt a severe blow by recent Irish experience in both its European and independence claims. For example, Lord Forsythe argued that the bill's proposals should be put to a referendum, claiming that the bill is unlikely to work, will be damaging to Scottish interests and makes it hard to dispute nationalist calls for full fiscal autonomy 'when you have conceded the principle' (Barnes, 2010). On the other hand, as one would expect, the SNP claimed that only full fiscal autonomy can address Scotland's needs and that the bill is an incoherent compromise, simply justifying Treasury control in the language of 'equity'. The SNP, having dropped from its own legislative programme the promised referendum on independence, has adopted a strategy of linking criticism of the bill with opposition to the Coalition's spending plans. The object is to secure electoral support for even more radical constitutional change. According to Alex Salmond, the only alternative 'to a decade of despair, of Tory Westminster cuts, is to have the financial independence for the parliament to generate more revenue, more wealth for Scotland and give us a better future' (Carrell, 2010). Independence, blocked by unionist parties at Holyrood, is now for the people to decide.

The Comprehensive Spending Review specified that current expenditure in Scotland would fall in real terms by 6.8 per cent and capital spending by 38 per cent by 2015. The debate, as it is elsewhere, is not about the requirement for spending reductions but about their pace and extent. In his appearance at the Scottish Parliament's finance committee Chief

Secretary to the Treasury, Danny Alexander, put the Coalition's case that the pace of deficit reduction was necessary to stabilize public finances for the benefit of both Scotland and the UK (Scott, 2010b). For the SNP and for Labour, albeit for different reasons, the Coalition's strategy is destructive of economic growth and both are competing to play the Scottish card. In the appeal to Scottish public opinion it appears that the old cry of 'Tory cuts' still resonates. A ComRes poll found that 53 per cent of Scots thought expenditure reductions went too far and 60 per cent thought they were unfair (the highest criticism of Coalition policy across the UK territories). That response shows the difficulty of persuading Scottish opinion of the virtue of the Coalition agenda and the opportunity for its opponents to play both the democratic and the national cards in opposition to it.

Wales

The Coalition commitment to introduce a referendum on further Welsh devolution represented both continuity with previous policy and also consensus among the parties in the Welsh Assembly and at Westminster. Gillan – on the recommendation of the Electoral Commission – agreed with the First and Deputy First Minister in September 2010 the wording of the referendum question. It was more than a mere question, also an explication of current practice. It noted how the Assembly has powers to make laws on 20 subject areas, such as agriculture, education, health, housing and local government, but that in each policy area it can make laws on some matters but not on others: 'To make laws on any of these other matters, the Assembly must ask the UK Parliament for its agreement. The UK Parliament then decides each time whether or not the Assembly can make these laws.' If in the referendum most voters vote 'yes', then the Assembly will be able to make laws in those areas for which it has responsibility without Westminster's agreement. The question then is: 'Do you want the Assembly now to be able to make laws on all matters in the 20 subject areas it has powers for?' The referendum was scheduled for 3 March 2011 and the relevant Orders were laid before Parliament on 21 October. These orders were then voted through the Assembly on 9 November 2010 – with all-party support – by 47 votes to none.

The wording of the Programme for Government on the future financing of Welsh devolution was a curious composite. The Coalition recognized the concerns about the system of devolution funding but stated that 'at this time, the priority must be to reduce the deficit' though, depending on a positive vote in the referendum, the Coalition promised to 'establish a process similar to the Calman Commission for the Welsh Assembly'. A long-standing Welsh grievance has been that the formula for allocating spending across the devolved parts of the UK – the so-called Barnett formula – has unfairly disadvantaged Wales, currently underfunding it by about £300 million per year. All Welsh parties have been united in pushing for reform, with even the leader of the Conservatives in Wales, Nick Bourne, enunciating the 'Bourne Doctrine' – a preparedness to oppose Coalition policy where public expenditure reductions target Wales unfairly (Williamson, 2010a). In the spending review, Wales did take a bigger percentage cut than Scotland and Northern Ireland – 7.5 per cent in current and 41 per cent in capital expenditure. However, unlike opinion in Scotland, the Welsh public was more likely to accept the necessity for reducing public expenditure, even if it thought Wales was still being treated less fairly (BBC, 2010b). When he appeared before the Assembly's finance committee in November 2010, Alexander was challenged by the committee's chair, Conservative Angela Burns, to replace the inequities of Barnett with a new, needs-based formula. The existing formula, she claimed, 'just merely emphasizes the great difference or lack of parity between us and Northern Ireland or us and Scotland', confirming that there exists no common position between devolved institutions on all policy issues. However, Alexander merely repeated the position outlined in the Programme for Government, that 'as a Government it is not our policy to reopen the question of the Barnett formula or the funding allocations within the United Kingdom whilst this very serious fiscal consolidation is going on' (for a record of the exchanges, see Williamson, 2010b). Nevertheless, he did leave open the door for fiscal powers to be devolved at a point in the future. Here was some acknowledgement of one of the recommendations made by the Welsh Assembly Government's Independent Commission on Funding and Finance (known as the Holtham Commission), which reported in 2010.

Gerry Holtham, who had chaired that Commission, argued that the lack of fairness which Welsh politicians claimed to characterize Coalition expenditure cuts did not mean that Wales had been deliberately 'diddled'. It was simply a consequence of the mechanical application of the Barnett formula. However, in Holtham's opinion the formula – which reads across 'consequentials' from expenditure in departments in England to the devolved block grants – is not governed by iron necessity. There is a degree of political choice and inertia is one such choice. While admitting that the ad hoc approach of the Treasury towards territorial finance had served the UK quite well in the past, he believed the time had now come for a rational, needs-based assessment. This would be a difficult case to make since 'Wales is by far the politically least influential part of the UK, with no credible threats to the centre, no senior politician in the Coalition Government, few Parliamentary seats, fewer marginals'. Westminster, which was 'extremely sensitive to the reaction of Scottish and Northern Irish politicians and give them the benefit of the doubt', simply had much less reason to do so when it came to Wales (Holtham, 2010). Holtham was calling for the Coalition to follow the reasoning of Cameron's thinking about Scotland – that there was no contradiction in an Assembly with greater powers being more both Welsh and more pro-Union, linking under the principle of accountability the power to spend money and some responsibility to raise it.

Northern Ireland

In an interview on *Newsnight* during the General Election campaign, Jeremy Paxman had asked Cameron: 'In some parts of the country you have said that the state accounts for a bigger share of the economy than the communist countries in the old Eastern bloc and that this is unsustainable. Which parts of the country?' Cameron's response had been: 'The first one I'd pick out is Northern Ireland, the size of the state has got too big' (Crichton, 2010). This proved to be a gift to UNCUNF's opponents even though there was widespread agreement locally about needing to rebalance the respective weight of public and private sectors. The issue was not whether this rebalancing should happen but how, and how swiftly it could be done. It was a theme to which the new Secretary of State for Northern Ireland, Owen Paterson, returned in his speech to the Conservative party conference in 2010. He reaffirmed the main lines of Coalition policy: that the overriding priority was the economy; that Northern Ireland had its part to play because 'we're all in it together'; and that, although spending decisions were a devolved matter, the UK Government had an interest to secure financial responsibility. The imbalance in Northern Ireland's economy was one such interest: 'After 13 years of Labour, public spending accounts for a staggering 77.6 per cent of the economy. This is simply unsustainable. It was the Coalition's business to help expand the private sector, even though this could take up to 25 years' (Paterson, 2010). One of the proposals, promised in the election and included in the Programme for Government, was to produce 'a government paper examining potential mechanisms for changing the corporation tax rate in Northern Ireland'. Speaking later to the Northern Ireland Grand Committee at Westminster, Paterson argued for dovetailing strategies between London and the Northern Ireland Executive and noted that there was increasing support from the business community and political parties for the devolution of corporation tax. He stated: 'I do believe that devolving powers over corporation tax could play a major role in attracting significant new investment into Northern Ireland and, over time, reducing its dependence on the public sector' (Northern Ireland Office, 2010).

The question of varying the corporation tax was not new. It had been considered by Sir David Varney under the previous Labour Government. Varney was critical of the proposal on two counts. For Northern Ireland, there was no clear case for a reduction to 12.5 per cent (and the main reason cited had been to compete for external investment on the same terms as the Republic of Ireland). Varney estimated a revenue loss of over £300 million with little expectation of recovering such a sum in the medium term. For the UK, the case against was even more marked because the likelihood was a displacement of capital and profits from Great Britain to Northern Ireland would result in an estimated loss to the Exchequer over ten years of about £2.2 billion (Varney, 2007). Calman had also considered the devolution of corporation tax for Scotland but rejected it on terms similar to Varney's. However, some ideas become fashions and a coalition of business organizations in Northern Ireland has assiduously lobbied for a cut in corporation tax as the great economic panacea, despite the fact that the trade union movement is opposed and the Northern Ireland Finance Minister unconvinced (Gordon, 2010; Murphy, 2010). In the light of the Coalition's narrative, it is difficult to understand how either UK or Northern Ireland interests are best served by devolving power over corporation tax.

A report by the Institute for Fiscal Studies predicted that proposed changes in welfare benefits would hit Northern Ireland harder than the other devolved territories, mainly because of the greater number receiving disability allowances and the higher number of households with children (Phillips, 2010). Although welfare expenditure is a UK matter, the Northern Ireland Executive has the competence to modify levels of social security benefit. It has never chosen to do so, content to maintain the Unionist principle of 'parity' since roughly £3 billion of the annual £8 billion UK transfer covers social welfare payments. The Minister for Social Development, Alex Attwood, did raise the possibility of resisting changes to housing benefit and Jobseeker's Allowance. Breaking parity, however, would involve financial consequences, which local politicians are reluctant to contemplate. The Assembly has been averse not only to reducing public expenditure but also to raising more of its own finances. Parties have failed on a number of occasions to introduce water charges that would bring in about £213 million per annum and the regional rate was frozen in 2007. Under the Coalition's plans Northern Ireland will face reductions of 6.9 per cent in current and 37 per cent in capital spending over the period to 2014–15. There was some political expectation that (as Holtham thought) Northern Ireland could play the 'sensitivity card' since the history of the peace process showed that supposed settlements were movable feasts. On this matter at least, the Coalition has been made of sterner stuff than its predecessor. Paterson restated that there could be no renegotiation of the allocation under the spending review: 'A settlement is precisely that – a settlement. It is not the opening round of a negotiation' (BBC, 2010c). Northern Ireland was the last of the devolved administrations to table its budget. Because of internal party divisions in the Executive, it was not until 15 December that agreement was finally reached. To the surprise of many it approved a draft budget for four years, whereas Wales's was for three and Scotland's only for one. For some, this indicated the Executive's 'coming of age' though a bitter wrangle over health cuts continued in 2011. However, water charges were again deferred, though the regional rate will now increase in line with inflation.

Conclusion

The Coalition's agenda addresses the question identified by Alan Trench (2010b) – how to ensure equity across the UK and to balance equity with devolved autonomy. There is significant continuity with Labour's own territorial politics, though the respect agenda could be said to provide the outlines of the sort of narrative Hazell requested in 1998. It intimates by necessity as well as design a new style of territorial politics conducted more openly between Westminster and the devolved governments and more formally through the JMC. Managing devolution in a cold economic climate is difficult and clashes of democratic mandate are inevitable. As the policy on higher education tuition fees show, the spillover of specifically English affairs into devolved politics is difficult to contain, and vice versa. Westminster's relations with Scotland, Wales and Northern Ireland will continue to require sensitivity and subtlety, as well as respect.

Note

The author gratefully acknowledges the support of a Leverhulme Major Research Fellowship in the writing of this chapter.

References

Barnes, E. (2010) Lord Forsyth Demands New Holyrood Referendum. *The Scotsman*, 28 December.

Barnett, A. (2010) Twelve Reflections Now We Have Coalition Government. www.opendemocracy.net/ourkingdom/anthony-barnett/twelve-reflections-now-we-have-Coalition-government (accessed 20 December 2010).

BBC News (2010a) Cameron Calls for Scots 'Respect'. news.bbc.co.uk/1/hi/scotland/8680816.stm (accessed 15 December 2010).

BBC News (2010b) 'Devolved Leaders' Cuts Pleas in Full. www.bbc.co.uk/news/uk-scotland-11493649 (accessed 16 December 2010).

BBC News (2010c) No New Negotiations On Spending Review Cash – Paterson. www.bbc.co.uk/news/uk-northern-ireland-11843527 (accessed 20 December 2010).

Bradbury, J. (2010) Wales and the 2010 General Election. *Parliamentary Affairs*, 63(4): 726–41.

Cabinet Office (2010) *The Cabinet Manual – Draft*. www.cabinetoffice.gov.uk/sites/default/files/resources/cabinet-draft-manual.pdf (accessed 20 December 2010).

Cable, V. (2007) Prospects for a Post-Blair 'Progressive Consensus'. *Public Policy Research*, 14(2): 119–25.

Cameron, D. (2006) Speech to Conservative party conference, 4 October. www.guardian.co.uk/politics/2006/oct/04/conservatives2006.conservatives (accessed 21 December 2010).

Cameron D. (2007a) I Support the Union for What it Can Achieve in the Future. Speech at Gretna Green, 19 April. www.conservatives.com/popups/print.cfm?obj_id=136389&type=print.

Cameron, D. (2007b) Stronger Together, Speech, Edinburgh, 10 December.

Cameron, D. (2009a) I would Govern Scots with Respect, 8 February. www.conservatives.com/news/articles/2009/02/david_cameron_i_would_govern_scots_with_respect.aspx?cameron=true (accessed 18 December 2010).

Cameron, D. (2009b) Speech to Scottish party conference, 15 May. www.conservatives.com/News/Speeches/2009/05/David_Cameron_Speech_to_Scottish_Party_Conference.aspx (accessed 18 December 2010).

Cameron, D. (2009c) Speech to Welsh Conservative party conference, 29 March. www.conservatives.com/News/Speeches/2009/03/David_Cameron_Speech_to_Welsh_Conservative_Party_Conference.aspx (accessed 20 December 2010).

Cameron, D. (2010a) Speech to Conservative party conference, 6 October. www.telegraph.co.uk/news/newstopics/politics/david-cameron/8046342/David-Camerons-Conservative-conference-speech-in-full.html (accessed 19 December 2010).

Cameron, D. (2010b) Control Passes Over to Where it Belongs – With the Voters of Scotland. *The Scotsman*, 1 December.

Carrell, S. (2010) Alex Salmond Postpones Plans for Scottish Independence Referendum. *The Guardian*, 6 September.

Crichton, T. (2010) Election 2010: David Cameron Left Squirming in Jeremy Paxman Interview. *The Daily Record*, 24 April.

Cutts, D., Fieldhouse, E. and Russell, A. (2010) The Campaign that Changed Everything and Still Did Not Matter? The Liberal Democrat Campaign and Performance. *Parliamentary Affairs*, 63(4): 689–707.

Denver, D. (2010) The Results: How Britain Voted. *Parliamentary Affairs*, 63(4): 588–601.

Gallagher, J. (2010) Why the Scotland Bill is Good News for England. *Daily Telegraph*, 30 November.

Gillan, C. (2010) Address to the National Assembly for Wales on the Queen's Speech, 16 June. www.walesoffice.gov.uk/2010/06/16/cheryl-gillans-address-to-the-national-assembly-for-wales-on-the-queen%E2%80%99s-speech (accessed 20 December 2010).

Gordon, D. (2010) Sammy Wilson is Sceptical of Tax Cut for Businesses. *Belfast Telegraph*, 12 May.

Hazell, R. (1998) Reinventing the Constitution: Can the State Survive? CIPFA/Times and Inaugural Lecture. www.ucl.ac.uk/spp/publications/unit-publications/33.pdf (accessed 18 December 2010).

HM Government (2010) The Coalition: Our Programme. www.direct.gov.uk/prod_consum_dg/groups/dg_digitalassets/@dg/@en/documents/digitalasset/dg_187876.pdf (accessed 19 December 2010).

Holtham, G. (2010) Why Wales Has Been Hit. www.clickonwales.org/2010/11/why-wales-has-been-hit (accessed 23 December 2010).

Jeffery, C., Lodge, G. and Schmuecker, K. (2010) The Devolution Paradox. In G. Lodge and K. Schmuecker with A. Coutts (eds.), *Devolution in Practice 2010: Public Policy Differences in the UK* (London: Institute for Public Policy Research), pp. 9–27.

Kirkup, J. (2010) AV Referendum Rebels Focus on Date. *Daily Telegraph*, 2 July.

Lodge, G. and Schmuecker, K. (2007) The End of the Union? *Public Policy Research*, 14(2): 90–6.

Mitchell, J. (2009) *Devolution in the UK* (Manchester: Manchester University Press).

Mitchell, J. and van der Zwet, A. (2010) A Catenaccio Game: The 2010 Election in Scotland. *Parliamentary Affairs*, 63(4): 708–25.

Mundell, D. (2010) We Want to Use Devolution to Take Scotland Forward, Not Keep it in the Past, 6 October. www.conservatives.com/News/Speeches/2010/10/David_Mundell_We_want_to_use_devolution_to_take_Scotland_forward_not_keep_it_in_the_past.aspx (accessed 20 December 2010).

Murphy, R. (2010) *Lowering Northern Ireland's Corporation Tax: Pot of Gold or Fool's Gold?* (London: TUC; Belfast: ICTU).

Northern Ireland Office (2010) Northern Ireland Grand Committee (Spending Review): Extracts from speech by Secretary of State Owen Paterson MP. www.nio.gov.uk/northern-ireland-grand-committee-spending-review-extracts-from-speech-by-secretary-of-state-owen-paterson-mp/media-detail.htm?newsID=16947 (accessed 15 December 2010).

Paterson, O. (2010) Working Flat out for Peace, 6 October. www.conservatives.com/News/Speeches/2010/10/Owen_Paterson_Working_flat_out_for_peace.aspx (accessed 19 December 2010).

Phillips, L. (2010) Northern Ireland Will Bear Brunt of Benefit Cuts. *Public Finance*, 10 December.

Scott, D. (2010a) Scotland Bill Gives Holyrood Tax Powers. *Public Finance*, 1 December.

Scott, D. (2010b) Alexander Warns of Steep Scottish Spending Cuts. *Public Finance*, 26 November.

Settle, M. (2010) Cameron Focused on Scotland after Poor Poll Results. *Herald Scotland*, 26 November.

Snowden, P. (2010) *Back from the Brink: The Extraordinary Fall and Rise of the Conservative Party* (London: HarperPress).

Trench, A. (2008) Introduction: The Second Phase of Devolution. In A. Trench (ed.), *The State of the Nations 2008* (Exeter: Imprint Academic), pp. 1–22.

Trench, A. (2010a) Labour's Failure to Understand Devolution. devolutionmatters. wordpress.com/2010/09/16/labours-failure-to-understand-devolution (accessed 21 December 2010).

Trench, A. (2010b) The Options for Devolution Finance: The Choices for the New Government. *Political Quarterly*, 81(4): 571–82.

Varney, D. (2007) *Review of Tax Policy in Northern Ireland*. webarchive. nationalarchives.gov.uk/+/http://www.hm-Treasury.gov.uk/media/1/3/ varney171207.pdf (accessed 22 December 2010).

Williamson, D. (2010a) Tory, Lib Dem Welsh Leaders to Fight 'Unfair' London Cuts. *Western Mail*, 13 October.

Williamson, D. (2010b) Treasury Minister Scuppers Barnett Reform. *Western Mail*, 23 November.

Part Three
Coalition Policies Abroad

12
The Con–Lib Agenda for National Security and Strategy

Christopher Martin

Introduction

Security is unlike any other aspect of government. It is subject to external pressures over which UK politicians have little control. Interests are generally fixed, as are the means to protect and extend them. It would be surprising if the Coalition attempted to radically change UK security and strategy policy. It does not. The policy of the Coalition is that of all UK governments since 1945: the UK is a global player with global interests. The policy is essentially economically driven. Potential points of friction are conveniently avoided. It is a pain today, jam tomorrow policy.

The Liberal Democrats, in their manifesto for 2010, made no grand statements about the UK's global role. Their emphasis was on the UK's responsibilities and international cooperation. The manifesto did commit to specifics on defence: cancellation of the Tranche 3B Typhoon; greater cooperation with France and the EU, particularly to facilitate procurement; an immediate Strategic Defence and Security Review (SDSR); and no like-for-like replacement for Trident (Liberal Democrats, 2010: 56–65).

The Conservatives, who raised security in the standard manifesto and an armed forces 'special', based everything on the UK's global status. The role of government, they claimed, is to protect the UK's interests: 'We are a global trading nation and home to the world's pre-eminent language.' Action on security was vital, they argued, because in a rapidly changing world the UK stood 'to lose a great deal of its ability to shape world affairs unless we act to reverse our declining status' (Conservative Party, 2010: 103). They committed to creating a National Security Council (NSC), an immediate SDSR and review of National Security Strategy (NSS) and a like-for-like replacement for Trident. They emphasized the importance of the UK's involvement in international organizations such as NATO, at the same time maintaining their usual Eurosceptical stance by arguing for a re-evaluation of the UK's role with the European Defence Agency. Most important was their reaffirmation of the official mantra espoused by every UK government since 1945, that the UK is a global player: 'Protecting [the UK's] enlightened national interest requires global engagement' (Conservative Party, 2010: 109). There were several areas in common: an immediate SDSR and a transformation of UK forces to meet modern conditions. Possible areas of conflict were obviously Trident's replacement and the degree of cooperation with the EU.

Between all the major British political parties since 1945 there has been a general consensus about security. This is not surprising as national security and strategy is generally a non-negotiable issue. Certain commitments, such as a NATO requirement that a minimum 2 per cent of GDP be committed to defence, defence contracts, fighting in Afghanistan and a general sensitivity to allies' concerns, mean that there is little room for manoeuvre for any government in this area. Additionally, although support services can be privatized, security is the one area of government that only the state can provide. This is not to claim that there is no debate; but it is more to do with how we secure, rather than what we secure. The one major continuity in UK security and strategy pursued by every government since 1945, despite massive changes in the UK's relative status, is a self-perception that the UK is a global player with global interests whose presence on the world stage is beneficent to the world and beneficial to the UK. The SDSR and NSS drawn up by the Coalition have not altered this perception.

Managing Security in Austerity

The SDSR and NSS that the Coalition undertook after taking office claimed that the Ministry of Defence (MoD) faced an unfunded deficit of £35 billion over ten years, £20 billion of which related to equipment and support:

> Nowhere has the legacy we inherited been more challenging than in the state of the defence budget our predecessors left behind. We have been left a litany of scandalous defence procurement decisions, which have racked up vast unfunded liabilities. (Cabinet Office, 2010: 5)

There is no doubt that a SDSR was required; the previous government had announced its decision to hold a review and had published a Green Paper in February 2010 to initiate the process. The Coalition's SDSR made numerous cuts to defence. The reason for these cuts, the Coalition claimed, was down to Labour, not the Coalition: 'the unanticipated scale of the budgetary over-extension has also made painful, short term measures [cuts] unavoidable' (HM Government, 2010a: 9). In effect, the Coalition claimed it would not be making these cuts if it were not for the financial situation left by Labour. On no fewer than 23 occasions in these two papers Labour is blamed for the Coalition's 'painful' decisions.

However, much has been made of the speed with which the NSS and SDSR were conducted: both the NSS and SDSR were produced within five months of the Coalition taking office. The previous defence review produced under George Robinson in 1998 took over 18 months. It is of sufficient concern for the House of Commons Defence Committee to have commented:

> The rapidity with which the SDSR process is being undertaken is quite startling. A process which was not tried and tested is now being expected to deliver radical outcomes within a highly concentrated time frame. We conclude that mistakes will be made and some of them will be serious. (HCDC, 2010: 4)

There is evidence that the NSS was produced even more quickly as the Defence Committee reported in September that the new NSS 'already exists in substantial outline' (HCDC, 2010: 13). The speed with which these papers were produced is all the more surprising given that the Coalition boasted: 'This work is historic: no government has previously carried out a detailed review of all its security and defence capabilities' (Cabinet Office, 2010: 9). The chief of the new NSC and the Prime Minister's national security adviser, Sir Peter Ricketts, claimed: 'we have allowed a genuine, strategic process' (Ricketts, 2010: 4). It is impossible, however, to divorce the SDSR and NSS from the spending review. The Conservatives made it clear that immediate action on the deficit was paramount. The Liberal Democrats were presumably not averse to a Treasury-driven SDSR as they had demanded as much in their manifesto (Liberal Democrats, 2010: 65). Ricketts claimed, in response to critics of the speed of the process and the cuts that followed, that:

> '[T]he one way of guaranteeing it [the SDSR] would have been a cut-throat process would be to have the spending round – to have

the budgets for all departments, including the MoD, settled – and then get down to an SDSR afterwards because we would then certainly have been starting from cuts and we would have been thinking about strategy afterwards. (Ricketts, 2010: 4)

But this is disingenuous. Ricketts claims that this put the process the right way round: strategy first, finance second. However, what it actually demonstrates is that the SDSR and NSS were completed in short time in order to meet the demands of the Chancellor's timetable. The Coalition was anxious to push through the spending review in order to stabilize the markets. The SDSR and NSS had to be completed in order to meet this timetable because the SDSR cut force sizes and equipment procurement: in other words, the MoD had to settle its budget within time, as did all other departments, and this required a settled SDSR as it was impossible to set budgets before determining force scales. Nowhere was the haste, lack of clarity in strategy and focus on finance better demonstrated that in the late decision to scrap the carrier capability. The NSS was published on 18 October, the SDSR on 19 October and the spending review on 21 October. All discussions within Cabinet had only the spending review as the focus. The debate over defence was particularly acrimonious but the Government was adamant: cuts were required and defence had to make its contribution. As the NSS made clear after setting out all the priority threats to the UK from terrorism to nuclear attack:

[T]he largest single challenge facing the Government affects both national security and all other areas of public policy . . . [o]ur most urgent task is to return our nation's finances to a sustainable footing . . . [w]e cannot have effective foreign policy or strong defence without a sound economy and a sound financial position to support them. (Cabinet Office, 2010: 14)

In effect, the Coalition regarded the nation's finance as a security issue. This should not be surprising; the British establishment has always understood that 'security and prosperity form a virtuous circle' (Cabinet Office, 2010: 22).

The NSS and SDSR are fundamentally financially driven. Whatever the Coalition's claims, the SDSR is not a normal security review; it is an interim measure designed to meet current financial problems. It is focused on immediate necessary decisions 'and left to 2015 those decisions which can better be taken in the light of further experience in Afghanistan and developments in the wider financial situation' (HM Government,

2010a: 9). Regrettably, if the Defence Committee's fears are confirmed, then serious errors will manifest when it is too late.

Fudging over Conflict in the Coalition

The possible areas of conflict within the Coalition on security were, as mentioned, Trident's replacement and the degree of cooperation with the EU. In the case of the latter, the SDSR makes considerable commitments to established partnerships and alliances, especially NATO and the EU, although no specific mention is made of the EDA. As for Trident's replacement, the issue is neatly sidestepped. The Coalition's *Programme for Government* commits the UK to renewing Trident like-for-like, while recognizing the right of the Liberal Democrats to 'make the case for alternatives' (HM Government, 2010b: 15). Particularly important is the deferral of the key stage of Trident renewal. 'Main Gate', the second investment decision point of renewal, has been deferred until 2016. This is the crucial point at which detailed acquisition plans, design of boat and number of boats must be made (HM Government, 2010a: 59). By deferring this decision, while presently committing to replacement, any potential conflict over the security agenda in this key area was avoided. Additionally, considerable costs were deferred until after the spending review period. Liberal Democrat opposition to Trident renewal is effectively deferred to the next election campaign.

As mentioned above, security is an area where we should expect little change. Unless the Coalition were to undertake a fundamental review of the role and place of the UK in the world, draw back and leave the running of the world to others, we should not expect change. The Coalition claims that the NSS is a 'hard-headed reappraisal of our foreign policy and security objectives and the role we wish our country to play' (Cabinet Office, 2010: 9). Having considered this the policy is transparent: 'The National Security Council has reached a clear conclusion that Britain's national interest requires us to reject any notion of the shrinkage of our influence' (Cabinet Office, 2010: 9–10). This decision is predicated upon what the Coalition calls 'Britain's distinctive role'. Despite the economic situation, the Coalition points out that the UK is the world's sixth largest economy. Future growth in what it calls the 'world knowledge economy' is an area in which the UK will excel, owing to its leading financial, creative and media services, as well as its world-class universities. The UK is at the centre of global activity, with London at the hub. Its global language and historical links to most of the world with millions of UK citizens living abroad creates interests for the UK globally. The UK plays a major role in NATO, the EU, G20, as a permanent member of the UN Security Council and leads the Commonwealth. Above all, through its 'enlightened national interest', the UK's presence in global affairs is one for good. In effect, the benefit the UK acquires through its global status brings interests, but also threats to those interests.

The UK cannot ignore this and abandon its position in the world (Cabinet Office, 2010: 21–3), or as Professor Julian Lindley-French stated in oral evidence to the Public Administration Committee: 'We're simply too big to hide from friction in the world' (Lindley-French, 2010: 11). The NSS breaks no new ground with this. In fact, it is identical in every way to the previous review of 1998 and every other security review carried out by UK governments since 1945. The SDSR and NSS maintain the need for the UK to be able to act alone, but a major focus is placed on alliances and partnerships. NATO remains the cornerstone of UK defence, with a commitment to continue to work with EU initiatives such as 'Operation Atalanta'. Even the much heralded agreement with France to engage in greater cooperation is not unique to the Coalition; Gordon Brown announced that the UK would seek such ties early in 2010. The Coalition is in complete continuity with the previous government as to the essential strategic capability of the UK's armed forces: a maritime-based capability with global reach, expeditionary with full spectrum of capability from war fighting to stabilization.

Further continuity with the previous administration is reflected in the immediate procurement plans for UK forces. This should be the case. Unless there is a paradigm shift in technology or rapid threat change, what and how states securitize doesn't change rapidly. The long-term nature of defence contracts also ensures continuity. The Coalition will build the two *Queen Elizabeth* carriers, although there are changes to the design so that they will have standard launch-and-recovery apparatus to allow cooperation with French and US aircraft. Seven new *Astute* class submarines will be built, as well as six Type-45 destroyers. New Typhoon aircraft as well as the carrier-capable variant of the F-35 Joint Strike Fighter will also be acquired. Finally, Trident will be replaced with a like-for-like system (HM Government, 2010a: 58). Afghanistan will remain a focus of activity until 2015, when it is expected that UK forces will end their fighting role. In the meantime, the spending review commits fully to fund the war in Afghanistan through the Special Reserve at roughly £3.8 billion per annum. The amount is not to be fixed, but will reflect requirements at the time (HM Government, 2010a: 86). Additionally, to conduct operations there, new helicopters will be provided, as will new armoured fighting vehicles, communications and strategic lift capability.

The Nature and Impact of the Cuts

As well as setting out procurement, the SDSR also set out cuts to the current equipment currently held by the UK's armed forces. The RAF was to operate a reduced fleet of Tornado aircraft. This is ostensibly to cover continuing operations in Afghanistan. The Harrier, a joint force capability, is to be withdrawn immediately from service. The maritime reconnaissance aircraft MRA4 is to be cancelled before coming into service. Other cuts to existing RAF equipment, such as the TriStar transport and VC-10, are deferred to 2013 when replacement equipment should become available (HM Government, 2010a: 26–7). The Army is to lose one of its six deployable brigades. In addition, it will lose 40 per cent of its Challenger 2 main battle tanks and 35 per cent of its AS90 self-propelled artillery (HM Government, 2010a: 25). It was the Royal Navy, however, that bore the brunt of the cuts to its existing equipment and capability. The Harrier was the sole fast jet capability owned by the Navy. Its immediate retirement leaves the Navy without such capability. Similarly, the immediate decommissioning of HMS *Ark Royal* leaves the Navy without any carrier capability. Four of the Navy's frigates will be withdrawn from service and either HMS *Ocean* or HMS *Illustrious* will be decommissioned once it is determined which provides the better facility as a helicopter platform. A *Bay* class amphibious support ship faces decommissioning and further eroding the Navy's amphibious capability, a landing and command ship will be placed at 'extended readiness' (HM Government, 2010a: 22).

The cuts to the Army's heavy equipment located in Germany make sense. However, the five multi-role brigades (plus 16 Air Assault Brigade) is more problematic. It is supposed to be the case that one brigade will be held in high readiness while four are held in support. All are supposed to be capable of deployment when needed for large-scale operations. However, some concern must arise as a result of the 'building-block' structure of the brigades. Comprising some 6,500 personnel, each brigade will have its own artillery, communications, engineer, logistics and medical support. Just how these will cooperate across brigade lines when in full war-fighting deployment remains to be tested.

The RAF also faces a problematic future. The retention of Tornado GR4 for the time being is determined by the Afghanistan war because of the aircraft's air-to-ground attack capability. What will happen when Afghanistan is no longer a focus is a worry. It is noteworthy that at the end of the Afghanistan war the newly acquired Sentinel R1 force will also be cut. Most concerning, and not just for BAE Systems, is the cancellation of the maritime reconnaissance aircraft, the MRA4. This is a major blow to the RAF's ability to provide long-range reconnaissance and command and control. The MRA4 was a major joint asset, the loss of which will affect all services. Particularly damaging to the RAF will be the permanent loss of its anti-submarine capability, its deterrent protection role, as well as its search and rescue missions. Should it be the case, for example, that a major tanker incident occurs in UK waters, the UK will have to call on France or Norway to substitute for the RAF's lack of the MRA4.

It is the cuts to the Royal Navy which caused the greatest shock and must be regarded as most serious. The Coalition argues that at present fast jet support overseas can be best provided by eliciting 'host nation support'. The unreliability of host nation support, however, is exactly the reason the previous government decided to build the two *Queen Elizabeth* carriers. The fact that the UK will be without its own fast jet capability at sea, and will have to rely on friendly states to permit deployment of air cover for ten years, is of considerable concern. The Coalition calls for interoperability with allies as well as a 'whole of government' approach to security. This is all well and good. However, until the carrier is fully equipped with its strike capability in ten years' time the UK has a serious capability gap. A capability gap of this nature is not confined to the Royal Navy; as the UK is a maritime state it affects the capability of all UK forces. Simply put, without the aid of others, the UK is now unable to deploy its military capability overseas in defence of its interests. This is the worst possible scenario: we are dependent on the goodwill of others: friends and enemies.

Who or What Drives this Strategy?

The UK, according to the former Chief of Defence Staff, Jock Stirrup, has 'lost an institutionalized capacity for, and culture of, strategic thought' (Stirrup, 2009). The UK has traditionally been very good at conducting grand strategy: our diminished ability in this area is probably driven by inter-service rivalry which, since 1945, has centred on the services fighting over ever-dwindling resources. What matters here is that despite the Coalition's focus on the financial situation, a SDSR is supposed to be driven by *strategy*, but as described above, this SDSR is driven by *finance*. One 'innovation' championed by many is the creation of the NSC. The NSC is chaired by the Prime Minister and is based within the Cabinet Office. Members include the Deputy PM, the Chancellor, the Defence, Foreign and Home Secretaries, the Secretary of State for Overseas

Development and the Security Minister. Other ministers and the Chief of Defence Staff attend as required.

The NSS is, in truth, broader in scope than the predecessor organization the National Security, International Relations and Development Committee (NSID) of the Cabinet. That body rarely met and even less often did the Prime Minister chair it. The role of the new NSC is crucial to understanding the NSS and SDSR as this body was central in the creation of both. The SDSR made clear that the financial situation drove decisions to cut particular areas of capability 'that are less critical to today's requirements' (HM Government, 2010a: 16). However, the NSS determined the priority threat areas and the NSC created the NSS. Because the Coalition's focus and priority were on budget deficit one is bound to ask whether financial issues determined the selection of threat priorities. The relevant lack of status of the CDS on the NSC must be a concern: of course, security is more than a military matter but there have been many complaints about the lack of consultation of the military in the SDSR process, particularly given the scale of capability reduction. Some concern has been expressed as to whether this large body can effectively conduct strategy given the power of the permanent member ministries (Lindley-French, 2010: 7). Of particular concern is that the Public Administration Select Committee is not too impressed in its assessment of the NSC which, it claims: 'functions more like a clearing house [for ideas] than as an organ of critical assessment'; also that, 'It appears . . . that national strategic thinking is divided and uncoordinated' (HCPASC, 2010: para. 56). Sir Peter Ricketts is clear about who is at the helm of the NSC taking decisions on national security: it is David Cameron (Ricketts, 2010: 3).

The impact of the fiscal deficit is particularly noteworthy in the translation of the strategy set out in the NSS in the form of capabilities as set out in the SDSR. The NSS sets out the threat priorities, the SDSR determines force structures. As the NSS correctly explains, a national strategy comprises several aspects: **ends** – the *objectives* a state wishes to attain: the **ways** – *how* it will go about attaining those objectives: finally, **means** – the *available resources*. The NSS sets out the first two, the SDSR the third. The two core objectives of the NSS are *a secure and resilient UK* and *shaping a stable world*. These objectives are enduring; there is nothing new.

In order to determine the allocation of resources, the NSC determined what it regards as the key threats facing the UK now and for the next five years. It arranges the threats into three 'tiers' which are determined by a cross-tabulation of likelihood of event against likely impact of the event. The four top 'tier one' threats are:

- 'International terrorism affecting the UK or its interests, including a chemical, biological, radiological or nuclear attack by terrorists; and/or a significant increase in levels of terrorism relating to Northern Ireland.
- Hostile attacks on UK cyberspace by other states and large-scale cybercrime.
- A major accident or natural hazard which requires a national response, such as severe coastal flooding affecting three or more regions of the UK, or an influenza pandemic.
- An international military crisis between states, drawing in the UK and its allies as well as other states and non state actors' (Cabinet Office, 2010: 27).

A quick scan of these threats instantly throws up the obvious point: the military (the expensive part of security) has little role here. Even in the case of the latter threat, the NSS is careful in setting the scenario with allies, other states and non-state actors. It is also well short of war and, one presumes, envisages a very limited commitment from the UK which will be determined by the degree of UK interest, the commitments by other allies and states and the means available to the UK. As for the terror threat, this is largely a police and intelligence issue. The scenario of terrorists having and being able to deploy in the UK a CBRN threat seems most unlikely, unless the Coalition has intelligence it is unwilling to disclose. Without CBRN capability, terrorism is certainly an issue, but it does not constitute the principal major national security threat. The UK dealt with 30 years of Irish terrorism: it did not replace the Warsaw Pact as the focus of defence. The issue of natural events relating to the environment or health is, again, a civil issue, and it is impossible to be certain of the likelihood of such events. As for the emphasis on cyber-threats, the response of Microsoft founder Bill Gates to the Coalition's newly discovered emphasis on this threat best sums it up:

> [Y]ou won't have to spend like you spend on an Army. It's just a group of experts spreading best practices. So with the right approach it shouldn't be something that people will have to worry about. (Gates, 2010)

In any event, the UK will probably piggy-back on much of what the United States is doing in this field (US Government, 2010: 27). In effect, of the top 'tier one' threats, none really turns out to be much of a threat at all. The question remains then, how did they became top threats? The

NSS states clearly that 'the risks prioritized in Tier One also drive the prioritization of capabilities' (Cabinet Office, 2010: 34). This should be so; however, as has been demonstrated, none of these threats requires much in the way of financial support. Surely no government would prioritize threats to national security in a way that met its drive to deal with a fiscal deficit? Consider what the NSS states about the basis of strategy:

> A strategy is only useful if it guides choices. This is particularly true as the UK, like many countries, has a pressing requirement to reduce its fiscal deficit . . . national security cannot be exempt from these pressures...it is vital that decisions on civilian and military capabilities, which may have consequences for decades to come, are taken on the basis of careful prioritization of the risks we may face so we can make the most effective investments we can to deal with them. (Cabinet Office, 2010: 10)

Or, as it continues:

> The ways and means by which we seek to achieve our objectives must be appropriate and sufficient, and the objectives, must be realistic in light of the means available. (Cabinet Office, 2010: 10)

Sir Peter Ricketts explained: 'in an era of constrained resources . . . we have not got the resources to treat all risks equally' (Ricketts, 2010: 6). The point must be, however, that it is the Coalition Government in the SDSR that has determined the means available, based on its threat assessment. However, what really is happening here is that we are determining our national strategy on residual capabilities. This is placing the proverbial cart before the horse. It seems certain that the capability cuts announced in the SDSR were financially driven not strategically driven and this had led to a prioritization of threat according to the means available. Professor Julian Lindley-French, in evidence to the Public Administration Committee, warned of this when he said: 'if it's another exercise in recognizing only as much threat as we can afford, which is always the danger of these exercises, then it will fail.' (Lindley-French, 2010: 18–19). The words of Sir Peter Ricketts here offer little inspiration:

> with the National Security Strategy setting out ends and identifying ways and then the SDSR setting out means...we have produced a strategic whole here and that we have a planetary alignment which *allows us to call it a strategy*. (Ricketts, 2010: 6, emphasis added)

Future Force 2020

What the Coalition would argue is that the SDSR and NSS can only be understood fully when Future Force 2020 is taken into account. As has been discussed above, the current 'painful' decisions are the result of fiscal problems: they would not be taken otherwise. The current decisions are supposed to be based on threat assessments of what the UK is likely to face in the next five years. What the SDSR is about is generating future capabilities:

> We must therefore give priority over the next decade to recovering capabilities damaged or reduced...This takes time and investment but is needed to rebuild the strength and restore the capability of our armed forces. (HM Government, 2010a: 15)

The keys to understanding the future military capability are the National Security Tasks (which sets out the contribution the armed forces will be expected to make), more detailed Defence Planning Assumptions (the size of operations) and the Military Tasks (what the Government will expect the armed forces to undertake). The latter are of importance and are as follows:

- 'Defending the UK and its overseas territories.
- Providing strategic intelligence.
- Providing nuclear deterrence.
- Supporting the civil authorities in crisis.
- Defending interests by power projection through expeditionary operations.
- Providing a defence contribution to UK influence.
- Providing security for stabilization' (HM Government, 2010a: 18–19).

With Future Force the SDSR has not departed from the 1998 SDR. It remains essentially maritime-focused, notwithstanding the major reduction in contemporary naval capability. The Military Tasks set out above demonstrate that, essentially, Future Force 2020 is global in scale. The global nature of the maritime component and the ability of the maritime element to support operations overseas are demonstrated in what Future Force 2020 expects of the Royal Navy of the future:

- Continuous at sea nuclear deterrence.
- Maritime defence of the UK and its South Atlantic overseas territories.

- Enduring presence in unstable regions to provide deterrence and threat containment.
- Powerful intervention capabilities from the sea in the air and over-the-beach with specialized vehicles and ships.
- The capability of commanding UK and allied forces up to Task Force level'. (HM Government, 2010a: 21)

The ability to conduct and support operations such as this requires a sea-based capability centred on at least one large and capable (measured by the capability of its strike wing) aircraft carrier. This is in essence a carrier strike force. The SDSR makes a strong case for such a capability – *in the future*. Carriers provide military flexibility and capability, as well as potent political flexibility to impress friends and enemies alike. It has been mentioned above that the Coalition is building the two *Queen Elizabeth* class carriers contracted for by the previous government. It is intended that one carrier will be operational, with the other kept in extended readiness. It has been suggested that the second carrier might be sold. However, that would be a foolish move as it would remove flexibility and the ability to provide an enduring presence and would leave the UK reliant on allies. The SDSR is essentially an interim paper which cuts force levels today to meet the demands of fiscal problems, and promises more tomorrow when the economy is recovered.

Problems and Issues

The UK armed forces today can scarcely be regarded as having any real global capability. A major issue for any future government will be to ensure that sufficient funding is allocated to safeguard that the equipment needed to recover the lost capability is provided and maintained. This in turn will no doubt be determined by the economic situation. The Commons Defence Committee has already raised concerns as to whether the SDSR will be fully funded. For example, the proposed new Type 26 Frigates planned for 2020 and beyond are already under financial pressure. The projected £500 million cost per vessel has prompted the Government to order a specification redesign (to a simpler vessel) to cut each platform cost to £250 million–£300 million. This is driven by two factors: the requirement to provide more vessels; and the desire to make the vessels exportable in support of the defence industry. The concern here must be that there is pitiful evidence of post-1945 governments reviving lost capabilities. Indeed, what ought to be a useful proposal, a review every five years, might be problematic. Future governments might well take this as an opportunity to fail to invest in necessary equipment on the basis that the immediate threat scenario doesn't warrant expenditure. It could operate like the ten-year rule, which massively undermined UK defence capability in the 1920s and 1930s.

The Coalition is willing to assume a lot of risks. In effect, the Coalition is hoping that before 2020 no major incident occurs that threatens UK interests. The lack of a fixed wing carrier capability simply means that the UK will be unable to respond properly: we are hardly able to threaten the use of the deterrent. Of course, the Coalition would argue – and this is a point made in the SDSR – that we are tightening ties with allies, seeking interoperability and a common security approach. However, our allies would be right to ask just what use we are. It is all very well claiming that we'll be back in 2020, but in the interim, the SDSR effectively leaves leadership of European defence to France, especially in the maritime field. Particularly damaging is the loss of the MRA4, which would have provided the capacity to coordinate and command allied efforts overseas. Given the strong emphasis on international partnership in the SDSR, this is the wrong message to send to our allies.

Conclusion

The SDSR is a jam tomorrow promise. In the short term it cuts severely into UK military capability while in the long term aims at restoring the UK's capability to act globally, with a full expeditionary capability providing the means from war-fighting to peace-support operations. It is certainly not strategic in the military sense and allows capability to drive strategy, but the capability is financially driven and this is the wrong way round for any military strategic approach. Fundamentally, the whole long-term strategy rests on the assumptions that have driven every UK defence review since the end of the Second World War: that the UK is a global player with global responsibilities and interests. Essentially what it states is that, presently, we simply do not have the economy to be a global player; we are cutting our capability to match our bank balance, but we will be back.

Unfortunately, the record of post-Second World War governments is woeful in restoring lost or reduced capability. If this record is maintained and lost capability is not restored, then this SDSR will probably be the end of any UK pretensions to be an actor in serious global politics for all that will entail for UK influence and prosperity. This would be disastrous for, as the SDSR and NSS rightly point out, all serious strategic analysis for the twenty-first century indicates that it will be more, not less, unstable and violent. Failed states, terrorism, international crime (including piracy), intra- and inter-state wars, unstable and vulnerable supplies of energy – all will feature strongly in the near to long term. If future UK governments do not fulfil the promise of Future Force 2020 as a minimum, then the UK could be vulnerable to massive economic and military shocks.

The SDSR, over the next 10–15 years, accepts potentially major risks, but hopes that major crises will not occur. However, the record of the past ten years does not bear that hope out. There is a window of opportunity for states that have unresolved issues with the UK. Additionally, the absence of the UK military from many parts of the world gives others the opportunity to establish their own presence at the UK's expense. The Royal Navy, which has suffered a significant cut to its platform numbers, is the vehicle to 'show the flag' but does not have the ship numbers to meet the demands of government and maintain a global presence. This is bad for the UK politically and economically. Unless capability is restored, allies will look suspiciously on a UK which places reliance on partnerships and interoperability. The UK will be forced ever more to bandwagon with the United States and France. The value of the UK to alliances and partnerships will be sorely tested with the cuts.

It is certain that, if the cuts are not restored as planned under Future Force 2020, then the claims made by UK politicians to a global role will be mere pretence. The great concern is that if the promise of the SDSR is not fulfilled, then the UK could become, as one analyst has put it, 'a Belgium with a nuke'.

References

Cabinet Office (2010) *Securing Britain in an Age of Uncertainty: The National Security Strategy* (London: The Stationery Office).

Cameron, D. (2010) *The Prime Minister's Statement on Strategic Defence and Security Review*, 19 October 2010. www.number10.gov.uk/news/statements-and-articles/2010/10/sdsr-55912 (accessed 29 October 2010).

Conservative Party (2010) *An Invitation to Join the Government of Britain* (London: Conservative Party).

Conservative Party (2010) *A New Covenant for our Armed Forces and their Families: The Conservative Armed Forces Manifesto* (London: Conservative Party).

Forissier, Admiral P-F. (2009) The French White Paper Goes Navy Blue. *RUSI Defence Systems*: 45–7.

Gates, B. (2010), *Expertise Will Keep Internet Secure*, 18 October. www.bbc.co.uk/news/technology-11564020 (accessed 19 October 2010).

Lindley-French, J. (2010) 'Who Does UK Grand Strategy? Ev 1, 9 September, in Public Administration Select Committee, *Who Does UK National Strategy?* First Report of Session 2010–11, HC 435 (London: The Stationery Office).

HCPASC (2010) *Who Does UK National Strategy?* First Report of Session 2010–11, HC 435 (London: The Stationery Office).

HCDC (2010) *The Strategic Defence and Security Review, (DC), Report of First Session 2010–2011*, House of Commons Defence Committee, 15 September (London: The Stationery Office).

HM Government (2010) *The Coalition: Our Programme for Government* (London: The Cabinet Office).

HM Government (2010a) *A Strong Britain in an Age of Uncertainty: The Strategic Defence and Security Review* (London: The Stationery Office).

HM Government (2010b) *The Coalition: Our Programme for Government* (London: The Cabinet Office).

HM Treasury (2010) *The Spending Review*, Cm 7942 (London: The Stationery Office).

Liberal Democrats (2010) *Liberal Democrat Manifesto* (London: Liberal Democrat Party).

Ministry of Defence (2010) *Future Character of Conflict, Strategic Trends Programme, Ministry of Defence*, DCDC, 3 February. www.mod.uk/NR/rdonlyres/00CD3C81-8295-4B79-A306-E76C370CC314/0/20100201Future_Character_of_ConflictUDCDC_Strat_Trends_4.pdf (accessed 5 May 2010).

Ministry of Defence (2010) *Spending Review 2010*, Defence Internal Brief, 2010DIB/81, 20 October.

Stirrup, Sir J. (2009) Annual Chief of Defence Staff Lecture, Royal United Services Institute, London, 3 December.

Ricketts, Sir D. (2010) *The Role of the National Security Council in Developing the National Security Strategy and Strategic Defence and Security Review: (CH)*. Transcript of a speech by Sir David Ricketts, UK National Security Adviser, London, Chatham House, 21 October.

Taylor, C. and Lunn, J. (2010) *Strategic Defence and Security Review*, SN/IA/5592, International Security and Defence Section (London: House of Commons Library), 16 August.

Taylor, C. and Lunn, J. (2010) *Strategic Defence and Security Review*, SN/IA/5592, International Security and Defence Section (London: House of Commons Library), 13 October.

US Government (2010) *National Security Strategy*, May (Washington, DC: United States Government). www.whitehouse.gov/sites/default/files/rss_viewer/national_security_strategy.pdf (accessed 10 November 2010).

13
The Con–Lib Agenda for Foreign Policy and International Development

Rhiannon Vickers

Introduction

It is inevitable that in the area of foreign policy the ability of any incoming government to make radical changes is extremely limited by the constraints of existing policies, alliances, commitments, capabilities and the actions of other states and, increasingly, non-state actors. In addition, foreign policy for the Coalition Government is being made within the context of the budget deficit and the Comprehensive Spending Review (CSR). However, the Coalition Government has signalled its intention to make changes and implement a foreign policy that is distinct from its Labour predecessor's. These are a desire to improve foreign policy-making in the UK; a desire for an enhanced global role for the UK; a focus on building stronger relationships with 'emerging economies'; a greater sense of working in the national as opposed to international interest; and an end to the liberal interventionism carried out by Tony Blair, with a greater focus on conflict prevention instead. International development has been refocused very slightly to promote human security rather than poverty alleviation, but the budget has been protected and excluded from the CSR.

This chapter begins by providing some context to the foreign policy situation in the run-up to the 2010 General Election. It then moves on to outline the agenda for change in terms of the Government's overhaul of foreign policy-making, the renewed focus on the 'national interest', which has been conceived as enhancing Britain's global role. It then focuses on the new National Security Strategy (NSS) and the Strategic Defence and Security Review (SDSR), and concludes with an overview of the Government's approach to international development. While it is too early to be able to reach any conclusion on how successful the Government has been in terms of implementing its agenda for foreign policy and international development, it is clear that there is a new economic focus to foreign policy, with the desire to expand Britain's global reach and influence in a time of changing global economic fortunes. The approach that the Government is taking to achieve this is to place enhanced emphasis on economic objectives within British foreign policy, especially by building stronger relationships with the 'emerging economies', in particular India and China, as power shifts from the West to the East. The new Government does not wish to change the world, but does wish to maintain Britain's global reach across it at a time of economic constraints.

The Foreign Policy Context in the Run-Up to the 2010 Election

At the turn of the twenty-first century there was a renewed confidence in Britain's role in the world and optimism about global politics. Prime Minister Blair felt that he had resolved one of the traditional dilemmas in British foreign policy, namely whether to focus on the Atlantic relationship or Britain's role within Europe. The Cold War was firmly in the past and for Blair, his liberal internationalist approach to the world seemed to be vindicated with the success of Kosovo. His strategy of intervention and engagement seemed to be reaping rewards. He had embraced globalization as a positive force for gradually expanding shared norms and values. However, 9/11 changed all that. Fear and pessimism replaced the optimism of the 1990s. The globalized interdependent world, far from bringing new benefits, now seemed to herald new threats: al-Qaeda and transnational terrorist groups; the threat of the proliferation of weapons of mass destruction; failed states and humanitarian crises. It now appeared that Britain's role was to provide support for – and hopefully in return gain some influence over – the US in its 'war on terror'. To a large extent, Blair staked his reputation on the way that his Government responded to a disordered world.

Labour MPs had hoped that by getting rid of Blair, British foreign policy would change track and that once he was Prime Minister, Gordon Brown would take an approach that was more independent of the US.

However, Brown never stated that this would be the case. There were major differences between the approach being outlined by Brown and that of his predecessor. First, whereas Blair's approach to foreign affairs had been to place emphasis on the efficacy of the use of force, Brown's approach placed faith in the use of economic measures: aid and economic development for Africa, economic reconstruction for conflict zones in the Middle East and sanctions against transgressors such as Iran. Second, Brown mentioned Iraq only briefly and said nothing about radical Islam or 9/11. Brown was signalling very clearly that Britain had moved on from the immediate post-9/11 era which had been defined by the 'war on terror', a phrase that Brown was careful not to use. Brown's foreign policy was to be slightly less ambitious in its expectations of changing the world than Blair's had been. With Brown's premiership, Britain had left the immediate post-9/11 era behind. Instead, Britain entered an era of unprecedented financial uncertainty and the threat of global recession.

Rather surprisingly, it was David Cameron who made the case for a foreign policy that would be more independent of the US. In a speech on foreign policy and national security on the fifth anniversary of 9/11, Cameron emphasized his belief in the importance of the Anglo-American relationship, but said that 'we will serve neither our own, nor America's, nor the world's interests if we are seen as America's unconditional associate in every endeavour'. He argued that by slavishly following the US, Britain had risked combining 'the maximum of exposure with the minimum of real influence over decisions'. Over the last five years, foreign policy had been too warlike and had lacked 'humility and patience', which were 'two crucial qualities which should always condition foreign policy-making' (Cameron, 2006). This was the message that the Labour Party had wanted to hear from Brown, not from the leader of the opposition, and demonstrated that Cameron was capable of moving outside the usual boundaries of diplomatic speak.

However, notwithstanding this rather unusual speech, Cameron, like all Conservative leaders (with perhaps the exception of Edward Heath), is personally committed to the Anglo-American relationship and views this as the cornerstone of British security. In a speech on NATO, Cameron said that 'Atlanticism is in my DNA and the DNA of the Conservative Party' (Cameron, 2008). With a staunch commitment to NATO comes a less positive view of the European Security and Defence Policy (ESDP), a development under the Labour governments that the Conservatives had opposed, with a concern with the potential for 'politically inspired duplication of effort'. As Cameron said: 'I believe that NATO remains as essential to Britain's security, and to Western security, in the age of global terrorism as it was in the era of Soviet expansionism' (Cameron, 2008).

Despite this difference between the parties, foreign policy featured very little during the 2010 General Election campaign; it was almost as if all the party campaign teams were slightly worried about making commitments on Britain's foreign and security policy and so chose to say as little as possible. The Conservative manifesto promised a 'liberal Conservative' foreign policy:

> A Conservative government's approach to foreign affairs will be based on liberal Conservative principles. Liberal, because Britain must be open and engaged with the world, supporting human rights and championing the cause of democracy and the rule of law at every opportunity. But Conservative, because our policy must be hard-headed and practical, dealing with the world as it is and not as we wish it were. (Conservative Party, 2010: 109)

A Conservative government would 'Promote our enlightened national interest', which would require 'global engagement' and would champion a 'distinctive' British foreign policy. Interestingly, in terms of relationships, the manifesto said that Conservatives will 'work to establish a new special relationship with India' and 'seek closer engagement with China while standing firm on human rights'. The relationship with the US was mentioned further on in the manifesto and then relatively briefly: 'We will maintain a strong, close and frank relationship with the United States' (Conservative Party, 2010: 109–10). The Conservative Party manifesto actually included more detail than did Labour's on foreign policy and international development. Both promised a Strategic Defence Review.

One key foreign policy theme that was present in the Conservative manifesto but that did not appear in either the Labour or the Liberal Democrat manifestos was a concern with declining British influence. The Conservatives warned that while Britain possesses great assets and advantages, in the next decade or two:

> [P]owerful forces of economics and demography elsewhere in the world will make it harder for us to maintain our influence. All this in a world that is becoming more dangerous, where threats as diverse as state failure, international terrorism and new forms of warfare are being amplified by the impact of climate change and the spread of nuclear weapons technology. In a world of shifting economic power and increased threats, the UK stands to lose a great deal of its ability

to shape world affairs unless we act to reverse our declining status. (Conservative Party, 2010: 103)

While Conservative governments have tended historically to warn against the dangers of a declining Britain, this was to become a major theme for the new Coalition Government and was at odds with the self-confidence of the New Labour Governments.

The Coalition Government and Foreign Policy-Making

In an echo of Robin Cook's 'mission statement' to the Foreign and Commonwealth Office (FCO), the Foreign Secretary, William Hague, outlined his strategic vision for British foreign policy in a speech to his department on 1 July 2010, entitled 'Britain's Foreign Policy in a Networked World'. This was the first of four linked speeches in which Hague said that the Government would 'set out how we will deliver a distinctive British foreign policy that extends our global reach and influence'. He promised that 'for the first time in years in my view Britain will have a foreign policy that is clear, focused and effective' (Hague, 2010c). Indeed, a key criticism that the new government made of its predecessor was that 'Labour have failed to deliver a unified and coherent approach to national security' (Conservative Party, 2010: 105) and that 'the previous government had neglected to lift its eyes to the wider strategic needs of this country, to take stock of British interests' (Hague, 2010c). The belief was that the Labour governments had failed to analyse Britain's strategic interests and needs, and had failed to determine how best to meet these in a rapidly changing world. Indeed, both Cameron and Hague came into power believing that British foreign policy not only required a new vision, but also needed to be overhauled in terms of policy-making, which under New Labour had become too informal and disjointed. The new Foreign Secretary said that the FCO would now be 'back where it belongs at the centre of Government'.

One of the goals of the new government was to 'reform the machinery of government in foreign policy' (FCO, 2010: 2). On his first day in office, Cameron set up an American-style National Security Council (NSC) to bring together the key figures in foreign and security policy, and appointed Sir Peter Ricketts (Permanent Under-Secretary at the FCO) to the newly created post of National Security Adviser. It was stated that:

The Council will coordinate responses to the dangers we face, integrating at the highest level the work of the foreign, defence, home, energy and international development departments, and all other arms of government contributing to national security. (Downing Street, 2010)

An early priority for the NSC was to oversee the drawing up of a new version of the NSS (Gordon Brown had initiated Britain's first NSS in 2008) and contribute to the promised Strategic Defence and Security Review. All this was to occur within the context of the Government's CSR with its remit of determining where spending cuts could be implemented.

Thus, the Government launched a number of early initiatives aimed at improving the machinery of foreign policy-making. It is too early to determine whether these have been successful, but it is interesting to note that on 18 October the House of Commons Public Administration Committee published a report, *Who Does UK National Strategy?* This concluded that 'no one' appeared to be in control of an overarching UK strategy. It said that a lack of strategic thinking at the heart of government threatened UK's national interests (Public Administration Committee, 2010). It pointed to a lack of strategic rationale and preparation in Iraq and Afghanistan, and a reactive approach to foreign and security policy, with no capacity to assess potential risks (Public Administration Committee, 2010: 10 and 14). It concluded:

> The new Government's aspiration to think strategically is most welcome, but we have yet to see how this marks any significant improvement in qualitative strategic thinking from its immediate predecessors. Apart from the creation of the NSC, which we go on to discuss below, **we have found little evidence of sustained strategic thinking or a clear mechanism for analysis and assessment. This leads to a culture of fire-fighting rather than long-term planning**. (Public Administration Committee, 2010: 15, bold in original)

In addition, on 4 November the House of Commons Foreign Affairs Committee announced that it would be conducting an inquiry into 'The Role of the FCO in UK Government' in light of the above claim, and in light of the changing environment provided by the CSR, the new National Security Council, and SDSR, and the NSS (Foreign Affairs Select Committee, 2010). While the findings of this inquiry are not yet known, it will be interesting to compare these with the claims of the Coalition Government.

As part of the Government's reform agenda, each department published a business plan in November 2010, outlining key priorities, actions to be undertaken to achieve them, with start and end dates for the delivery of these actions. The Government's key foreign policy priorities were to protect and promote the UK's national interest; to contribute to the success of Britain's effort in Afghanistan; to reform the machinery of government in foreign policy; to pursue an active and activist British policy in Europe; and to use soft power to promote British values, advance development and prevent conflict (FCO, 2010: 2).

Britain's National Interest: An Enhanced Global Role

This of course raises questions of what exactly the new government believes that Britain's national interest is. The New Labour governments had sought to move beyond this traditional foreign policy language, arguing that its foreign policy actions were in the *international* interest. In contrast, the new government has indicated a return to a more *Realpolitik* focus on the national interest, though Hague has often softened this by referring to Britain's 'enlightened national interest' and frequently discusses the pursuit of British values. According to Cameron:

> Our national interest requires our full and active engagement in world affairs. It requires our economy to compete with the strongest and the best. And it requires too that we stand up for the values we believe in. Britain has punched above its weight in the world. And we should have no less ambition for our country in the decades to come. But we need to be more thoughtful, more strategic and more co-ordinated in the way we advance our interests and protect our national security. (Cameron, 2010b)

He stated in his speech to the Lord Mayor's Banquet that 'Our national interest is easily defined. It is to ensure our future prosperity and keep our country safe in the years ahead' (Cameron, 2010c).

Both Cameron and Hague have taken issue with the view that Britain is in relative economic decline and have argued that it is in Britain's national interest to expand its global role. For Hague, 'My vision is of a distinctive British foreign policy promoting our enlightened national interest while standing up for freedom, fairness and responsibility. It should extend our global reach and influence and be agile and energetic in a networked world' (FCO, 2010: x). Indeed, Hague had argued while in opposition that despite Britain's economic problems, or 'economic shrinkage' as he referred to it, relative to the rest of the world, a Conservative government would reject the notion that there needed to be any subsequent 'strategic shrinkage'. He stated: 'We have not waited thirteen years to return to office simply to oversee the management of Britain's decline in world affairs' (Hague, 2010a) and reiterated this in the House of Commons on 26 May when he said that while 'It is no secret that we live in a world where economic might is shifting to the emerging economies and that the relative size of the economies of Britain and the rest of Europe are declining in relation to those powers.' However, 'there can be no suggestion that it is in our national interest for our role in the world to wither and shrivel away. This Government reject the idea of strategic shrinkage. We believe that this would be to retreat as a nation at the moment when a more ambitious approach is required' (Hague, 2010b).

What is most interesting about this is that Cameron and Hague have chosen to resurrect the debate about Britain's declining status. There are clear parallels here with the incoming Thatcher Government. When still in opposition, Thatcher's speeches indicated a new direction in foreign policy. She promised that, if returned to power, the Conservatives would pursue Britain's interests more vigorously, in contrast to what was seen as the 'half-heartedness and implicit defeatism of much of British foreign policy in the 1970s' (Riddell, 1988: 230). Thatcher heralded change in that, unlike the political leaders of the 1960s and 1970s, she did not see British statecraft as the management of national decline. However, it is significant that Cameron and Hague have made so much of this issue, for Britain's declining status and world role have not been a popular topic of debate in British politics for some time, and Britain today has self-confidence about its global role that was missing in the late 1970s. The problem might arise that the more that Cameron and Hague mention Britain's declining status, the more the British people become aware of it and see it as a problem than needs to be tackled successfully.

In Hague's first major speech as Foreign Secretary, he outlined five key ways in which the world had changed and argued that 'if we do not change with it Britain's role is set to decline with all that that means for our influence in world affairs'. These were first, a shift in economic power and opportunity to countries in the East and South, with the emerging powers of Brazil, India and China. Second, the circle of international decision-making had become wider and more multilateral, with the G20 rather than the G8. Third, ensuring security had become more complex in the face of new threats. Fourth, the nature of conflict was changing, with intra-state rather that state-to-state conflict. Fifth, there had been the emergence of a 'networked world'. He argued that all these developments meant that Britain needed a new foreign policy approach. While Hague did not go into much detail as to exactly how Britain and British foreign policy needed to change, there have been several substantive developments to British foreign policy initiated by the new government as a response to the challenges posed by a changing international system.

First, under the new government there has been an enhanced emphasis on economic objectives within British foreign policy. When asked by the Public Administration Committee what the Government's overall strategy was, Hague replied: '*there is a national strategy . . . which the Prime Minister and the Cabinet discuss together and pursue together, central to which is the deficit reduction without which we will not have a credible national position in the world on very much at all*' (Public Administration, 2010: 15). If the overall strategy is to reduce the deficit in order to enhance Britain's position and resist relative economic decline turning into a declining role in the world, how is this to be achieved? Well, the first 'action' in the FCO's 2010 business plan is that the FCO must become 'more commercially minded' and 'lead that thinking across government, working with domestic departments to lobby for British business overseas and inward investment into the UK' (FCO, 2010: 5). At Hague's second keynote speech on the new government's approach to foreign policy, which was given in Tokyo, Hague said:

> [O]ur new government believes that British foreign policy needs to support the UK economy to a greater degree if we are to ensure our economic recovery and long-term growth for the future. We will make economic objectives a central aspect of our international bilateral engagement alongside our other traditional objectives. (Hague, 2010d)

In order to do this, 'we will inject a new commercialism into the work of our Foreign Office and into the definition of our country's international objectives', with the Foreign Office giving new emphasis to providing direct support to the UK economy (Hague, 2010d). To this end, a commercial diplomacy taskforce has been established within the FCO.

Second, there is a new focus on developing stronger links with what the Government calls 'emerging powers', in particular China, India and Brazil. This focus was seen with Cameron's trip to China in November 2010, which he described as a 'vitally important trade mission', and which consisted of four Cabinet ministers and 43 business leaders. Cameron promised 'close engagement' with China and said that 'banging the drum for trade' was key to UK foreign policy. 'Our message is simple: Britain is now open for business, has a very business-friendly government, and wants to have a much, much stronger relationship with China' (BBC, 2010). Cameron also visited India and Turkey, both growing economies identified by the Government as targets for increasing trade, pleasing the former by criticizing Pakistan and the latter by criticizing Israel. Whether engagement with China and India will result in a resurgent Britain is unclear, but what is in no doubt is that for Cameron, 'Our national security depends on our economic strength, and vice versa' (Cameron, 2010b: col. 797). This was message of the NSS and SDSR which were presented in October 2010.

Britain's National Security Strategy in an Age of Austerity: An End to Liberal Interventionism?

The Coalition Government's National Security Strategy (NSS), which had been drawn up by the National Security Council, was unveiled by Hague on 18 October. The aim was to set the scene for the Strategic Defence and Security Review (SDSR) and to outline the major risks to British security which had been identified by the Coalition Government. The foreword to the NSS stated: 'We are entering an age of uncertainty' and 'This Strategy is about gearing Britain up for this new age of uncertainty.' It stressed the need to move away from the Cold War mind-set of tanks and heavy artillery and in invest more in building up defences against cyber-attacks and terrorism (NSS, 2010: 3–5).

The NSS outlined four 'first tier' risks to the UK, namely those that were identified as being most likely and having the biggest impact. These were first, international terrorism affecting the UK or its interests, including an increase in the threat posed by residual terrorist groups in Northern Ireland; second, hostile attacks on UK cyberspace by other states or cyber-criminals; third, a major accident or natural hazard, such as severe flooding or an influenza pandemic; and fourth, an international military crisis between states which draws in Britain and its allies (NSS, 2010: 25). This list generated a great deal of attention, especially the focus on cyber-attacks, which was seen as a new and somewhat esoteric threat by many in the media, but in many ways the threats outlined by the Coalition Government reflected those outlined in Brown's NSS of 2008. This had also focused on the threats posed by transnational terrorism and crime, failed states and civil emergencies, but had placed more emphasis on the danger of the proliferation of weapons of mass destruction (NSS, 2008).

One notable shift from the NSS of the previous Labour Government was that the 2010 strategy focused on preventing rather than on intervening in conflict, and appeared to herald the end of liberal interventionism so that if a Kosovo-type situation arose, the new government might take a different approach from Blair's. This message was made clear in

Cameron's statement to the House of Commons on the SDSR the next day, when he said that there would be more focus on conflict prevention not intervention, as 'Iraq and Afghanistan have shown the immense financial and human costs of large-scale military interventions, and although we must retain the ability to undertake such operations we must get better at treating the causes of instability, not just dealing with the consequences' (Cameron, 2010b: col. 798). The SDSR stated:

> [G]iven the direct linkages between instability and conflict, our Department for International Development will double its investment in tackling and preventing conflict around the globe, consistent with the international rules for Official Development Assistance. Our approach recognises that when we fail to prevent conflict and are obliged to intervene militarily, it costs far more. And that is why we will expand our ability to deploy military and civilian experts together to support stabilization efforts and build capacity in other states, as a long-term investment in a more stable world. (SDSR, 2010: 3)

It was announced that there would be more 'joined-up thinking across government' on how to improve security, the suggestion being that the Department for International Development (DFID) might use its role more strategically. Hague also said that aid would be used strategically, and gave the examples of aid going to Pakistan and Yemen to prevent terrorism from being planned there (NSS, 2010: 25). This was reiterated by Cameron, who said that DFID must focus on conflict prevention.

International Development

When Thatcher came to power in 1979 she reduced the value of overseas aid and shifted its distribution away from poverty alleviation to supporting British strategic objectives. The separate Ministry of Overseas Development, which had been established by Harold Wilson in 1964, was abolished and its work taken over by the Foreign and Commonwealth Office. In direct contrast to this approach, the 2010 Conservative manifesto promised that a new Conservative government would be fully committed to achieving the UN target of spending 0.7 per cent of gross national income as aid by 2013, that is, the same year pledged by Labour in its 2005 and 2010 election manifestos. Furthermore, this would be enshrined in law in the first session of the new Parliament. The Conservatives also promised that they would work towards the UN's Millennium Development goals and towards greater effectiveness and transparency on aid expenditure (Conservative Party, 2010: 117). The manifesto complained that, under Labour, aid had not been spent in a focused way, and had been spent on countries that should be looking after their own citizens. Under the Conservatives, Britain would stop giving aid to China and Russia; instead, 'We will focus more on the poorest.' The manifesto also promised 'a more integrated approach to post-conflict reconstruction where the British military is involved – building on the Stabilization Unit in Whitehall and creating a new Stabilization and Reconstruction Force to bridge the gap between the military and the reconstruction effort' (Conservative Party, 2010: 118).

These commitments were elaborated in the DFID Business Plan, in which Andrew Mitchell, the Secretary of State for International Development, stated:

> We will concentrate our efforts on supporting achievement of the Millennium Development Goals, creating wealth in poor countries, strengthening their governance and security and tackling climate change. The prize, in doing so, is huge: a better life for millions of people, and a safer, more prosperous world for Britain. (DFID, 2010: 1)

The Millennium Development Goals have at their heart a human security perspective, focusing on the need for access to education and health as well as on direct poverty alleviation, and in particular on the need for women's rights. Mitchell stated: 'We want to see girls and women, who so often hold the key to development, becoming empowered members of their communities. We will work to strengthen women's voice and engagement in decision making' (DFID, 2010: 1). Thus, the Government is taking an approach to international development that builds on the work of the Blair and Brown governments, though with a greater focus on conflict prevention, but which signals a clear break with previous Conservative Governments. However, it was left to Nick Clegg to address the UN General Assembly during the Millennium Development Goals Summit, which Cameron did not attend.

The Coalition Government has signalled its intention to link strategic interests with development need, in that one of the key goals outlined in DFID's business plan is that DFID is to 'strengthen governance and security in fragile and conflict-affected countries', in particular with a focus on Afghanistan and Pakistan (DFID, 2010: 13). In terms of the new focus on conflict prevention, the SDSR had maintained that one of Britain's major security tasks was to 'tackle at root the causes of instability' (SDSR, 2010: 11) because:

Recent experience has shown that instability and conflict overseas can pose risks to the UK, including by creating environments in which terrorists and organised crime groups can recruit for, plan and direct their global operations. Groups operating in countries like Somalia and Yemen represent a direct and growing terrorist threat to the UK; criminal gangs use West Africa for smuggling goods into the UK; and conflicts overseas disrupt our trade and energy supplies. (SDSR, 2010: 44)

The SDSR pointed to the nexus between a lack of effective government, weak security and poverty, which can all cause instability and which will be exacerbated in the future by competition for resources (SDSR, 2010: 44).

The SDSR had argued that in order to be able to tackle this, Britain required first, 'an effective international development programme making the optimal contribution to national security within its overall objective of poverty reduction, with the Department for International Development focusing significantly more effort on priority national security and fragile states'. Second, civilian and military stabilization capabilities that can be deployed together early to help countries avoid crises or deal with conflict. And third, targeted programmes in the UK, and in countries posing the greatest threat to the UK, to stop people becoming terrorists (SDSR, 2010: 11). In order to further these aims, DFID has revised its strategies for Afghanistan and Pakistan in line with the National Security Council's objectives, and a cross-government board has been established bringing together DFID, the FCO and the Ministry of Defence to develop and support the implementation of the Building Stability Overseas strategy of the SDSR. However, Cameron did not endear himself to the Pakistani Government when, during his trip to India, when asked about Pakistan and terrorism, replied:

We should be very clear with Pakistan that we want to see a strong and a stable and a democratic Pakistan, but we cannot tolerate in any sense the idea that this country is allowed to look both ways and is able in any way to promote the export of terror, whether to India or whether to Afghanistan, or anywhere else in the world. (Cameron, 2010a)

Conclusion

While signalling that the Coalition Government has an agenda for change in foreign policy and international development, the main shift has been an enhanced emphasis on economic objectives in British foreign policy.

This is due to the desire to expand Britain's global reach and influence in a time of changing global economic fortunes, and the concern that:

> In a world of shifting economic power and increased threats, the UK stands to lose a great deal of its ability to shape world affairs unless we act to reverse our declining status. (Conservative Party, 2010: 103)

Before gaining power, Hague and Cameron determined that the way to do this was to build stronger relationships with the 'emerging economies', in particular India and China, as power shifts from the West to the East. The goal is to enhance Britain's global role, to be in effect a mini-superpower, though whether this is achievable in an era of budget cuts and spending restraint remains to be seen. In terms of international development, there has not been a shift from the priorities of the previous Labour governments, but there has been a significant shift in terms of the adoption of a human security agenda which is at odds with previous Conservative governments.

One area where there is a shift away from the previous administration is over Cameron's diplomacy. Cameron has at times been surprisingly outspoken in some of his comments and has risked controversy. In a speech to business leaders during his trip to Turkey, he said that the Israeli blockade of Gaza was turning it into a 'prison camp'. This is a contrast to the New Labour governments, where Blair and Brown were so anxious to demonstrate that they could be trusted to govern, they were extremely careful over the language they used in order not to cause offence, and shied away from criticizing Israel in particular. As the journalist Simon Tisdale put it: 'With its mix of energy and determination, this is Cameron-style kick-and-run diplomacy. Call it naive. Or call it radical. But it's certainly different' (Tisdale, 2010).

References

BBC (2010) *Cameron Raises Human Rights in China Talks*, 9 November. www.bbc.co.uk/news/business-11715216 (accessed 14 November 2010).

Cameron, D. (2006) A New Approach to Foreign Affairs – Liberal Conservatism. Speech to the British American Project, 11 September. www.guardian.co.uk/politics/2006/sep/11/conservatives.speeches (accessed 14 November 2010).

Cameron, D. (2008) Crossroads for NATO. Speech at Chatham House, 1 April. www.chathamhouse.org.uk/files/11280_010408cameron.pdf (accessed 13 November 2010).

Cameron, D. (2010a) PM's Speech in India. Bangalore, 28 July. www.number10.gov.uk/news/speeches-and-transcripts/2010/07/pms-speech-in-india-53949 (accessed 4 November 2010).

Cameron, D. (2010b) Statement on Strategic Defence and Security Review, House of Commons, 19 October, HC Deb, cols. 797–801.

Cameron, D. (2010c) Speech to Lord Mayor's Banquet, 15 November. www.number10.gov.uk/news/speeches-and-transcripts/2010/11/speech-to-lord-mayors-banquet-57068 (accessed 13 November 2010).

Clegg, N. (2010) Deputy PM's speech at Millennium Development Goals Summit, UN, New York, 22 September. www.number10.gov.uk/news/speeches-and-transcripts/2010/09/deputy-pms-speech-at-millennium-development-goals-summit-55257 (accessed 4 November 2010).

Conservative Party (2010) *Invitation to Join the Government of Britain: Conservative Election Manifesto 2010* (London: Conservative Party).

Department for International Development (2010) *Business Plan 2011–2015* (London: Department for International Development).

Downing Street news briefing, Establishment of a National Security Council, 12 May 2010. www.number10.gov.uk/news/latest-news/2010/05/establishment-of-a-national-security-council-49953 (accessed 15 November 2010).

Foreign and Commonwealth Office (2010) *Business Plan 2010–2015* (London: Foreign and Commonwealth Office). www.fco.gov.uk/resources/en/pdf/about-us/our-publications/fco-business-plan-2011–2015 (accessed 13 November 2010).

Hague, W. (2010a) The Biggest Risk for Britain is Five More Years of Brown. Speech, 10 March. www.conservatives.com/News/Speeches/2010/03/William_Hague_The_biggest_risk_for_Britain_is_five_more_years_of_Brown.aspx (accessed 15 November 2010).

Hague, W. (2010b) 26 May, HC Deb, col. 174.

Hague, W. (2010c) Britain's Foreign Policy in a Networked World. Speech at the Foreign and Commonwealth Office, 1 July. www.fco.gov.uk/en/news/latest-news/?view=Speech&id=22472881 (accessed 10 November 2010).

Hague, W. (2010d) Britain's Prosperity in a Networked World. Speech in Tokyo, Japan, 15 July. www.fco.gov.uk/en/news/latest-news/?view=Speech&id=22551011 (accessed 11 November 2010).

HMG (2008) *The National Security Strategy of the United Kingdom: Security in an Interdependent World* (London: The Stationery Office).

HMG (2010) *A Strong Britain in an Age of Uncertainty: The National Security Strategy*, Cm 7953 (London: The Stationery Office).

House of Commons Foreign Affairs Committee (2010) Press release, 4 November. www.parliament.uk/business/committees/committees-a-z/commons-select/foreign-affairs-committee/news/the-role-of-the-fco-in-uk-government/ (accessed 14 November 2010).

Public Administration Select Committee (2010) *Who Does UK National Strategy?* First Report of Session 2010–11, HC 435 (London: The Stationery Office).

Riddell, P. (1998) *Parliament under Blair* (London: Politico's).

Strategic Defence and Security Review (2010) *Securing Britain in an Age of Uncertainty: The Strategic Defence and Security Review*, Cm 7948 (London: The Stationery Office).

Tisdale, S. (2010) Gaza Remark Signals Kick-and-Run Diplomacy. *Guardian*, 27 July.

14
The Con–Lib Agenda for Europe

Philip Lynch

The Conservative Party suffered serious divisions over the issue of Europe when in power in the 1990s. Since then, the Conservatives have become more Eurosceptic while integration has deepened. In opposition, the leadership had some success in detoxifying 'Europe', however, managing the issue will be more difficult in government. Having opposed the Lisbon Treaty, the Conservatives must now engage with a European Union (EU) operating under that treaty, while pacifying Eurosceptic backbenchers who are unhappy that the manifesto commitment to repatriate powers was not part of the Coalition Agreement with the pro-European Liberal Democrats.

The ideological differences between the Conservatives and Liberal Democrats are starker on Europe than most other policy areas. The Conservatives are a 'soft' Eurosceptic party (Taggart and Szczerbiack, 2008: 247–8) which supports membership of the EU but has, in the last 20 years, opposed key areas of integration such as Economic and Monetary Union (EMU), treaty reform and the extension of EU competence in social policy, justice and home affairs, and foreign and security policy. In the same period, the Liberal Democrats were enthusiastic advocates of European integration, favouring British membership of the euro and the extension of the EU's powers. David Cameron and Nick Clegg appeared in tune on many issues in the early months of the Coalition, but have very different views on Europe. Cameron is an instinctive Eurosceptic, but a pragmatic one who is wary of the damage that Europe has, and could still, pose for his party. Clegg worked in the European Commission and was a Member of the European Parliament (MEP) before entering the House of Commons. At the 2010 Conservative party conference, Cameron recalled discussions between the two leaders: 'when I told him what I really thought of the European Parliament he said "my God it's worse than I thought"'. In the second leadership debate, Clegg described the Conservatives' allies in the European Parliament as 'a bunch of nutters, anti-Semites, people who deny climate change exists, homophobes'.

Conservative Policy on Europe

When Cameron became Conservative leader in 2005, he maintained the party's commitment to a referendum on the Lisbon Treaty. This allowed him to make Europe an issue of trust by highlighting how Labour had denied voters a referendum on Lisbon, having pledged to hold one on the treaty establishing a Constitution for Europe (Lynch, 2009). Cameron over-egged the pudding, however, by claiming that his commitment to a referendum was a 'cast iron guarantee' (*The Sun*, 26 September 2007) because there was a significant caveat. If Lisbon had not been ratified by all 27 Member States when the Conservatives entered office, they would suspend ratification, hold a referendum on the treaty and lead the campaign for a 'No' vote. But if it had been ratified, the Conservatives promised only to 'not let matters rest there'.

After the second Irish referendum on Lisbon delivered a 'yes' vote and the Czech president signed the treaty, Cameron announced that a Conservative government would not hold a 'made-up referendum' (Cameron, 2009). The Conservatives would 'use the forthcoming General Election deliberately to seek a mandate to negotiate "British guarantees" on the application of the Lisbon Treaty and on seeking to restore key powers to Britain'. With this, a referendum would not be required. A referendum would have been a distraction and would not guarantee negotiating success. The Conservatives would also have run the risk of losing control of the agenda and reopening internal differences.

Cameron pledged action in the domestic arena and in the EU to prevent further powers being ceded without the consent of the British people, and address concerns about Lisbon. These were repeated in the party's election manifesto (Conservative Party, 2010). A 'referendum lock' would ensure that any future treaty handing further powers to the EU would be subject to a referendum, and a Sovereignty Bill would confirm that ultimate authority resides with the Westminster Parliament. Both originated from policies developed under William Hague's leadership.

A Conservative government would seek a 'full opt-out from the Charter of Fundamental Rights' and 'greater protection against EU encroachment into the UK's criminal justice system' (Cameron, 2009). The party believed that exemptions negotiated by Labour were insufficient (Lynch, 2009). The repatriation of social and employment policy was a long-standing Conservative demand, but it did not necessarily mean a rolling back of existing policy. Cameron spoke of seeking 'guarantees over the application of the Working Time Directive in our public services' rather than overturning it (Cameron, 2009).

The Liberal Democrats and Europe

The Liberal Democrat manifesto had a strong pro-European flavour, albeit one tempered by the economic crisis. This was most apparent on EMU – the party continued to believe that it was in Britain's long-term interest to join the single currency, subject to approval in a referendum, but recognized that 'Britain should only join when the economic conditions are right, and in the present economic situation they are not' (Liberal Democrats, 2010: 67). In the final leadership debate, held as the economic situation in Greece worsened, Clegg denied that he was 'advocating entry'. The party pledged to remain part of justice and home affairs measures, such as the European Arrest Warrant, and sought EU regulation of financial services and banking. The manifesto noted, however, that the EU is not perfect and promised campaigns to reform the EU budget and Common Agricultural Policy (CAP), and end European Parliament sessions in Strasbourg.

The Liberal Democrats also committed themselves to an 'in–out' referendum the next time that a British government signed up to 'fundamental change in the relationship between the UK and the EU' (Liberal Democrats, 2010: 67). The journey to this position had been a fraught one. The 2005 manifesto promised a referendum on the treaty establishing a Constitution for Europe, but the party later argued a referendum on Lisbon was not required. The then leader Menzies Campbell advocated a broader in–out referendum, a policy that Clegg maintained. When a Liberal Democrat amendment on an in–out referendum was not selected, Clegg ordered his MPs to abstain on a Conservative amendment on a Lisbon referendum. Three members of his Shadow Cabinet – David Heath, Alistair Carmichael and Tim Fallon – resigned their posts in protest, and 15 Liberal Democrats voted for a Lisbon referendum (Cowley and Stuart, 2010: 143–4). The rebels claimed that many MPs were uncomfortable with the party's strong pro-European stance, particularly those in marginal seats in south-west England and the Scottish isles, but no Liberal Democrats MPs rebelled on the substance of the Lisbon Treaty.

Coalition Policy on Europe

Europe was one of the Conservatives' red lines in the Coalition negotiations. They were unwilling to concede ground on the referendum lock and opposition to further European integration. But senior Conservatives were prepared to drop demands for the repatriation of powers and further guarantees on the Lisbon Treaty, recognizing that these were unpalatable for the Liberal Democrats and would strain relations with key allies in the EU. The Liberal Democrats wanted to ensure that the Government would play a constructive role in the EU, but had little problem in accepting that membership of the euro would not happen in the next five years. Their key concession was accepting that there would be no further transfers of power during this period. Both had advocated a referendum, but the Conservatives opposed an in–out referendum – a Liberal Democrat policy that many Tory Eurosceptics would have embraced – so the referendum lock survived. The Conservative commitment to a Sovereignty Bill was watered down, with the agreement merely promising to 'examine the case' for it.

The Coalition's *Programme for Government* claims that it 'strikes the right balance between constructive engagement with the EU to deal with the issues that affect us all and protecting our national sovereignty' (Cabinet Office, 2010: 19). Its positive statements on the EU are similar to those made in the Conservative manifesto on global competitiveness, global warming and global poverty. Compromises are evident on policy competences, where the Coalition promises to 'examine the balance of the EU's existing competences' and 'work to limit the application of the Working Time Directive'. European Commission proposals to amend the latter may address British concerns about the impact on the NHS of strict rules on on-call time and rest periods. The Coalition programme rules out participation in a European Public Prosecutor system, but other legislation on criminal justice would be handled on 'a case-by-case basis, with a view to maximizing our country's security, protecting Britain's civil liberties and preserving the integrity of our criminal justice system' (Cabinet Office, 2010: 19).

The policy agreed by the Coalition is not radically different from that of recent Labour and Conservative governments. All wished to play a positive role while defending the national interest, supported the Single Market and EU enlargement, demanded reform of the CAP and EU budget, and were cautious about EU social policy, criminal justice and defence proposals.

Conservatives took the key ministerial positions on Europe, William Hague becoming Foreign Secretary. But the appointment of the pragmatic David Lidington, a former adviser to Douglas Hurd at the Foreign Office, as Minister for Europe rather than the Eurosceptic Mark Francois, who had held the position in the Shadow Cabinet, calmed Liberal Democrat nerves.

Cameron had been a pragmatic Eurosceptic in opposition. In his first months as Prime Minister, his pragmatism on Europe became more apparent and his Euroscepticism less so. After the October 2010 European Council, Cameron described himself as a Eurosceptic, but a 'practical, sensible one at the same time.' (*The Telegraph*, 2010). Even before the Coalition took office, senior Conservatives had stressed that, although they would defend British interests robustly, they would not actively seek confrontation in the EU. Hague spoke of a 'strategic decision' to avoid early conflict with the EU: 'We have enough on our hands without an instant confrontation with the EU. . . . It will not be our approach to go and bang on the table and say immediately we demand A, B, C' (*Financial Times*, 2010).

The Conservatives would be 'active and activist in the European Union from day one, energetically engaging with our partners' (Hague, 2010). Relations between Cameron and German Chancellor Angela Merkel had been badly strained since the former's announcement that the Conservatives would leave the European People's Party-European Democrat Group (EPP-ED), in which Merkel's Christian Democrats were the largest party. Suggestions that Merkel would continue to cold-shoulder Cameron in government were far-fetched, but the new Prime Minister still had work to do to win over the most influential figure on the EU stage. Efforts would also be made to strengthen alliances with states in Eastern and Central Europe who tended to be more favourable to key parts of the British agenda. Clegg's experience in EU institutions helped to smooth potential tensions.

The Coalition's pragmatic approach surprised some commentators. Iain Martin proclaimed the 'strange death of Tory Euroskepticism' (Martin, 2010) and Steve Richards was surprised that 'Europe has ceased to be a toxic issue in British politics and the detoxification will last' (Richards, 2010). There were reasons for believing that relations with the EU would be relatively quiescent during the Coalition's first months in office. There was no major treaty revision on the horizon and the Franco-German motor of integration had been spluttering. But, there were also signs that Europe could become a difficult issue. As we shall see, discontent on the Conservative benches escalated by late autumn. The dynamism of European integration also means that new problems for British governments are never far away. Two key developments posed particular challenges. The Lisbon Treaty entered into force in December 2009 and new arrangements, such as the European External Action Service, were about to become reality. Second, the Greek economic crisis prompted a bailout and demands for greater EU action on economic governance.

EU Policy Developments

The Lisbon Treaty established the European External Action Service (EEAS) as a diplomatic service for the EU. It speaks on behalf of common positions on foreign policy and manages the EU's foreign relations, security and defence policies. The EEAS was created from a number of Commission and Council departments, and supports the High Representative for Foreign Affairs and Security Policy. The Conservatives had opposed the creation of the EEAS but now accepted it as a fact. The Coalition aims to shape the development of the EEAS so that it respects the competence of Member States in foreign policy and works in cooperation with their diplomatic services, but provides a cohesive voice in areas where the EU has an agreed common position.

Cameron maintained British support for Turkish membership of the EU, making the case forcefully in a speech in Ankara in July in which he said that he was 'angry' at the slow pace of negotiations and drew comparisons with de Gaulle's veto of British membership in the 1960s. Support for Iceland's membership application would, however, depend on it reimbursing the Government for the £2.3 billion it paid to investors after the collapse of Icelandic banks.

Justice and Home Affairs

The five-year Stockholm Programme of action in justice and home affairs indicates that this is an expanding field of EU activity. Lisbon extended EU competence in police and criminal justice, giving the Commission the power to propose legislation and the ECJ the power to implement law in this area. Britain has an opt-in arrangement that allows it to stay outside new legislation. Once a proposal is tabled, the British Government has three months to decide whether to opt in or opt out, but it may also opt in to the legislation at a later date.

The Coalition opted in to the draft EU Directive on the European Investigation Order (EIO) in July 2010. Home Secretary Theresa May told the House of Commons that it would help to tackle cross-border crime, the British police believing that it would be a speedier and more efficient system of obtaining evidence from overseas than existing arrangements (Hansard, 27 July 2010, col. 881). Signing up to the EIO did not, May claimed, involve a transfer of sovereignty and was purely a practical measure. Other police forces would not be permitted to instruct the British police on what operations to conduct or operate with law enforcement powers in the UK.

Conservative Eurosceptics and civil liberties groups warned that British police could be compelled to collect evidence on individuals for conduct that is not treated as criminal in the UK and where cases are viewed as trivial. By opting in while the directive was still at draft stage, the Government hoped to add a proportionality test and further safeguards on the collection of evidence. But the final decision on the directive will be taken by qualified majority voting, and the Government cannot reverse its decision to opt in.

In its first six months in office, the Coalition opted in to five other EU proposals in the area of justice and home affairs, including an EU–US agreement on the tracking of terrorist finance and draft directives on combating the sexual exploitation of children (HC Written Answer on EC Justice and Home Affairs, 30 November 2010, no. 27619). But it opted out of five measures, including draft directives on seasonal workers and human trafficking. Ministers claimed that much of what the latter proposed was already in operation in the UK and that the decision would be reviewed once the directive had been agreed. In autumn 2010, the Government announced that Sir Scott Baker was to chair an independent review of Britain's extradition laws, including the operation of the European Arrest Warrant (EAW). More than 1,000 people had been detained and extradited by British police under the EAW in 2009–10.

Economic Governance

In his first budget, Chancellor George Osborne announced the abolition of the Treasury's Euro Preparations Unit. This was a symbolic rather than dramatic break with the past because British entry into the euro had been off the agenda since Gordon Brown announced in 2003 that only one of his five economic tests had been met. While the Conservatives and Liberal Democrats were locked in Coalition negotiations, outgoing Labour Chancellor Alistair Darling tied their hands by agreeing to an EU bailout for Greece, a temporary European Financial Stability Mechanism (EFSM) funded by all Member States, and a smaller European Financial Stability Facility to which only euro zone states contribute. The treaties include a 'no bailout' clause (Article 125) but Member States agreed to use Article 122(2), which allows financial support in exceptional circumstances, to come to the aid of Greece. Britain will contribute 8.6 per cent of the

EFSM funds and will be part of the temporary bailout mechanism until 2013. Cameron opposed this at the time but, when in office, said that the Government would have to live with it. Conservative ministers reminded domestic and European audiences that they had warned of the dangers of EMU, but argued that the break-up of the euro zone was not in the national interest. Britain also contributed £3.25 billion in a bilateral loan to Ireland as part of an international bailout, as well as providing assistance through the IMF and the EFSM.

A Task Force on Economic Governance, led by Herman van Rompuy, proposed a permanent bailout facility. At the December 2010 European Council, Member States duly agreed to establish a permanent European Stability Mechanism from 2013 which may be used to bail out states, subject to 'strict conditionality', if their debt problems threatened the stability of the euro zone. Germany pressed for a treaty revision to make such bailouts legal. The British Government accepted an amendment to Article 36 because its provisions will only apply to Member States whose currency is the euro and will not involve a transfer of power from the UK to the EU. Treaty change will occur through the Simplified Revision Procedure. If the European Union Bill is enacted, ratification in the UK will require an Act of Parliament but not a referendum (see below).

The Task Force also proposed greater economic surveillance. Member States agreed an 'EU semester': they will send their national budgets to the Commission in spring, which will then check that their plans are consistent with EU guidelines on fiscal policy and deficit reduction. The Commission will issue an opinion and draft budget plans will be discussed at Ecofin in early summer before they are approved by national parliaments. The Coalition agreed to this, but insisted that the budget would be heard first by the Commons and warned that it would veto any proposal that required the British budget to be cleared by the Commission. As Cameron put it: 'co-ordination and consultation, yes; clearance, no, never' (Hansard 21 June 2010, col. 36). The UK is exempted from the sanctions and enforcement measures because of its EMU opt-out. Despite government assurances that the economic governance measures did not involve any transfer of power from Britain to the EU, Eurosceptics warned that the measures marked a significant expansion of the EU's power in economic policy.

The credit crunch also led to EU action to regulate financial services and the banking sector. In September 2009, the Commission proposed a new European system of financial supervisors. Osborne agreed to the creation of a European Systemic Risk Board to monitor risks to financial stability, and three new EU regulators which started work in 2011 – a

European Banking Authority based in London, a European Insurance and Occupational Pensions Authority and a European Securities and Markets Authority. They will work with national authorities, but have the power to draw up rules and take action (e.g. ban short selling) in emergencies.

EU Budget

The Government rejected a demand by the Commission and European Parliament, exercising its post-Lisbon budgetary powers, for a 5.9 per cent increase in the EU budget for 2011. Cameron led calls for the budget to reflect the economic conditions and public spending cuts being made across Europe, a position supported by eleven other Member States including France and Germany. If no deal was reached, the 2011 budget would remain at the previous year's level – a prospect that many Eurosceptics welcomed. The Government's initial demand for a budget cut or freeze did not garner sufficient support and a compromise 2.9 per cent increase was agreed. This will cost Britain an additional £450 million. Cameron had talked tough then settled for a deal which others were already willing to accept and failed to deliver what Eurosceptics hoped for.

Negotiations on the EU's financial framework for 2014–20 began in 2011. Britain, France, Germany, Finland and the Netherlands agreed a text in December 2010 calling for the 2012 and 2013 budgets to reflect national spending cuts and for a real-term budget freeze for 2014–20. Cameron again claimed that his Government was leading the initiative. The proposal angered Poland, a key British ally in other policy areas. The Government will also come under intense pressure to give up the British budget rebate, but maintains that it will not do so. Ahead of negotiations on major reform of the CAP, Environment Secretary Caroline Spelman wanted to 'make the new CAP fundamentally different', with a reduction in subsidies and a greater emphasis on the environment (Spelman, 2011). But Britain's unwillingness to give ground on the EU budget and its rebate makes CAP reform less likely.

Overall, the European policy of the Coalition Government has not departed significantly from that of its predecessor. In part, this reflects policy commitments that it inherited. The Conservatives were far from enthusiastic about the European External Action Service, new EU measures on economic governance and an increase in the EU budget, but were prepared to live with these, subject to assurances that they would not transfer powers from Britain to the EU, rather than provoke an early confrontation with the EU. Both the Labour and Coalition Governments supported the Single Market, economic competitiveness and welfare reform (e.g. in the Europe 2020 strategy). The case-by-case approach to justice and home affairs mirrored that of the previous government, although Labour had been more favourable to EU action.

The European Union Bill

The European Union Bill introduced in autumn 2010 did mark a departure from the approach adopted by the Labour Government. The Bill sought to enact three commitments made in the Coalition programme: (i) a referendum lock; (ii) additional controls on the use of the ratchet clauses in the EU treaties; and (iii) a restatement of the sovereignty of Parliament.

The referendum lock will ensure that any future treaty that transfers power from the UK to the EU will be subject to a referendum before the Government can agree to it. Ministers must issue a statement to Parliament setting out whether a treaty change involves a transfer of power, with their decisions subject to judicial review if challenged. A referendum would occur after the treaty had been approved by Parliament and its result would be binding – it could not come into force unless a majority of those voting in the referendum were in favour of ratification. Separate questions would be required for each treaty change or decision requiring a referendum.

A referendum would also be required before the Government can agree to certain decisions provided for in the treaties that transfer competence or power to the EU. Whereas the competences of the EU are set out in the treaties, they do not define 'power'. The bill thus stipulates that a transfer of power occurs when unanimity is replaced by qualified majority voting and when an EU institution gains the power to impose an obligation or sanctions on the UK. The treaties include various procedures that allow Member States to agree to modify the existing treaties without recourse to formal treaty change. The Simplified Revision Procedure allows decisions currently taken by unanimity (except on defence) to be decided in future by a majority vote if all Member States must agree to this by unanimity and all national parliaments also give their approval. Enabling clauses and *passerelles*, known as 'ratchet clauses', allow the transfer of an area of competence to the EU without treaty change.

The European Union Bill proposes additional controls on the use of the Simplified Revision Procedure and specified ratchet clauses. As there is no clear definition of what constitutes a ratchet clause, the bill lists the treaty articles and stipulates what action must be taken before the Government can use them. Some will require an Act of Parliament and a referendum, some an Act of Parliament and others a vote in both the House of Commons and House of Lords before the Government can agree to them. The bill specifies that a referendum is required before a decision to give up the veto in a 'significant' area. Among the decisions that would automatically require an Act of Parliament and a referendum are joining the euro, participating in a European Public Prosecutor system, the removal of UK border controls and areas of social policy, EU finance and social security and foreign and security policy. The accession of new Member States does not involve a transfer of competences, so a referendum would not be required. Where the use of a ratchet clause would alter what can be done in an existing area of EU competence (e.g. on criminal law), approval by an Act of Parliament will be necessary. A vote in both Houses will be required where, for example, a ratchet clause modifies the rules of procedure or composition of EU institutions.

Sovereignty Clause

Clause 18 of the bill states:

> It is only by virtue of an Act of Parliament that directly applicable or directly effective EU law (that is, the rights, powers, liabilities, obligations, restrictions, remedies and procedures referred to in section 2(1) of the European Communities Act (1972) falls to be recognised and available in law in the United Kingdom. (European Union Bill, 2010–11, Bill 106, p. 11)

This is a declaratory clause which does not change the relationship between the UK and the EU or affect the primacy of EU law. By creating a statutory reference point for the principle that EU law only takes effect in the UK through the will of Parliament, the Government argues that the clause counters claims that EU law constitutes a higher autonomous legal authority derived from the EU treaties which has become an integral part of UK law independent of statute, and thus assist the courts by providing clarity about the intentions of Parliament (European Union Bill 2010–11, Explanatory Notes, para. 106: 24–5). The latter claim was made in *Thoburn v Sunderland City Council* [2002] but was rejected by Lord Justice Laws. Clause 18 would, the Government claims, put the matter beyond speculation (Lidington, 2010).

The European Union Scrutiny Committee, chaired by veteran Eurosceptic Bill Cash, conducted pre-legislative scrutiny on the sovereignty clause. Constitutional experts who gave evidence agreed that the clause was not required in a legal sense and had no practical effect. Clause 18 reaffirms the principle of dualism – that a treaty agreed by the Executive does not come into effect domestically until incorporated into law by

Parliament – but does not, the Committee claims, say anything about the relationship between UK and EU law in the event of a clash between the two. The Committee was critical of claims made by the Government about parliamentary sovereignty. Its report expressed concern that the Government's assertion that the legislative supremacy of Parliament originates from common law leaves it open to revision by the courts. As Clause 18 only concerns EU law, the report also warned that the courts may interpret legislative supremacy in this narrow sense. The Committee concluded that 'Clause 18 is not a sovereignty clause in the manner claimed by the government, and the whole premise on which it has been included in the Bill is, in our view, exaggerated' (European Scrutiny Committee, 2010, para. 86: 31). The government made a limited concession in early 2011 when it agreed to amend the Explanatory Notes to state that the government did not endorse the opinion that Parliament's authority derives from common law.

The coupling of the sovereignty clause and the referendum lock is an uncomfortable one. The doctrine of parliamentary sovereignty states that Parliament cannot bind its successors – a future Parliament may amend or repeal any existing legislation. However, the European Union Bill attempts, if not to bind its successors, at least to make it difficult for a future government to overturn the requirement to hold a referendum if powers are transferred to the EU. This might, in time, become a constitutional convention, but no previous EU treaty has been put to a popular vote.

Potential for Divisions

The European Union Bill passed its Second Reading without a vote. But the debate illustrated the unease felt by Eurosceptic Conservatives about both it and Coalition policy on Europe. They argued that the bill's provisions on sovereignty were toothless and that the referendum lock was too restrictive because a referendum would not be required if a transfer of power was not judged 'significant'. There were five rebellions during the Committee stage of the Bill, the most significant seeing 27 Conservative MPs supporting an amendment to Clause 18 reaffirming the sovereignty and 20 Conservatives voting for an in-out referendum.

Eurosceptic dissent had been relatively muted at the outset of the Coalition but gathered momentum in the autumn. Seven Conservative MPs voted against a motion in July 2010 taking note of EU documents establishing the European External Action Service. The House debated the draft 2011 EU budget in October when a majority backed a motion

supportive of the Government's efforts to maintain it at a level equivalent
to the 2010 budget. Also approved, with the support of the whips, was an
amendment by Cash calling for the Government to reject the European
Parliament's proposal to increase the budget. Economic Secretary to the
Treasury, Justine Greening, stated that she shared the sentiments behind
an alternative amendment proposed by Douglas Carswell, which urged
the Government to reduce Britain's contribution to the EU, but could
not support it because withdrawing money would be illegal (Hansard,
13 October 2010, col. 410). Despite intensive activity by the whips,
the Carswell amendment was supported by 37 Conservative MPs (12
others had signed the amendment but abstained or were absent from
the vote). The following month, MPs approved a motion supporting the
Government's position that sanctions proposed by the Task Force on
Economic Governance should not apply to the UK but 25 Conservatives
opposed it, registering their concern about the extension of EU powers.
These were the largest Tory rebellions of the Parliament.

Senior Eurosceptics estimate that more than 100 Conservative
backbenchers are unhappy with Coalition policy on Europe. A total of 53
Conservative MPs had rebelled on European votes by March 2011. Among
the rebels were veteran Eurosceptics like John Redwood and Richard
Shepherd, as well as members of the 2005 intake such as Carswell, who
had quickly established a reputation for independence. The 2010 intake
is primarily Eurosceptic, with most favouring the repatriation of powers
and a significant minority advocating withdrawal. By March 2011, 26
of the new intake of Conservative MPs had defied the whips on Europe.

Eurosceptic rebels (and potential rebels) fall into three broad groupings.
First are 'hard' Eurosceptics who support British withdrawal from the EU
(Taggart and Szczerbiack, 2008: 247–8) and have criticized the leadership
for dropping commitments to a referendum on Lisbon and the repatriation
of powers. The MEP Roger Helmer captured their anger when he claimed
that 'we've been handing powers to Brussels under the Coalition arguably
faster than Labour did' (Helmer, 2010). Many in this grouping, including
Carswell, Philip Davies and Philip Hollobone, are supporters of the Better
Off Out campaign and have been serial rebels on Europe and other issues.
The second grouping consists of Eurosceptics who support a significant
rebalancing of the relationship with the EU – including the repatriation
of powers on social policy, justice and home affairs, and fisheries – and
are unhappy that the commitment to repatriation was dropped. MPs in
this grouping, like Redwood and Cash, believe that the European Union
Bill is too timid and have criticized the Government for accepting treaty
change on economic governance without demanding a repatriation of

powers or further opt-outs in return. They will call for a referendum when the new EU treaty comes before Parliament and will press the Government to use the negotiations on the next financial perspective to demand policy repatriation and EU reform.

The final grouping includes pragmatic Eurosceptics who initially accepted the Coalition's position on Europe, albeit with reservations, but are concerned that its pledge that there would be no further integration during the current Parliament is not being adhered to rigorously. To date, MPs in this grouping have generally accepted government assurances that measures on economic governance and justice and home affairs will not entail a transfer of powers. It will be a cause for concern to the whips that many MPs from the second grouping have already rebelled; if those from the third grouping lose patience with the Government's approach, serious dissent on Europe is likely.

The dissent seen in 2010 lacked the organization and coherence of the Maastricht rebellions. The new breed of Eurosceptics has not (yet) formed an organized group, and they differ on strategy and objectives. With no defining moment, such as a major treaty change, on the horizon it will be difficult to mobilize sufficient numbers to defeat the Government. However, if Labour opposes the European Union Bill or the treaty amendment on economic governance, then defeat becomes a real possibility.

Dissent on Europe has come solely from Eurosceptics. Not a single Liberal Democrat rebelled on Europe in the first nine months of the Government. Pro-Europeanism is now a minority position in the Conservative Party and those who remain have accepted its Eurosceptic position, Kenneth Clarke being the prime example. On the backbenches, one-time pro-Europeans like Stephen Dorrell have tempered their enthusiasm, while the handful of pro-Europeans in the 2010 cohort, such as Robert Buckland and Laura Sandys, are unlikely to rock the boat. All three spoke in favour of the European Union Bill at its Second Reading.

Conclusion

The European policy of the Coalition Government has not been as different from that of the previous Labour Government as some had expected. Its policy on the euro, the EU budget, CAP, the Single European Market, social policy, EU foreign policy and justice and home affairs is broadly consistent with that of recent British governments. Effective working relations have been forged with other EU Member States. The most significant break in European policy has come in the domestic arena with the European Union Bill's referendum lock and sovereignty clause, although these are not as radical as Eurosceptics had hoped.

The pragmatic approach adopted by the Coalition reflects the compromises required for agreement between the soft Eurosceptic Conservatives and the pro-European Liberal Democrats. But the Conservative leadership had already determined that it would avoid confrontation with the EU in its first months in office. As in opposition, Cameron's instinctive Euroscepticism was trumped by his political pragmatism and desire to detoxify the issue. Managing the European issue was, however, going to be more difficult in government than in opposition because, given that they were uncomfortable with key aspects of the EU, the Conservatives would nevertheless have to deal with proposals for further integration. The escalation of Conservative dissent shows the difficulty that faces Cameron in striking the right balance between pragmatism and Euroscepticism.

Further difficulties in Brussels and at Westminster await the Government. It is unlikely to gain significant CAP reform or a budget freeze for the 2014–20 financial framework, especially if it refuses to give ground on the British rebate. Eurosceptics will demand that the Government uses the negotiations to seek one of their core objectives: policy repatriation. The financial situation in the EU remains bleak and, should Portugal or Spain require a bailout, Britain remains liable for payments until 2013. The treaty amendment establishing a permanent bailout mechanism will require approval by the Commons and Eurosceptics will take this opportunity to push for their second key objective: a referendum. The Commission is also expected to propose new EU taxes, while Germany and France favour further harmonization of economic policy in the euro zone. Such measures would not apply to the UK, but Liberal Democrats who harbour long-term ambitions to join the euro will be concerned if Britain appears to be being left on the side lines as an 'inner core' of states proceed with further integration.

References

Cabinet Office (2010) *The Coalition: Our Programme for Government* (London: The Cabinet Office).

Cameron, D. (2009) A European Policy that People Can Believe In. Speech, London, 4 November. www.conservatives.com/News/Speeches/2009/11/David_Cameron_A_Europe_policy_that_people_can_believe_in.aspx

Conservative Party (2010) *Invitation to Join the Government of Britain: The Conservative Manifesto 2010* (London: Conservative Party).

Cowley, P. and Stuart, M. (2010) Where Has All The Trouble Gone? British Intra-Party Divisions during the Lisbon Ratification. *British Politics*, 5(2).

European Scrutiny Committee (2010) *The EU Bill and Parliamentary Sovereignty*, 10th Report of the Session 2010–11, Vol. 1, HC 633-I, House of Commons.

Financial Times (2010) Hague Proffers EU Olive Branch, 9 March.

Hague, W. (2010) The Foreign Policy Framework of a New Conservative Government. Speech to the Royal United Services Institute, London, 10 March, www.rusi.org/events/ref:E4B91259F1741D.

Hansard, 21 June 2010, col. 36.

Hansard, 27 July 2010, col. 881.

Hansard, 13 October 2010, col. 410.

Helmer, R. (2010) 'We've Been Handing Powers to Brussels Faster than Labour', 4 October, conservativehome.blogs.com/centreright/2010/10/has-the-Coalition-lost-the-plot-on-the-eu.html.

HC Written Answer on EC Justice and Home Affairs, 30 November 2010, no. 27619.

Liberal Democrats (2010) *Liberal Democrat Manifesto 2010* (London: Liberal Democrat Party).

Lidington, D. (2010) Speech to the UK Association for European Law, 25 November. www.fco.gov.uk/en/news/latest-news/?view=Speech&id=249892682.

Lynch, P. (2009) The Conservatives and the European Union: The Lull Before the Storm? In S. Lee and M. Beech (eds.), *The Conservatives under David Cameron. Built to Last?* (London: Palgrave Macmillan), pp. 187–207.

Martin, I. (2010) The Strange Death of Tory Euroskepticism. *The Wall Street Journal*, 22 September. http://online.wsj.com/article/SB100014240527487041292045755062003468203 56.html.

Richards, S. (2010) For the First Time in Four Decades, 'Europe' is No Longer Poisonous. *The Independent*, 4 November. www.independent.co.uk/opinion/commentators/steve-richards/steve-richards-for-the-first-time-in-four-decades-europe-is-no-longer-poisonous-2124615.html.

Spelman, C. (2011) Speech to the Oxford Farming Conference, 5 January. ww2.defra.gov.uk/news/2011/01/05/spelman-speech.

Taggart, P. and Szczerbiack, A. (2008) Theorising Party-Based Euroscepticism: Problems of Definition, Measurement and Causality. In P. Taggart and A. Szczerbiack (eds.), *Opposing Europe. The Comparative Party Politics of Euroscepticism*, Volume 2 (Oxford: Oxford University Press), pp. 238–61.

Telegraph (2010) David Cameron Says He is a 'Eurosceptic' Following EU 'Deal', 29 October.

Part Four

A Coalition Built to Last?

15

A Leap of Faith and a Leap in the Dark: The Impact of Coalition on the Conservatives and Liberal Democrats

Tim Bale and Emma Sanderson-Nash

The parties which, in May 2010, formed Britain's first peacetime Coalition Government since the 1930s had both undergone considerable change during Labour's 13 years of office under Tony Blair and Gordon Brown. David Cameron's Conservative Party had done much to move on and to move on out of the populist cul-de-sac into which it had been driven under the leadership of William Hague, Iain Duncan Smith and Michael Howard, none of whom managed to do much to alter the negative perceptions of the party that had hardened during Margaret Thatcher's and John Major's time in Number Ten. Likewise, Nick Clegg's Liberal Democrats were a very different party from the one Paddy Ashdown attempted to lure towards Labour in 1997, and different again from the one Charles Kennedy led in opposition to Blair's war in Iraq in 2003. Indeed, it was the changes to both parties, as well as the parliamentary arithmetic, which meant they were able to come to an agreement in May 2010.

Precisely how much the Conservative Party had changed before the 2010 General Election and the one that it lost so badly in 1997 is a matter for debate (see Beech, 2009; Bale, 2011; Dorey et al., 2011) – and not just among academics. One of the reasons that Cameron, despite being considerably more popular (and arguably much more capable) than his immediate predecessors as Tory leader, was unable to achieve an outright victory in May 2010 was that too many voters remained unconvinced that he had fundamentally changed his party. Its membership had continued to shrink despite his best efforts and, rightly or wrongly, was still routinely portrayed as a bunch of knee-jerk right-wingers. True, most of the parliamentary party he had inherited when he took over as leader in 2005 seemed supportive of (or at least resigned to) his efforts to 'decontaminate' the Tory brand by stressing new themes like the environment, a renewed commitment to the centre ground of British politics and to a more liberal outlook, as well as the promotion of new-look women and ethnic minority candidates. However, some of the policies the party espoused, in contrast to the poses its leadership liked to strike, seemed not so very different from those traditionally associated with Conservative governments in the not very distant past. This was less serious when it came to Europe, law and order and immigration, where traditional Tory positions retained their popularity, but potentially damaging on economic issues and public services – as Cameron found to his cost when he began to talk not just about a 'big society' but also about the need for an 'age of austerity'.

Cameron's changes, real or apparent, were carried out in the full glare of the media spotlight. Most journalists, however, failed fully to appreciate the scale of the gradual transformation of the Liberal Democrats during the first decade of the twenty-first century. The activists have for the most part dumped their beards and sandals, and emerged as a professional, ambitious and determined political force. The parliamentary party doubled in size in 1997 and, helped by a significant increase in state and private funding, were able to begin building a more professional machine (Evans and Sanderson-Nash, forthcoming). The party's political position altered too. In Parliament the party became more accustomed to voting with the Conservatives and against Labour year on year (Cowley 2009). Internal reforms have changed the relationship between HQ and the parliamentary party, and have strengthened the new leader's hand. The social profile of support for the party also changed to resemble more closely that of the Conservatives (Russell and Fieldhouse, 2005). Ideologically, the party has also undergone subtle shifts. In 2003 David Laws, MP for Yeovil, and Paul Marshall, a multi-millionaire and philanthropist, conceived of a project to produce *The Orange Book*, a collection of essays by prominent parliamentarians, in which Laws and others made the case for a more market-friendly liberalism and a move away from the more state-centred social democracy that the party had adopted under the leadership of Kennedy. Their left-leaning opponents then gathered under the banner of the Social Liberal Forum (SLF), making for tensions that were still unresolved by the General Election (Hickson, 2010). That said, Clegg had no problem satisfying the party's so-called 'triple lock' requirement to get at least 75 per cent of the support of the parliamentary party and the federal executive for Coalition, overwhelming approval for which was also voiced at a hastily convened (though constitutionally unnecessary) special meeting of the membership.

Having outlined where the two parties stood by the time of the 2010 General Election, this chapter goes on to discuss how they have more or less adapted to the advent of the Coalition Government that it produced. While it discusses both parties in turn, beginning with the Conservatives, it does so under the same headings for each party – headings which conform to an approach first suggested by the seminal comparative project on parties run by two political scientists: Richard Katz and Peter Mair (1994). We discuss, first, 'the party in public office' (which for our purposes covers the parliamentary party), then 'the party in central office' (its largely professionally staffed headquarters) and finally 'the party on the ground' (its ordinary members and activists). In a brief conclusion we summarize the impact of the Coalition on both parties and speculate a little about what the future holds for them.

The Conservatives[1]

In Parliament

The Tory MPs elected in 2010, both old and new, aren't very different from those elected in 2005 and before, with one or two obvious differences. After the 2005 election there were 17 Tory women; after 2010 there were 49. May 2010 also saw the election of 11 Tory MPs from ethnic minorities – an increase of nine on the previous election. The majority of these new faces came from highly paid occupations in the private sector, such as business, banking and the law, which makes them much more like other Conservative MPs than the general population. Almost half the parliamentary Conservative Party elected in 2010 had backgrounds in business, accountancy and PR; 20 per cent of them were lawyers, with the third biggest group (at 10 per cent) being gainfully employed in politics before becoming an MP; only two Tory MPs could claim to have worked in a manual occupation (one of them the highly respected and able Chief Whip, Patrick McLoughlin, a former miner). More worryingly for a party with big plans for the reform of education and the NHS, there were no teachers or lecturers on the Conservative benches after 2010 and fewer than ten people with backgrounds in the health professions. That said, 2010 continued the trend towards a more state than privately educated parliamentary party: now only just over half of Tory MPs went to independent schools, even if this still makes them untypical of the population as a whole, where the figure is well under 10 per cent.

Just under half (147 out of 306) of those elected in 2010 were first-timers and therefore a largely unknown (or at least unmeasured) quantity ideologically. However, there is no reason to believe that they are, in the main at least, any less committed to market-based, state-shrinking solutions than their predecessors. Certainly, if the elections to the Executive of the 1922 Committee (the body that represents the interests of ordinary Tory MPs and has sometimes proved a thorn in the side of the leadership) are anything to go by, the new intake may indeed be 'Thatcher's children'. The same impression is given by the results of the contests to choose the chairs of the party's newly configured backbench subject committees (covering economic, home, and foreign affairs, public services, and the environment) and the three MPs who represent the parliamentary party on the Party Board. Such results were something of a reaction to Cameron's unwise attempt to neuter the '22 by bouncing his MPs into allowing frontbenchers as well as backbenchers as full voting members – something he sensibly drew back from. But they were also testimony to the vigour, and newfound willingness to work together, of various right-wing clubs – the '92 group, Cornerstone and No Turning Back. The same qualities may also have helped ensure the success of the internal campaign to limit the rise in capital gains tax (CGT) announced in George Osborne's first budget to just 28 per cent rather than the 50 per cent that the Liberal Democrats hoped to get.

Feelings on CGT, it should be said, ran high through the parliamentary party, going beyond the nucleus of around a dozen right-wing irreconcilables and even the 10–15 MPs prepared on occasion to join them in defying the whips, especially on Europe. The latter is still the issue which looks set to cause party managers their biggest headaches, with rebellions which began very early on in the Parliament likely to continue well into the foreseeable future. Moreover, many of the new intake are doughty local campaigners who might easily be persuaded that their best hope of holding on to their marginal seats is being seen to be acting independently and according to their principles – an approach that might also appeal to those Tories concerned about losing out as a result of the reduction of parliamentary constituencies. It is also the case that the generally (and, perhaps surprisingly, genuinely) cordial relationships that most Tory MPs enjoy with their Liberal Democrat counterparts may come under considerable strain if and when the Cabinet is seen to promote policies that go against the Conservative grain, not only on

Europe but on, say, criminal justice or immigration. And while it will be tempting for Liberal Democrats to try to preserve their independence by distancing themselves from government policies they don't like, this will – hypocritically or otherwise – go down very badly with Conservative MPs, as will any sign of a return to what many of the latter regard as vicious and highly personal campaigning by the Liberal Democrats at the local level.

Following the formation of the Coalition, most Tory MPs were simply glad to be back in government, even if quite a few of them were critical of the leadership's failure to secure an overall majority and still smarting at what, at best, was a lack of consultation and, at worst, an outright untruth told them by Cameron about Brown's offer to Clegg on the Alternative Vote during the Coalition negotiations. For many, especially those who went on to receive preferment, however lowly, relief will continue to trump disappointment, resentment and suspicion. Even those Tories who saw their hopes of an immediate ministerial job evaporate because of the need to bring Liberal Democrat MPs into the Government seem to have been persuaded to bide their time and bite their tongues for the greater good – and in the hope that, as normally happens, some of those who did make it onto the frontbench will fairly soon fail to prove they have what it takes, thus making way for those who were disappointed. The downside of that, however, will be the return to the backbenches of MPs with no reason to feel grateful to Cameron and no longer obliged to avoid speaking ill of his Deputy, Nick Clegg, and his Liberal Democrat colleagues.

Millbank

A seemingly inescapable consequence of the Conservative Party going into government is a decline in the attention paid by the leadership, now surrounded by civil servants and preoccupied with national rather than party problems, to its administrative, organizational and research capacity. Funding can also prove a problem because of the loss of the state funding that automatically flows to opposition parties, although in the case of the Conservatives any shortfall can normally be made up from donations and loans from a business community which is either ideologically inclined towards the party or simply keen to keep in with whichever party is in office. Unfortunately, such funding does have the potential to bring the party into disrepute. Within months of the Coalition being formed, for instance, the Tories were facing awkward questions about fundraising activities that seemed to offer privileged access to ministers and about the business dealings and tax affairs of some of their wealthiest donors. As a result, the man announced as the Party's new Treasurer, David Rowland, never took up the role, which would instead continue to be played by Stanley Fink, who has for some time used his vast wealth, accumulated in part through hedge funds, to fund the party centrally and to make donations to, for example, Boris Johnson's successful campaign for the London mayoralty.

The task of ensuring that, despite such stories, the party in central office maintained its capacity and its morale would be down to Andrew Feldman and Sayeeda Warsi, appointed as co-chairman – a division of responsibility that has been tried before under Michael Howard's leadership (when Maurice Saatchi and Liam Fox shared the job) but didn't work out very well. Feldman (a long-term personal friend of Cameron's and very much a backroom figure rather than a public face) wasted little time in authorizing managerial reform, some of which – as occurs after most elections – involved job losses at the margins as well as some initially disruptive reorganization of roles and responsibilities between both individuals and departments at CCHQ (Conservative Campaign Headquarters, formerly Central Office). Stephen Gilbert, the Director of Campaigning, wasted no time, for instance, in restructuring his department so that its field operations are organized into four large zones, while new Voluntary Party Managers were introduced to develop and improve the party organization in constituencies. More generally, back office functions at CCHQ were almost immediately streamlined and the new post of Chief Operating Officer created to oversee them, although whether this will see an improvement in the party's chronically chaotic membership operation and its Merlin IT system is open to debate. The same sense of urgency applied with regard to candidates, with an application deadline of November 2010 imposed and initial selection panels being held in the first half of 2011. The Coalition's declared preference for a fixed term of five years is well known, but it would seem the Conservatives are keen to ensure they are ready if the election has to come earlier.

The main responsibility for maintaining morale and front of house until that election is still largely the responsibility of the co-chairman, Warsi – one of the few women, and the only person from an ethnic minority, sitting around a Cabinet table largely occupied on the Conservative side by colleagues who were largely white (95 per cent), male (80 per cent), independently educated (60 per cent) and extremely wealthy (if press reports that all but four of them are worth over a million are true). Inevitably this gave rise to whispers, within the party as well as without, about tokenism – whispers that only grew louder after Warsi failed to impress early on in the other essential task of the Party Chairman – handling the media. Cameron's decision to appoint Michael Fallon MP (a shrewd and smooth media performer) as Deputy Chairman suggested he sensed there was indeed a gap that badly needed filling.

The Party in the Country

A survey conducted in July 2009 found that the average age of the grassroots Conservative Party member (three-quarters of whom are in occupational groups ABC1) was 55, although those who were 55 and older made up 60 per cent of the total membership. Although generally right-wing (on a scale of 1–7 they rated themselves on average at 5.62), those members were by no means all the 'swivel-eyed' extremists of legend, either on the state–market (i.e. left–right) dimension or the authoritarian–libertarian dimension used to tap into attitudes on issues like Europe, crime, immigration and attitudes to gender, morality and sexuality. About a quarter could be described as liberal (pro-market but outward-looking and tolerant of difference), with the rest equally divided between what one might term Thatcherites (pro-market with little time for, say, Europe, immigration and 'progressive' policies on crime and the environment), on the one hand, and 'traditionalists' (quite authoritarian but centrist on public spending and taxation), on the other. It is this ideological balance, along with the good deal Cameron managed to get and the fact grassroots members were simply glad to be back in government, that helps explain why he had relatively little trouble convincing them that the decision to enter Coalition was the right one.

That said, 'Team Cameron' made a concerted effort from the start to reassure both Tory members and voters (and probably MPs as well) that, as Cameron stressed in numerous newspaper articles and interviews over the weekend of 21–23 May, he was still a *Conservative* Prime Minister delivering an agenda on immigration, Europe, spending cuts and education and health reform, of which they could be proud. Most were prepared at least to 'suck it and see', even if they had some reservations, especially on constitutional reform, community sentences and a lack of tax cuts. ConservativeHome's reader surveys showed a growing but not necessarily universal belief that the Coalition was good, not only for the country (because of the need to cut the deficit in a way that a minority government could not have pushed through) but also for the party itself.

Senior Tories need not worry, then, at least for the moment, that the inevitable grumbling about this or that policy will turn into a grassroots revolt against the Coalition. But they are concerned – understandably so – about their on-going failure to attract new members and hold on to existing ones: the party lost approximately 80,000 members between 2005 and 2010, by which time the total had dropped to around 177,000. The 2009 membership survey suggests that no more than a third of party members consider themselves active – and even that figure would come a surprise to many of those who actually deliver leaflets and knock on doors. Moreover, there is no sign of a new generation of young Conservatives falling over each other to sign up or, having signed up, to do much, although this may change as the young and ambitious are attracted to what, at least initially, looks like a party that may stay in government for some time. The problem, however, is that being in office – a period when traditionally British parties do little to reform or rebuild their grassroots organization – is unlikely to help the Tories reverse the long-term trend, even if that trend has nothing to do with Coalition *per se*.

The Liberal Democrats[2]

In Parliament

The Liberal Democrats in Parliament no longer all fit into one taxi but can still just about squeeze in to the Whips' Office. Whether, however, they continue to see themselves as one big happy family is debateable – especially after the three-way split that occurred over the raising of the cap on university tuition fees in December 2010. At the General Election the party held 49 seats, lost 13 and gained eight, a net loss of five. The most notable change was the loss of some of the party's most colourful characters, including Lembit Opik, whose extra-parliamentary activities were blamed for losing the previously safe Lib-Dem seat of Montgomeryshire to the Conservatives, and Evan Harris, who lost his Oxford West & Abingdon seat to the Conservatives by 176 votes, after his pro-euthanasia stance earned him the nickname 'Dr Death'. The parliamentary party remains all white and 88 per cent male (Cracknell, 2010). The party fielded fewer women than in 2005, female candidates dropping to 22 per cent of the total, and had just four ethnic minority candidates in the top 100 target seats. Of the 57 MPs the majority are from business backgrounds, closely followed by those from the political, PR and charity sectors, the rest working in education. Non-graduates and non-professionals can be counted on the fingers of one hand and the MPs' educational profile is close to that of the Conservatives, with 40 per cent of its MPs having attended private school and 28 per cent with degrees from Oxford or Cambridge (Sutton Trust, 2010). In keeping with the flavour of the 1997 intake, over half the current parliamentary party have at some time been elected as local councillors.

While the election had little significant impact on the party's inability to reflect its electorate, it represented a seismic shift in other ways. Nick Clegg effectively tried to change the Liberal Democrats from a party of opposition to a party of government – a move with immediate, but also potentially far-reaching, practical consequences. Most obviously, the party has lost its right to 'Short money' – state funding to opposition parties to support the cost of their official duties, calculated using a combination of money per seat won and money per votes cast. The injection of funds the party received in 1997, when it more than doubled its number of MPs, enabled it to organize and mount a significantly more professional operation at Westminster and at its headquarters in Cowley Street. The party introduced specialist researchers attached to parliamentary portfolios and began to operate a Shadow Cabinet as well as improving the party's press and media function. Reliance on this income, amounting to approximately £2 million a year and representing around a third of the party's overall annual income, should not be underestimated. The party now has to rely entirely on membership subscriptions and private donations in order to survive.

One way in which the party is adapting to this is to have staff 'seconded' from companies that share an interest and expertise in complex policy issues. Individual MPs continue to employ non-specialist research and secretarial support in Westminster and in their constituencies, paid for by their individual office costs allowance. The Parliamentary Office of the Liberal Democrats (POLD), which provided specialist researchers and support to the parliamentary party, has, however, undergone a profound change. In the days that followed the Coalition Agreement, POLD was forced to take immediate action to make more than half its staff redundant, reducing the party's press and research function dramatically. The reduction of the POLD operation has all the more significance when combined with the impact of a large growth in professional support offered to Liberal Democrat ministers through government-paid Special Advisers, most drawn from the parties own ranks – obvious examples include Alison Suttie, a long-term member of party staff and now Clegg's Special Adviser, and Duncan Brack, former long-term chair of the party's federal conference committee and director of policy and member of the Policy Committee, now Special Adviser to Chris Huhne. Liberal Democrat MPs without a government position, however, are left without the research and the media support they might need, for instance, to scrutinize legislation brought by those departments in which the party has no representation. It also places serious constraints on their ability to develop policy independently of government in preparation for future election campaigns.

This feeds into a potential rupture between the team in government, who meet on a weekly basis, both with and without their Conservative partners, and the parliamentary party. The Leader's Office, once an important centre off the committee corridor in the Palace of Westminster, is now virtually deserted. Occupying their new offices, and less likely to bump into party colleagues and exchange pleasantries, has distanced the leader and his team of ministers from the rest of the parliamentary party. This would be common practice for larger parties, already at a distance from their leader, but in a party of just 57 MPs, whose survival tactics in the late 1980s and 1990s produced a tight-knit and defiant political unit, it comes as something of a culture shock. The hope – not altogether forlorn – was that electing Simon Hughes as deputy leader would offset all this. But he will find it difficult to counter any division that opens up between Liberal Democrat MPs based on who they are challenged by in their constituencies – Conservatives or Labour: the tuition fees debacle demonstrated that even those MPs traditionally on the radical wing of the party are prepared to back the Coalition if they are in constituencies that face little real threat from Labour.

Cowley Street

The party's headquarters in Cowley Street have also undergone significant change. Chris Fox, a man with considerable experience in corporate communications, joined Cowley Street as Director of Communications in 2008, and succeeded Chris Rennard as Chief Executive in 2009. His predecessor was well known in the party as a by-election and campaign chief, credited with much of the party's revival in the 1980s and 1990s, but whose skills at overseeing party HQ were less obvious. Fox, by contrast, has professional experience outside the party and a reputation for disliking the culture of 'martyrdom' that has pervaded HQ. He has recruited from outside party ranks, supported by HQ Operations Director Ben Stoneham, previously HR Director at News International, and has been successful in transforming the fundraising, candidates and conference departments. Cowley Street has been slowly but surely shifting away from its volunteer culture, towards a more professional and business-like operation. How far this transformation can proceed given the reduction in funds and staff, and the potential to depend once again on amateur volunteers, remains to be seen. In addition to this, the real test for party HQ – now less concerned with policy research and media, and more with campaigning and membership – is how successful it will be in devising a campaign that both supports the Government with which it is in partnership, while campaigning against the party with which it shares power.

The Party in the Country

The Liberal Democrats are a federal party, created in 1988 out of the merger of the Liberal Party and SDP, with a lengthy constitution which commits the party, in theory at least, to internal democracy. In practice the grassroots members elect the leader, members of various internal committees and the party president, as well as voting on policy at the twice yearly federal conference. Ordinary members provide income, local campaigners, Focus leaflet deliverers, prospective candidates and councillors. The party has learned that without ordinary members it may not have survived at all. For a time after May 2010 the party reported a significant increase in numbers. In the weeks that followed Coalition, party sources indicated that for every one member leaving eight were joining, which slowed in the months following the election and six months later was reported to be levelling out at two. The Welsh party, for whom figures are available, reported a 12 per cent increase in membership overall between October 2009 and October 2010, a figure supported by anecdotal evidence from individual constituency parties. This was important not only as an indicator of the party's overall support but will, if it continues, have an impact on the character of the party, with the disaffected former Labour supporters it picked up in the mid-2000s leaving, replaced by soft Conservatives. This may, of course, not continue.

Prior to Coalition the Liberal Democrats were already in the throes of change. In his 'first 100 days' Clegg commissioned a wide-ranging and radical review of the party, known as the Bones Commission. Its eventually diluted recommendations have proved bureaucratic and difficult to implement. However, the establishment of a Chief Officers Group (COG) has taken power away from the directly elected Federal Executive (FE) and is responsible for the overall management of the party. The FE nevertheless continues to be the vehicle through which the party's ordinary membership can at least demonstrate its views. Biennial elections to the FE and Federal Policy Committee were conducted in November 2010 and show the first example of the grassroots operating factional 'slates' against the leadership. Although not uniformly convened on this basis, the make-up of the new FPC is weighted in favour of those considered to be on the social liberal wing of the party, and the result hailed as a triumph by the party's leftist Social Liberal Forum. The immediate post-Coalition resignation of the Party's President, Ros Scott, also raised a few eyebrows, although the election of her successor, Tim Farron, tipped eventually to replace Clegg, came as no surprise.

The party is proud of its policy-making tradition at federal conference but the autumn conference in particular has become more important to the party as a fundraising and training event than for policy debates in the main hall. The opportunity remains, though, for representatives to use the conference to voice opposition to the leader if they so wish. As the debate over tuition fees has demonstrated, policy passed at conference, which becomes the manifesto on which MPs are elected, is now supposedly subordinate to the Coalition Agreement into which Clegg led his party. And the mood at the 2010 autumn conference was that the policies contained in that document, and the things that were left out, were necessary compromises. The party faithful were quiet, earnest, slightly swooning and largely in agreement. The notable rise in the numbers of lobbyists, media and increased security added to the more serious, largely cooperative atmosphere. How long this will last remains a moot point, especially after the tuition fees row and with other issues – notably control orders and the cutbacks in local government spending – bound to provoke grassroots suspicion.

Conclusion

The Conservative–Liberal Democrat Coalition was a gamble for both parties, but perhaps a bigger gamble for Clegg than for Cameron. Clegg and his colleagues calculated that their party would ultimately gain more by putting an end to the argument that a vote for the Liberal Democrats was a vote wasted than they would by sitting on the sidelines and then facing a second, unaffordable election. Clegg has also taken a leap of faith in hoping that the public (especially in those northern cities that came over to the Liberal Democrats under Kennedy) will be sufficiently impressed by his taking governmental responsibility to forgive him – at least in time – for cuts in public services and for abandoning various pre-election commitments. So far, the biggest 'hit' has been taken in the opinion polls. The immediate impact on the party itself has not proved as catastrophic as some predicted, and the leader still has some aces to play. He has already promoted 19 of his 57 parliamentary colleagues to office and held all but three of them to the Coalition Agreement on policies they oppose, such as tuition fees. He enjoys the professional might of the civil service, the title of Deputy Prime Minister and the profile the party has long craved. If opposition inside the party grows, it may turn to Hughes as deputy leader and/or Farron as Party President, but they have little real power. Party HQ now has a largely perfunctory role and is weakened by dwindling resources, while the party conference and elected federal committees can voice opposition, but do little to effect change. Clegg's task is to play to these strengths and play the long game, relying in the meantime on his supporters within the party to win over their more reluctant colleagues, as well as on a tradition of coalition at the local level making people realistic about what can be achieved in a tight financial environment. The stakes could not be higher. If Clegg succeeds, he will have broken the two-party monopoly but, if he fails, he risks relegating the Liberal Democrats to opposition for decades. With that in mind, most in the party will try to remain supportive.

For Cameron, too, the decision to aim for, and stay in, a coalition was clearly not without risk. But it was by far the least worst option. A minority government (assuming it had been allowed to form in the first place) would have found it difficult to get its programme – especially its deficit reduction programme – through. A coalition with the Liberal Democrats not only provided political cover for cuts and other contentious measures. It also undermined the long-cherished aspiration (assumption even) among so-called progressives that one day a Lib-Lab Coalition would mobilize the supposedly natural 'anti-Tory' majority in the electorate to lock the Conservatives out of power, possibly forever. In so doing Cameron has won the grudging admiration rather than the undying gratitude of his parliamentary party, parts of which remain suspicious that he will use the demands of Coalition as an excuse to thwart their Thatcherite ambitions. Some grassroots Conservatives share those suspicions, but most, like their parliamentary counterparts, are glad to be back in government and have, if anything, warmed to the idea of Coalition – a development that should surely come as a surprise given the party's gloomy predictions of what would happen to the country were a hung parliament ever to materialize. As for party staffers, their main hope is that the leadership does not, as so often occurs in government, ignore the continued need to maintain the Conservatives' research and campaigning capacity, especially at a time when, because of the inevitable dip in popularity and the seemingly inexorable decline in membership, money may be tight.

The outcome of any leap in the dark is by definition hard to predict, and commitment to the Coalition varies not only between but within the two parties that make it up. For the Liberal Democrats at Westminster, and indeed in the party in the country, although individual policies, such as tuition fees, may create division and unease, commitment to the Coalition appears solid, and factionalism is not (yet) in the party's nature. Most genuinely believe – and will probably continue to do so unless the party's poll rating stays resolutely stuck in single figures – that it is in their best interest to hang on in there for what they hope will be their just reward. That said, the loss of the referendum on AV could be hard to bear and, together with simultaneous losses at elections in Scotland and Wales, might precipitate an exodus of members and even calls to end the Coalition. An alternative response – closer cooperation with the Conservatives, whether it be through a merger or simply a deal not to field candidates against one another – is likely to be a step too far for the party's activist base. Likewise, Conservative constituency associations are unlikely to take kindly to CCHQ telling them they may not select and stand their own man (or woman) in 2015. It is the sincere belief and hope among many Tories, after all, that Cameron's embrace of the Liberal Democrats will prove fatal to the latter, leaving the country no option, unless it is prepared to give Labour another try, to elect a Conservative majority government next time round.

Notes

1. Although full sources for the following account can be found in the Afterword to Bale (2011), we would nonetheless like to acknowledge here our debt to Byron Criddle for the data on MPs, Sarah Childs and Paul Webb for the data on party members, and ConservativeHome for information on grassroots opinion and on developments at CCHQ.
2. Evidence for changes to the Liberal Democrats are based on a series of non-attributable interviews conducted in 2009 and 2010 by Emma Sanderson-Nash and Elizabeth Evans, which are examined in greater detail in their forthcoming paper in the *British Journal of Politics and International Relations*.

References

Bale, T. (2011) *The Conservative Party from Thatcher to Cameron* (Cambridge: Polity).

Cowley, P. and Stuart, M. (2009) A Long Way from Equidistance – Liberal Democrat Voting in Parliament 1997–2007. *revolts.co.uk*. www.revolts.co.uk/A%20long%20way%20from%20equidistance.pdf.

Dorey, P., Garnett, M. and Denham, A. (2011) *From Crisis to Coalition: the Conservative Party from 1997 to 2010* (Basingstoke: Palgrave Macmillan).

Evans, E. and Sanderson-Nash, E. (forthcoming) Sandals to Suits – Professionalization, Coalition and the Liberal Democrats. *British Journal of Politics and International Relations*.

Hickson, K. (2010). *The Political Thought of the Liberals and Liberal Democrats since 1945* (Manchester: Manchester University Press).

Katz, R. and Mair, P. (1994) *How Parties Organize: Change and Adaptation in Party Organizations in Western Democracies* (London: Sage).

Lee, S. and Beech, M. (2009) *The Conservatives under David Cameron: Built to Last?* (Basingstoke: Palgrave Macmillan).

Russell, A. and Fieldhouse, E. (2005) *Neither Left nor Right? The Liberal Democrats and the Electorate* (Manchester: Manchester University Press).

16
The End of New Labour?
The Future for the Labour Party

Kevin Hickson

Introduction

The purpose of this chapter is to assess the impact of the Conservative–
Liberal Democrat Coalition on the Labour Party. What future is there
for the Labour Party? Any conclusions made in this chapter must be
tentative for much depends on how long the Coalition lasts. In early
December 2010, at the height of the university fees issue, it looked as if
the strains of the Coalition were starting to tell, among Liberal Democrats
at least. However, for a number of reasons it seems that the Coalition may
last. What is perhaps surprising about the Coalition Government is how
radical and ideologically unified it has been. Other chapters in the book
have addressed this in more detail, but it seems that for the time being
at least the so-called *Orange Book* Liberal Democrats have taken charge
of the party and that they share much in common with contemporary
Conservatism in terms of a sceptical attitude towards the central state and
a strong preference for localism, markets and voluntary activity. David

Cameron and Nick Clegg have developed a strong working relationship and neither of the Coalition partners would seek to end the Coalition early for fear of electoral defeat in an ensuing General Election.

Added to this is the fact that the 2010 General Election result was the second worse defeat for the Labour Party since 1922, eclipsed only by the 1983 result under the leadership of Michael Foot with the 'longest suicide note in history' as the manifesto was famously termed by Gerald Kaufman. Gordon Brown had staggered from crisis to crisis as Prime Minister, appearing to lack direction despite wanting the job for over a decade (Seldon and Lodge, 2010). If anything, the bias in the voting system helped the Labour Party and changes to parliamentary boundaries proposed by the Coalition to make constituencies an equal size based on electoral registers will end this pro-Labour bias.

All of this would suggest that an evaluation of the future prospects of the Labour Party ought to be pessimistic. It would seem that the Coalition is here to last, and even if there were to be an early General Election, the Labour Party does not appear to be in a financial position to contest it effectively (Fisher, 2010). Thus appears the Labour Party's fate.

However, the tone of this chapter is more optimistic for reasons that will become clear in the course of the discussion. The Labour Party is actually in a much better position than may at first appear to be the case. Despite constant sniping in the press and attempted coups to replace him as leader, Brown actually managed to avert an electoral wipe-out. The Labour Party managed to remain united through a long leadership contest that was essentially a choice between two brothers and the unpopularity of the Coalition was readily apparent by the end of 2010. The cuts in public expenditure and increases in VAT could further erode the popularity of the Coalition in 2011. The chapter will begin with an analysis of the nature of New Labour and then discuss the outcome of the 2010 General Election for Labour, the leadership contest and the ways in which Ed Miliband has sought to respond to the Coalition.

Fatalism and Labour Politics

Andrew Gamble has made a distinction between politics and fate (Gamble, 2000). Fatalism is the opposite of politics. Fate is associated with arguments that there is no fundamental choice to be made in politics any more. It is concerned with 'endism' – the idea that we are at an end state which is irreversible. Such end-state arguments include the idea that we are at the end of history in terms of the end of the broad clash of ideologies. Moreover, the nation-state is also said to be at an end with the triumph of globalization. Capitalism has won and those ideologies, notably socialism, which seek to challenge capitalism are defeated permanently. We are fated to live under neoliberal, global capitalism. This marks the death of politics, which is about making fundamental choices about the kind of government, economy and society under which we wish to live. Gamble rejects such end-state arguments, arguing that there are still fundamental choices in both the national and international political arenas.

In British politics, fatalism is a feature principally of traditionalist conservatives who have argued for generations that civilization, as they appreciate it, is coming to an end. Such was the argument made by Lord Salisbury in the nineteenth century, when he argued that the forces of democracy and liberalism were leading to the disintegration of civil society. Some leading Conservative intellectuals in the middle of the twentieth century argued that the postwar welfare state was destructive of traditional morality and, more recently, Roger Scruton has argued that 'England' as a political idea has died. Such pessimistic Tory notions contrast with more combative strands within Conservative thought (Scruton, 2000; Aughey, 2005).

What has this to do with the Labour Party? After all, the Labour Party is surely based on political optimism – the desire to build the 'new Jerusalem', a crusade for social and economic reforms leading to a more inclusive, equal and just society. However, I shall argue that the Labour Party is in fact also infected with such a fatalistic attitude.

The essence of this fatalism is to argue that there is a trade-off between political principle and electoral success. The Labour left often regarded itself as the 'keeper of the faith', the ideologically pure within the party untainted by a desire to sacrifice its principles in order to win elections. Such was the argument by leading figures on the Labour left in the two long periods of Opposition after 1945: 1951–64 and 1979–97. In the 1950s Richard Crossman argued that it was better for the Labour Party to remain in opposition as eventually there would be a moment of crisis and the demand for socialism would be overwhelming, so that the Labour Party could win without sacrificing its principles (Beech and Hickson, 2007). The Bevanites claimed that they were seeking to preserve the Labour Party as a socialist movement against the electoral expediency of the Revisionists, especially at the time of the Clause Four controversy. Tony Benn made a similar argument, that he and his followers were also seeking to defend the cause of socialism against the modernization under the leadership of Neil Kinnock, with some even arguing that the Labour Party lost the 1992 General Election because it wasn't socialist enough, despite the absence of any evidence to support this claim (Heffernan and Marqusee, 1992).

The Labour right often obliged by saying that without abandoning its more radical policies the party could not win. The starkest example of this was New Labour, which was essentially an exercise in political fatalism. The New Labour leadership argued that in order to win a General Election it needed to abandon its socialist, or some would even argue its social democratic, aspirations.

There were three irreversible forces at work which political argument could not change. The first was the power of the press in determining election outcomes. The significance of the 1992 General Election outcome in shaping the attitude of the modernizers within the Labour Party cannot be overstated. The opinion polls famously got it wrong and showed that Labour was on course for victory. On polling day, the *Sun* warned voters of the consequences of a Labour victory and then claimed that it had won the election for the Conservatives. Academic analysis has always been sceptical of this claim, but the New Labour elite were convinced that they could not win without the support of Rupert Murdoch and went a long way to obtain his support. In 1997, the *Sun* supported Labour and this appeared to confirm the strategy of the Labour leadership. However, it was more likely that the *Sun* was following public opinion rather than shaping it. Much of New Labour politics from 1997 onwards was framed in terms of appealing to what remained an essentially right-wing press, and this explains the dominance of the 'spin doctors'.

Second, New Labour politics was shaped by focus group findings of what 'middle England' wanted. This seemed sensible enough. There was an attempt to appeal to what Anthony Downs termed the 'median voter' and the centre ground of public opinion was firmly to the right of where it had been prior to 1979 (Downs, 1957). However, New Labour appeared to rule out the possibility that through the presentation of socialist or overtly social democratic arguments, public opinion could be moved decisively. Again, this constituted a form of political fatalism. It was not that there were no social democratic successes – clearly there were – but that these were not expressed in an overtly social democratic *narrative*, to use the fashionable term. Social democratic policies such as redistribution were often done more by 'stealth' and increased public expenditure was financed largely by the fiscal dividends of economic growth than by more progressive forms of taxation, which would have required a political strategy to win people over by force of argument. The consequence of this was that when economic growth ended abruptly, as it did in 2007, there was a sharp increase in the public sector deficit

(Smith, 2010). When faced with a much more formidable opposition in the form of David Cameron and his plan for a 'big society', New Labour was found lacking in its social democratic defence of the central state.

Finally, New Labour accepted the fate of the nation-state in the face of globalization. Indeed, Brown's economic policy was strongly supportive of a deregulated financial sector as Simon Lee has shown in numerous publications (notably Lee, 2007).

All of this calls into question the extent to which New Labour succeeded in its 'politics of dominance' (Beech, 2008). Of course, it was dominant electorally. Blair won handsomely in 1997 and again in 2001. Even the 2005 result can be regarded as a fairly comfortable win given the legacy of the Iraq War. It seems unlikely that any other leader could have secured the victory on the scale that Blair did in 1997. However, it is worth pointing out that Labour's lead in the opinion polls pre-dated Blair's election as leader, in fact dating from Black Wednesday in September 1992. Despite the claims of the *Sun* it seems more likely that Labour lost in 1992 as the Conservatives were still more trusted to manage the economy (along with concerns over Labour's tax pledges). This trust was shattered when Britain was forced to withdraw from the Exchange Rate Mechanism, despite the fact that the British economy actually improved once free from this European entanglement. It therefore seems fair to conclude that had Labour had another leader and had not become 'New Labour' it could well have won in 1997, by which time the feeling that it was 'time for a change' was overwhelming, especially as John Major's Government was damaged by allegations of sleaze. Successive Conservative leaders failed to respond effectively to Blair and the party was split over Europe for a long time after 1997, to the extent that it rejected the one person who might have had a reasonable chance of challenging the dominance of Blair – Kenneth Clarke. The argument above suggests that in terms of policy, and even more so governing philosophy, New Labour was never dominant.

The 2010 General Election and the Challenge for the Labour Party

The results of the 2010 General Election have been analysed elsewhere in this book and in at least two other significant studies published in the months after the Election (Geddes and Tonge, 2010; Kavanagh and Cowley, 2010). The purpose here is not to repeat this analysis, but to point to the relevant facts on which the Labour Party must begin its recovery.

The results of the 2010 General Election are set out in Table 16.1.

Table 16.1 2010 General Election Results

Party	Votes (%)	Net Change from 2005	Seats won	Net change from 2005 (%)
Conservative	36.1	+3.8	307	+97
Labour	29.0	−6.2	258	−91
Liberal Democrat	23.0	+1.0	57	−5

Source: BBC (2010a).

This represents Labour's second worse electoral result since the 1920s (surpassed only by 1983) on a swing from Labour to the Conservatives of 5 per cent. Labour's total vote was down to 8,609,527. Labour performed worse in all electoral regions apart from Scotland. Although this may be thought to be because of its decline in support among the middle-class voters it had won over in 1997, it was largely due to a decline in C1/C2 voters (lower middle/upper working-class voters) (Geddes and Tonge, 2010: 284).

Although these results were undoubtedly poor for the Labour Party they were not as bad as had been feared at the height of one of the many crises of confidence the party had during Brown's leadership, with the last plot to overthrow him taking place at the start of 2010. They were also not as good as Cameron's Conservatives had hoped, failing to secure an overall majority, but at the same time ensuring that they were by some margin the largest party and the only one to significantly improve its share of votes and seats. The Liberal Democrats had a net loss of seats despite a 1 per cent increase in votes. Although disappointing for Clegg, who had failed to build decisively on the 2005 performance by Charles Kennedy, he found himself in the position of holding the balance of power. Although there was speculation of a 'rainbow Coalition' dominated by Labour under Brown or an alternative leader, the parliamentary arithmetic favoured a Conservative–Liberal Democrat Coalition, which was the eventual outcome.

After earlier election defeats, the Labour Party faced deep and damaging ideological splits between its left- and right-wing factions, such as those that occurred after 1951 and 1979. One reason for the Labour Party to be optimistic was that this did not occur after the 2010 defeat and is unlikely to do so. The leadership contest (discussed below) highlighted the degree of ideological unity within the party, certainly compared to the earlier periods.

The result is that the Labour Party has been able to bounce back quickly from defeat, at least in terms of its opinion poll ratings. Since Ed Miliband was elected leader on 25 September 2010 the Labour and Conservative Parties have been very close in the opinion polls and by the end of the year, Labour had a small lead. For instance, on 20 December a poll recorded Labour on 42 per cent, the Conservatives down to 40 per cent, the Liberal Democrats (having slumped since entering the Coalition) 9 per cent and all others on 9 per cent. Translated into seats on current parliamentary boundaries this would give Labour 357 seats, the Conservatives 257, the Liberal Democrats 11 and the others 25, thus giving Labour an overall majority (BBC, 2010b). John Curtice has argued that the traditional defence of the first-past-the-post electoral system – namely, that it produced 'strong' government with a large overall majority in the House of Commons – had not worked in 2010 and that it was unlikely to do so in the future for a number of reasons (Curtice, 2010). However, should the unpopularity of the Coalition last, then it seems likely that the traditional role of the current electoral system, assuming that the referendum in 2011 does not result in a change in the electoral system, will reassert itself at the next General Election. It seems sensible on the current polling evidence for Labour to seek to govern by itself after the next General Election rather than adopt a pluralist approach as some have argued it now should, taking votes from the Conservatives and the Liberal Democrats (Rawnsley, 2010).

The Leadership Contest and Beyond

Brown's decision to resign as leader of the Labour Party immediately after the General Election was not a surprise. There was a sense that his leadership always lacked authority because of the way in which he was appointed rather than elected leader. There was therefore a need for a thorough leadership contest to decide his successor. One outcome of such a high-profile and long drawn-out leadership contest, combined with fallout from the Coalition Agreement, was for Labour Party membership to increase substantially after a period of decline under Blair's and Brown's premierships.

The initial favourites were David Miliband and Ed Balls. Both had been prominent within the rival Blairite and Brownite factions. Miliband had been Blair's chief policy adviser before the 1997 General Election, having previously worked for the centre-left think tank the Institute of Public Policy Research (IPPR), including serving as Secretary to the Commission on Social Justice, established by John Smith in 1992. He became Head of the Number 10 Policy Unit and shortly after being elected as an MP in 2001, became a Cabinet Minister. He rose to the position of Foreign Secretary upon Brown becoming leader in 2007. He was frequently associated with plots to remove Brown, although the extent to which he orchestrated such moves is doubtful, and he lost support among the other leading Blairites after failing to grasp the challenge. However, as there was no other leading Blairite candidate in the leadership contest, he won the support of the Blairites, developing such momentum that he was the clear initial favourite, winning the nominations of a substantial number of MPs (81 nominations) and significant financial support.

Ed Balls had long been associated with the Brown camp, indeed he was probably the most loyal Brownite. He served as economic adviser to Brown prior to 1997 and at the Treasury. He became an MP in 2005, was appointed as a Minister in 2006 and became a Cabinet Minister the following year. In a straight contest with Miliband, Balls would have expected to obtain the support of the Labour left, including the majority of the trade unions, although he only secured the minimum number of nominations from MPs required under party rules.

The decision of Ed Miliband to stand for the leadership was therefore a blow to both of the initial frontrunners. It was seen as highly unlikely that he would challenge his older brother, who had been quick off the blocks. However, not only did he do so but was to set out a different stall from that of his brother, which would see him challenge from the 'left' obtaining much of the trade union support that had been expected to go to Balls. The difficulty for the older Miliband and for Balls was that they were too closely associated with the rival factions that had so destabilized New Labour. This was despite that fact that Ed Miliband had also been a close associate of Brown's. However, he was less antagonistic to the Blairites, who apparently viewed him as the 'emissary from planet "fuck"'(the way in which the Brown camp was described) (Brady and Shields, 2010). He had also been prepared to speak out against the tactics of the party leadership during the Crewe and Nantwich by-election in 2007, when the Tory candidate, Edward Timpson, had been labelled a 'toff' (Seldon and Lodge, 2010: 100). He was much less associated with plots than was Balls, and he was also seen as a better communicator and less 'geeky' than his older brother.

Ed Miliband obtained the support of prominent left-wing members of the Brown Cabinet (to the extent that there were any recognizable ideological camps) including Hilary Benn and Peter Hain, together with the support of Neil Kinnock and Roy Hattersley (Hattersley, 2010) and six of the major trade unions. The consistent theme of Ed Miliband's leadership campaign was that there was cause for the Labour Party to be optimistic, as the opening quote to this chapter demonstrates. Above all, he appeared more able to break free of the New Labour mind-set on key issues such as the Iraq War, where he stated in his acceptance speech that it had been a mistake, leading to the famous exchange between David Miliband and Harriet Harman, which really demonstrated how the older Miliband was much less flexible in his intellectual outlook.

Of the other potential candidates, no one really stood a serious chance of winning. Andy Burnham, who had been Health Secretary under Brown, ran an effective campaign and attracted significant local following but was squeezed out by the main contenders. Diane Abbott stood as the left-wing candidate, but only after a deal had been struck whereby John McDonnell would not stand (despite having more support among MPs) and when some notable right-wing MPs such as David Miliband and Jack Straw decided to support her so she would meet the required number of nominations. She failed to make inroads into the support of the other candidates during the long campaign. Jon Cruddas may well have proved to be a popular candidate among party members and trade unionists, but decided not to stand and later supported David Miliband. Yvette Cooper, who some regarded as a leader in waiting, decided to support her husband, Balls. Alan Johnson also refused to stand, despite being far more experienced than the other candidates.

The results are set out in Table 16.2. The leadership was decided by a complex voting system, whereby the candidate obtaining the least votes would be eliminated and their next preference votes reallocated until one candidate emerged with 50 per cent of the vote. The electoral college, consisting of MPs and MEPs, party members and trade unionists and other affiliated socialist societies, was the consequence of deals struck in 1993 when John Smith had introduced 'one member one vote'. In fact, it turned out that one member may have several votes as they could be an MP, a trade union member and a member of various other affiliated socialist societies. The initial lead was held by David Miliband, with Diane Abbott, Andy Burnham and Ed Balls being eliminated in that order. It was only in the final round that Ed Miliband took the lead, and therefore won. The nature of this victory has been an issue facing Ed Miliband. David Miliband was ahead in the first two categories even in the last round, with Ed Miliband only winning the contest on the trade union/affiliates section. It could be argued in Ed Miliband's favour that the electoral college reflects the reality that Labour is a broad movement, representing the fact that it was born out of the trade union movement around the start of the twentieth century. It was also possible to argue that Ed Miliband was the clear winner in terms of the total number of votes cast. Finally, in his defence it would be possible to show that the trade unions allowed for one member, one vote rather than casting a block vote as in some past leadership elections.

Table 16.2   Results of the Labour Party Leadership Contest 2010 (winning figure in each round in bold font)

	Round 1 %	Round 2 %	Round 3 %	Round 4 %
Diane Abbott	7.42			
Andy Burnham	8.68	10.41		
Ed Balls	11.79	13.23	16.02	
David Miliband	**37.78**	**38.89**	**42.72**	49.35
Ed Miliband	34.33	37.47	41.26	**50.65**

Source: *Sunday Telegraph* (2010).

However, the results remain a difficulty. First, Ed Miliband obtained less support among MPs than his brother, even in the final round. This may well be because many MPs came out for David before Ed declared he was a candidate, and it is unlikely that there will be much antagonism directed towards the leader from the backbenches for the foreseeable future. It did mean, however, that there was considerable media attention given to the early performances of Ed Miliband at Prime Minister's Question Time. Cameron had proved to be an effective parliamentary performer as leader of the Opposition at the end of Blair's premiership and also against Brown, who frequently came off worse from the exchanges. Ed Miliband, surprisingly for some, did well at his first attempt at Prime Minister's Question Time and, even though Cameron improved somewhat after the initial exchange, continued to have some success in the run-up to Christmas.

The other problem was that Ed Miliband could be presented as a figure of the 'left' – 'Red Ed' as he was labelled by the Conservative Party and the media (d'Ancona, 2010). He will increasingly be presented as someone under the control of the trade unions in the run-up to the next General Election. For some in the Labour Party this has also been a problem. Shortly after being appointed Shadow Chancellor (see below), Alan Johnson issued a statement saying he was in favour of revisiting the rules for electing party leaders. Other Blairites also spoke in favour of reforms that would allow for only MPs and party members to vote in future leadership contests, with some saying that Blair had missed an opportunity to break the link with the trade unions before the 1997 General Election (Sylvester and Baldwin, 2010). Such statements may sound like sour grapes on the part of those who supported David Miliband, and could not bring themselves to accept the result. There is no doubt a lot of truth in this, but it would seem that Ed Miliband would need to address the nature of Labour Party organization, and not just policy, including the awkward question of how best to revise the rules for the election of party leader under which he was himself elected. The trade unions remain a key source of funding for the Labour Party and any attempt to reduce their influence may well be opposed, so one possible solution would be to have a reduced membership fee for trade union members, while allowing the unions to have an input into policy reviews.

The first challenge for Ed Miliband as leader was to appoint a new Shadow Cabinet (Watt and Wintour, 2010). After some delay, David Miliband decided not to seek election to the Shadow Cabinet. Other long-serving members of the previous Labour Cabinet decided not to seek election (the Cabinet is fully appointed, but the Shadow Cabinet is elected by MPs with a number appointed by the leader), including Jack Straw and Alistair Darling. Two candidates emerged for the important position of Shadow Chancellor: Ed Balls and Yvette Cooper. However, in a surprise move Ed Miliband decided to appoint Alan Johnson to that position. His thinking was no doubt that Johnson had a lot of experience in the previous Labour Cabinet (more than anyone else following the decisions of Straw and Darling not to seek re-election) and that he had been a close supporter of David Miliband, so that his appointment would help to unite the party. He could also show that he was independent and would not have his agenda fixed by the media. The appointment was widely regarded by journalists as a wise one, not least because Johnson would make a stark contrast with the privileged Chancellor and Prime Minister, who were embarking on massive cuts in public expenditure. However, Johnson lacked the economic analysis of Balls and Cooper. Of all the leadership contenders, Balls had spoken most fluently on the economy and had adopted a policy position to the left of all those apart from Abbott (Fabian Society, 2010). Balls had previously been seen to differ from Darling over the speed and scale of public expenditure cuts, while both disagreed with Osborne, who wanted to cut deep and quickly. Cooper had not had the same exposure, but was thought to hold similar opinions.

The issue of the economy, especially public expenditure reductions, will be the major strategic policy dilemma for Ed Miliband. The cuts proposed by Osborne in the Comprehensive Spending Review, just days after the Shadow Cabinet appointments, exposed the thinking that the new Labour leadership has to do on the issue. Osborne argues that cuts in public expenditure are needed to avoid a financial crisis like those seen in Greece and Ireland. The cuts are painful, but unavoidable following the economic 'mess' left behind by the Brown Government. Britain has one of the largest public sector deficits, meaning that if action was not taken to reduce it, then the confidence of the financial markets would be lost. Moreover, public expenditure reductions were needed to free up resources for the wealth-creating private sector, an argument reminiscent of the 'crowding-out' thesis articulated by the economic analysts Bacon and Eltis in the 1970s (Bacon and Eltis, 1976). Although there will be some increases in taxation, the majority of the deficit reduction would come in the form of cuts to public expenditure.

As Chancellor, Darling had argued that the deficit was a natural consequence of the banking crisis, where private sector debt had been taken on by the public sector; and the subsequent recession, where higher spending was needed to kick-start the economy. Reductions in spending would be required, along with tax increases, in order to reduce this deficit, but that this should be at a slower pace than that proposed by Osborne. To cut quickly as the Conservatives were proposing, Darling argued, would lead to a double-dip recession. This was the essence of the debate between the two parties at the General Election. Neither side proposed a radical departure in economic policy, merely disagreeing over how deep and at what speed cuts should be made.

Prior to the General Election, the Liberal Democrats had sided with Labour in this debate. However, this policy was abandoned in favour of Osborne's strategy as part of the Coalition agreement. Clegg and Vince Cable later argued that the more immediate deficit reduction strategy was necessitated by events in Greece, occurring around the time of the Coalition negotiations.

The strategy of Balls, and apparently Cooper, was to argue that the deficit reduction strategy should occur even more slowly than Darling had proposed. This case was made in Government, with Brown apparently in agreement. However, Labour policy was settled in line with the case made by Darling, thus showing the weakness of Brown as Prime Minister. Balls continued to make his case in the leadership contest and appointing him as Shadow Chancellor would have been seen as Ed Miliband endorsing this more radical position, whereas Johnson was known to favour the strategy of the previous government. The essence of the case made against cuts is that the nature of British debt is different from other economies such as Greece, in that the overall debt burden as a proportion of GDP is lower; that public sector debt is a consequence of the banking crisis and recession; that Britain does not face the problems of other EU countries as it is not part of the euro zone; and, finally, that cuts in public expenditure would lead to a situation like that faced in the Republic of Ireland. The deficit should be reduced largely through increases in direct taxation and once economic growth is restored. Arguably, the economic case made by Balls is sound, indeed it is rather reminiscent of the Keynesian-style defence of public expenditure made by Tony Crosland against the proposals of Denis Healey during the 1976 IMF crisis (Hickson, 2005).

On this occasion, the Labour Party does not have to make policy, but it does have to have a clear strategy in 2011 in order to convince the electorate to support it. The problem for the Labour Party is that, first, although it makes economic sense, the case put forward by Balls during the leadership contest is open to the charge of 'deficit denial'. Second, the record of Johnson in opposing the economic policy of the Coalition proved largely ineffective. This at first appeared to be because of his limited understanding of economics, but may well have had something to do with his personal circumstances which led to his surprise resignation in January 2011. The Labour Party needs to develop a clear policy capable of being both rigorous and popular if it is to advance from its perceived economic incompetence in government under Brown. The appointment of Balls as Shadow Chancellor was accompanied with comments from the Labour leadership that there was agreement between the two Ed's. Balls should prove to be a tougher opponent to Osborne but at the same time may be easier for the Coalition to attack given his close association with Brown in government from 1997 onwards and more difficult for the leader of the Opposition to control.

A similar ambiguity over Labour policy is evident when we examine the response to tuition fees. Labour opposed the decision to implement many of the proposals contained in the Browne Review into the future of higher education, despite the fact that it had set up the Browne Review in the first place. It struggled to come up with a clear response to the key decision to raise tuition fees by up to £9,000 per year. This was because Ed Miliband was known to favour a 'graduate tax', but Johnson had previously opposed this and favoured the introduction of tuition fees under the Labour Government. It was therefore relatively easy for the Coalition to expose the weaknesses in Labour's case as they lacked an agreed alternative, despite the fact that the Liberal Democrats were fundamentally split on the issue, with a majority of Liberal Democrat MPs failing to support the measures (there were also several Conservative rebels, including David Davis).

What these two policy issues demonstrate is that it is necessary for the Labour Party to develop a clearer sense of ideological direction under its new leader and also to present a more unified policy position of current issues, while at the same time leaving detailed policy formulation until later in the Parliament. If there was a criticism of Ed Miliband by the end of 2010 it was that he lacked a sense of direction. This was not particularly serious at such an early stage of his leadership but it would become so if he did not articulate such a vision during the early months of 2011. Perhaps the best example to draw from is not the over-emphasized 'Clause Four' moment of Blair's leadership of the Opposition, which was merely symbolic of earlier, much more hard-won reforms to Labour Party ideology, policy and organization. A better example would appear to be the largely forgotten 'Statement of Aims and Values' written by Roy Hattersley, with considerable input from Raymond Plant, in 1988 which led to the Policy Review but which provided a sense of ideological purpose while that Review took place. That Labour went on to lose the 1992 General Election perhaps does not bode well, but the Labour Party finds itself in a much stronger position to engage in such reform than it was in 1987. Moreover, Ed Miliband articulated a different approach from New Labour orthodoxy on foreign policy (notably on Iraq, as stated above) and on civil liberties and showed a sense of ideological direction and an ability to appeal to disillusioned Liberal Democrats. Again, the challenge for Miliband as leader is to develop this further.

Conclusion

In short, what this chapter has argued is that there are grounds for cautious optimism over the future of the Labour Party. The current economic situation, which will be likely to reduce public support for the Conservative-led Coalition in the coming months combined with the Liberal Democrat decision to become a party of the centre-right, thus leaving Labour as the only major 'progressive' party in British politics all bode well for Ed Miliband's leadership. The Labour Party did not undergo the ideological splits that it went into after defeats in 1951 and 1979 and bounced back quite quickly after the 2010 defeat. It is therefore the necessary task of Ed Miliband to formulate a clear ideological vision based on the optimism he consistently emphasized in the leadership contest and to formulate clearer policy positions on the big issues of the day. Such is the nature of contemporary British politics and the traditional fatalism of the Labour Party, and in particular New Labour, which said that there was a trade-off between socialist values on the one hand and electoral popularity on the other seems no longer relevant. It may well be possible to formulate radical policies on the economy, education and civil liberties, to name but a few, which are based on social democratic values and are also popular with the electorate.

All of this must of course be tentative since the longer-term consequences of the Coalition's policies, particularly on the economy, are unknown. Should the Coalition survive until, and the economy improve by, 2015, then the Labour Party may well remain in Opposition. If it does, then the future of the Labour Party looks bleak, but for now at least there is cause for optimism.

Note

I am very grateful to Lord Kinnock for granting me a long interview, held in the House of Lords on 23 November 2010 on which this chapter draws.

References

Aughey, A. (2005) Traditional Toryism. In K. Hickson (ed.), *The Political Thought of the Conservative Party since 1945* (Basingstoke: Palgrave Macmillan).
Bacon, R. and Eltis, W. (1976) *Britain's Economic Problem: Too Few Producers* (London: Macmillan).
BBC (2010a) news.bbc.co.uk/1/shared/election2010/results (accessed 20 December 2010).
BBC (2010b) news.bbc.co.uk/1/hi/uk_politics/election_2010/8609989.stm (accessed 20 December 2010).
Beech, M. (2008) New Labour and the Politics of Dominance. In M. Beech and S. Lee (eds.), *Ten Years of New Labour* (Basingstoke: Palgrave Macmillan).
Beech, M. and Hickson, K. (2007) *Labour's Thinkers* (London: I.B. Tauris).
Brady, B. and Shields, R. (2010) The Meek vs. the Geek: brothers Miliband Battle it out. *The Independent*, 16 May.
Curtice, J. (2010) So What Went Wrong with the Electoral System? The 2010 Election Result and the Debate about Electoral Reform. In A. Geddes and J. Tonge (eds.), *Britain Votes 2010* (Oxford: Oxford University Press).
d'Ancona, M. (2010) David Cameron Has Just Won the Next General Election. *The Sunday Telegraph*, 26 September.
Downs, A. (1957) *An Economic Theory of Democracy* (New York: Harper & Row).
Fabian Society (2010) *The Labour Leadership* (London: Fabian Society, online pamphlet).
Fisher, J. (2010) Party Finance: Normal Service Resumed? In A. Geddes and J. Tonge (eds.), *Britain Votes 2010* (Oxford: Oxford University Press).
Gamble, A. (2000) *Politics and Fate* (Cambridge: Polity).
Geddes, A. and Tonge, J. (eds.) (2010) *Britain Votes 2010* (Oxford: Oxford University Press).
Hattersley, R. (2010) Britain Will Back a Genuinely Radical Party with an Unapologetically Radical Leader. *The Observer*, 26 September.

Heffernan, R. and Marqusee, M. (1992) *Defeat from the Jaws of Victory: Inside Kinnock's Labour Party* (London: Verso).

Hickson, K. (2005) *The IMF Crisis and British Politics* (London: I.B. Tauris).

Kavanagh, D. and Cowley, P. (2010) *The British General Election of 2010* (Basingstoke: Palgrave Macmillan).

Lee, S. (2007) *Best for Britain? The Politics and Legacy of Gordon Brown* (Oxford: Oneworld).

Rawnsley, A. (2010) You Thought Fighting Your Brother Was Tough. That Was the Easy Bit. *The Observer*, 26 September.

Scruton, R. (2000) *England: An Elegy* (London: Chatto and Windus).

Seldon, A. and Lodge, G. (2010) *Brown at 10* (London: Biteback).

Smith, M. (2010) From Big Government to Big Society: Changing the State–Society Balance. In A. Geddes and J. Tonge (eds.), *Britain Votes 2010* (Oxford: Oxford University Press).

Sunday Telegraph (2010) How a Three Time Loser Snatched Victory at the Last. 26 September: 4.

Sylvester, R. and Baldwin, T. (2010) Miliband is Urged to Loosen Union Ties. *The Times*, 18 November.

Watt, N. and Wintour, P. (2010) Leader Shows Ruthless Streak over Shadow Chancellor Post. *Guardian*, 9 October.

17
A Tale of Two Liberalisms

Matt Beech

We share a conviction that the days of big government are over; that centralization and top-down control have proved a failure. We believe that the time has come to disperse power more widely in Britain today; to recognize that we will only make progress if we help people to come together to make life better. In short, it is our ambition to distribute power and opportunity to people rather than hoarding authority within government. That way, we can build the free, fair and responsible society we want to see. (Cameron and Clegg, 2010: 7)

Introduction: Bath and Manchester

The Conservative–Liberal Government represents a new period in British politics. The Coalition brought to an end 13 years of New Labour rule and reintroduced the idea of inter-party cooperation in government. The United Kingdom has not experienced such politics since the 1940–45 National Government of Winston Churchill. The major policy event of the Coalition's tenure and most likely of the decade was the Comprehensive Spending Review (CSR) on 20 October 2010. The CSR sought to radically reduce the national deficit by dramatically cutting public expenditure annually by 14.4 per cent and by 46.4 per cent over the next five years (Crawford, 2010). However, it also had another purpose – to curtail the size and the responsibilities of the central state. Whether Nick Clegg's Liberal Democrats as partners in the Coalition endorse the concept of the 'big society' is not known; nevertheless, it is the clearest expression of what David Cameron hopes will supplant Labour's 'big state'. What the public have in this new era of British politics is an accord between two political parties that espouse two types of liberalism and contain similarities as well as stark differences. And yet, at the heart of this accord is opposition to the social democratic state that has presided at the epicentre of British politics since the premiership of Clement Attlee and an opposition to the organization that has sustained this model of the state, namely the Labour Party. In short, the story of these times in British politics is a tale of two liberalisms.

The tale of two liberalisms refers to the ideological traditions that Cameron and Clegg come from within the Conservative Party and Liberal Democrat Party respectively. It is not economic liberalism versus social liberalism but rather, liberal Conservatism and *Orange Book* Liberalism. A full understanding of Cameron's liberal Conservatism is tricky to decode but it certainly contains four distinct elements.

First, the neoliberal economic philosophy of free markets, competition, the primacy of the profit motive, a dominant private sector, low levels of income tax and a de-socialized state all maximize individual liberty and lead to the most efficient way to provide goods and services in a free society (Beech, 2009). It ought to be said that his neoliberalism is not as unrelenting and hard-line as it can sometimes be, especially if one thinks of the United States. For example, state provision of health care and public pensions via the old age pension persist and appear to be supported by Cameron's liberal Conservatives.

Second, liberal Conservatism is a political instrument which acts as a marker of differentiation between the Cameronites and the recent leaderships and governing elites in the Conservative Party that haled from the Tory right (Beech, 2009). Under Cameron the Conservatives tacked to the centre ground of British politics on the environment; issues of UK funding and commitment to global development and anti-poverty strategies; and preserving (at least in theory) the National Health Service as the guardian of publicly provided health care.

Third, the social and ethical outlook of Cameron's Conservatives is accurately summarized as a social liberal outlook (Beech, 2009). Unlike many members of the Conservative Party both inside and outside of Parliament the Cameronites are not social conservatives or even moderate social conservatives. They endorse marriage but do not believe the state should prescribe what constitutes a family and they subscribe to New Labour's equalities agenda.

Fourth, a hybrid of the Liberal and the Conservative reading of international relations and Britain's place in the world sums up his liberal Conservatism abroad. Broadly speaking, this hybrid vision is a fusion of both idealist and realist assumptions and its practical outworking is the traditional Conservative conception of vigorously pursuing Britain's national interests, but one that is tempered by a Liberal commitment to human rights and democracy (Beech, 2011). This was the twin approach of Her Majesty's Government's delegation to the People's Republic of China in November 2010.

Whilst Cameron's liberal Conservatism is not a watertight ideology it sufficiently tells an ideological narrative about the present leadership of the Conservative Party and is therefore useful for students of British politics. Cameron first enunciated his political creed in a speech in Bath in 2007:

> I am a liberal Conservative. Liberal, because I believe in the freedom of individuals to pursue their own happiness, with the minimum of interference from government. Sceptical of the state, trusting people to make the most of their lives, confident about the possibilities of the future – this is liberalism. And Conservative, because I believe that we're all in this together – that there is a historical understanding between past, present and future generations, and that we have a social responsibility to play an active part in the community we live in. Conservatives believe in continuity and belonging; we believe in the traditions of our country which are embedded in our institutions. Liberal and Conservative. Individual freedom and social responsibility. (Cameron, 2007: 3–4)

Clegg contributed to the right-wing Liberal Democrat publication *The Orange Book* (Marshall and Laws, 2004) which sought to reconnect the party with free market liberalism (known as Manchester liberalism in the nineteenth century). Whilst not wishing to over-egg the pudding by suggesting a collection of essays is responsible for the development of a distinctive school of contemporary Liberal Democrat thought, it can be argued that the volume harnessed the views of a group of Liberal Democrats from the same generation that had experienced both Thatcherism and the politics of New Labour. The *Orange Book* liberals disdain the social conservatism and authoritarianism of the Conservative right; the interventionism and big state of the Labour Party; and were deeply critical of their own party's brand of social democracy. These Liberal Democrats desire to be consistently liberal in economic and social affairs as Clegg states:

> Marrying our proud traditions of economic and social liberalism, refusing to accept that one comes at the cost of the other. On that

point, if not all others, the controversial *Orange Book* in 2004 was surely right. (Clegg, 2008: 2)

The following quotation, again from Clegg's first major address as leader of the Liberal Democrats, is ideologically revealing; as an *Orange Book* liberal he takes aim simultaneously at both the conservative and the socialist or social democratic approach to politics. In no uncertain terms Clegg announces his conception of liberalism to the British public:

> There are two crucial dividing lines in British politics. First – the dividing line between progressives and conservatives – between those who believe in tackling inherited disadvantage and removing the scars of poverty, and those who don't. And second – the dividing line that splits liberals from the advocates of big government solutions – a dividing line that splits the progressive cause. Our party will always be on the progressive side of the argument...The split within the progressive cause is not about whether we wish to overcome social injustice, but how we want to overcome it. Socialism believes that Government knows best. Liberalism believes people know best. (Clegg, 2008: 3)

Thus, the tale of two liberalisms which seeks to explain how and why Conservative and Liberal Democrat politicians could form a political and ideological coalition can be understood with reference to a speech in Bath and a tradition from Manchester. As Cameron stated:

> But we recognised something really important, that we could work together. Not just lots of shared values, like wanting a country that is more free, more fair, more green, more decentralised. But a shared way of trying to do business. Reasonable debate, not tribal dividing lines. (Cameron, 2010: 3)

The shared outlook and values of these liberalisms is most appropriately termed an economic or neoliberal political economy and an attitude of social liberalism. The common enemies for these liberals are those who could be termed economic egalitarians and social conservatives. Economic egalitarians usually argue for a strong, centralized, social democratic state to distribute public goods and services. It is sustained through progressive taxation; develops redistributive public policy; and its approach to funding individuals, families and communities is prioritarian. This is the *modus operandi* of economic egalitarians; they are disproportionally found in the Labour Party and arguably the leading thinker of this school of thought in postwar Britain was Anthony Crosland with his social democratic thesis *The Future of Socialism* (Crosland, 1956).

Social conservatives are advocates of traditional conceptions of personal ethics, the family, law and order and individual responsibility within the public realm; they support polices which champion such perspectives and oppose libertarianism. Social conservatives are not necessarily religious but often they are sympathetic to the values and worldviews of the Judeo-Christian faiths. They believe that the state ought to be robust in its intervention in the public realm to uphold public ethics and that the dichotomy between public and private spheres is not always in the best interests of the nation. On the whole they tend to be members of the Conservative Party and in Parliament tend to be members of the Cornerstone group, but a significant minority are found in the Labour Party (including Christian socialists such as Frank Field). In decades past, many Labour members were Christian in mind-set, if not in practice, and combined economic egalitarianism with a brand of social conservatism which was peculiarly British. The Edwardian influence of Christian socialists such as R.H. Tawney and William Temple on the Labour Party was profound and to some extent still resonates today. Understandably very few if any Liberal Democrats are advocates of social conservatism. Therefore the liberalism of Cameron and Clegg is hostile to the type of economic egalitarianism and social conservatism outlined above. However, their liberalism emanates from deep political and ideological wells. They are respectively Tory and Liberal with reference to constitutionality, the European Union and the defence of the realm. It is difficult to measure, but is suggested here, that neither the liberal Conservatism of Cameron nor the *Orange Book* Liberalism of Clegg is indicative of the majority of card-carrying Conservatives and Liberal Democrats. It is argued that such Tories are more socially conservative than the Prime Minister and that most Liberal Democrats are more economically egalitarian than his Deputy.

The Austerity Debate

The debate surrounding the Comprehensive Spending Review is complicated and requires students of British politics to engage carefully with economics, political thought and public policy. In the following section I shall attempt to summarize this debate which characterizes the current ideological discourse in British politics. The Coalition asserts that New Labour squandered a benign economy inherited from the Major Government and mismanaged the economy by incurring a huge structural deficit predicated on extravagant expenditure and unnecessary, ill-conceived public policy programmes. This has placed the UK in an invidious position of relative economic weakness and leaves it exposed in a period of global economic uncertainty to further financial shocks:

> The Coalition Government inherited one of the most challenging fiscal positions in the world. Last year, Britain's deficit was the largest in its peacetime history – the state borrowed one pound for every four it spent. The UK currently spends £43 billion on debt interest, which is more than it spends on schools in England. (HM Treasury, 2010: 5)

The narrative contends that the level of personal and government debt has reduced the attractiveness of Britain as an economy for foreign investors which, in turn, greatly hampers the ability of the private sector to raise funds for investment and expansion. Financially, the situation is precarious and requires immediate and austere budgetary disciplines. In addition to this, the Coalition claim that New Labour presided over a culture of increased worklessness and welfare dependency which has spread to a significant minority of the population. This social dependency has trapped individuals and families in a cycle of poverty and a reliance on cash benefits which is socially corrosive and economically unsustainable. Scholars that appear sympathetic to the Coalition's approach, such as Patrick Minford, argue that significant cuts to public expenditure are justifiable prerequisites that will facilitate recovery and competitiveness:

> So the Coalition had no real choice but to be tough. It chose to be a little bit tougher than Labour. Probably too it chose to land the axe more on spending than to raise taxes than Labour in the end would have done. In the process it aims to tighten up on welfare benefits, to reform spending practices in education, health, the police and much else, to cut back public sector wages and net pensions, and in general to move away from the state-dominated society towards the 'big society'. (Minford, 2010: 5)

The Conservative–Liberal narrative continues by emphasizing that the onset of the credit crunch in September 2007 and the ensuing recession of 2008–9 was especially damaging to the British economy because of these structural weaknesses and large-scale indebtedness. In short, the Coalition's charge is that New Labour followed the tried-and-tested approach of Labour governments – tax and spend – which is path-dependent and as a result leads to an insatiable demand for higher and higher public sector budgets and has negative economic externalities on the private sector and society in general:

> The spending plans in the 2007 Comprehensive Spending Review were based on unsustainable assumptions about the public finances...from 2001 onwards public spending grew steadily as a share of the economy and a structural deficit began to emerge. Government measures to tackle this structural deficit did not begin to take effect until 2010, by which time the impact of the financial crisis had made an unaffordable situation unsustainable. (HM Treasury, 2010: 13)

The Conservative–Liberal Government has therefore had to embark upon a range of measures to substantially reduce the costs of the welfare state and public services. The short-and medium-term outlook is one of reluctant but yet enforced austerity in the hope that such a dose of retrenchment of the state will gradually enable entrepreneurs and private firms to engender growth and for the voluntary sector and businesses to begin to provide more goods and services to the British people where previously the state had dominated. The desired outcome is greater personal freedom, a smaller, less centralized state and financial rectitude.

Whilst the leader of Her Majesty's Opposition acknowledges that the deficit is of great import he does not assert that it is the single most pressing issue – that is reserved for stimulating healthy economic growth and recovery:

> I am serious about reducing our deficit. But I am also serious about doing it in a way that learns the basic lessons of economics, fairness and history. Economics teaches us that at a time of recession governments run up deficits. We were too exposed to financial services as an economy so the impact of the crash on the public finances was deeper on us than on others. We should take responsibility for not building a more resilient economy. But what we should not do as a country is make a bad situation worse by embarking on deficit reduction at a pace and in a way that endangers our recovery. The starting point for a responsible plan is to halve the deficit over four years, but growth is our priority and we must remain vigilant against a downturn. (Miliband 2010: 8)

Thus, the Labour Party under the leadership of Ed Miliband interprets the challenges facing the British economy in a contrasting way. They argue that the global credit crunch and the banking crisis that followed caused the recession of 2008–9. Gordon Brown's then Labour Government succeeded in preventing the UK from slipping into a depression due to a Keynesian stimulus plan which involved spending billions of pounds on public services and government-led projects to keep people in work. Similar stimulus plans were adopted by France, Germany and the United States. Simultaneously, the banking system was rescued through the nationalization of Northern Rock and the part-nationalizations of Lloyds-TSB, Halifax-Bank of Scotland and the Royal Bank of Scotland. This constitutes the mainstay of the existing budget deficit and without such government intervention much of the British banking sector would have collapsed and untold economic misery would have ensued. Furthermore, the then Chancellor Alistair Darling oversaw the Bank of England's policy of quantitative easing whereby billions of pounds were released into the financial system with the aim of increasing liquidity and enabling the banks to lend to each other and to businesses and individuals, which, in turn, aided consumption and growth. These combined measures led to a modest recovery which resulted in the economy exiting recession in January 2010. According to Labour's reading of recent economic events Darling managed to reduce the deficit from £178 billion in autumn 2009 to £155 billion by May 2010. This means that £23 billion was wiped from the deficit in eight months by investing in growth and helping combat unemployment and foreclosures.

Labour maintain that they too would embark on a period of expenditure cuts (halving the deficit by the next election) as one aspect of reducing the deficit but that the cuts would be slower and less deep than those outlined in the Comprehensive Spending Review. Moreover, Labour asserts that more revenue ought to be raised through taxation (in particular a levy on the banking sector) and by efficiencies made in government procurement. Labour's central thesis is that the Coalition's approach is a risk to economic growth and to a stable recovery because its austerity measures will cost 490,000 jobs in the public sector and approximately the same number in the private sector. This, they argue, will lead to a sharp rise in welfare payments and reduce spending as disposable incomes disappear. Labour's fear is that this 'remedy' may lead to a double-dip recession, cast millions of people into poverty and set back the prospects of economic growth.

How then do students of British politics navigate their way through the claims and counter-claims of the Coalition Government and the Opposition? Which of the interpretations of cause and effect is most accurate? To begin with one needs to look back beyond the recent past and the credit crunch to the start of New Labour's time in office. What became clear to some scholars of British political economy was that New

Labour was not challenging the City of London (Lee, 2007). In fact, in terms of their approach to the finance sector there was little alteration to the previous Major administrations and the laissez-faire mentality towards regulation persisted. New Labour was interventionist in social, foreign and some economic affairs but not when economics referred to the governance of the nation's key source of revenue. This 'light touch' approach to the City, coupled with the fact that the UK's economy is one of the world's most open and finance-oriented meant that it was especially vulnerable to the credit-crunch and the global banking crisis. Therefore, New Labour failed to regulate and govern the finance sector adequately. In contrast, the credit crunch was a failure of the banks. By banks one is referring to those engaged in financial speculation and trading rather than the high street arms of well-known banks. Part of the problem is that British banks are presently both investment houses and retail banks. Huge bonuses that rivalled or sometimes dwarfed salaries incentivized risk-taking on an enormous scale and eventually the banks became over-leveraged and uncertain of the state of their books. This unquantifiable debt incurred as products sold to those who often could ill-afford them has been termed 'toxic debt'.

Yet, the Labour Party's claim that the stimulus package moved Britain's economy out of recession and prevented depression with much greater levels of unemployment and poverty is indeed accurate. Furthermore, it does appear correct that the Brown Government's intervention to nationalize and part-nationalize much of the sector prevented a collapse and with it the concomitant loss of holdings. This came at a cost – approximately £80 billion – and took the British economy into a level of public indebtedness not seen since the Second World War.

This brings us to the most contentious issue in the debate about reducing the deficit – namely is it necessary to balance the budget and clear the totality of the debt within the next four financial years (2011–14)? The short answer is no. The idea that all of the debt built up due to the expansion and investment of public services, the banking bailouts and the stimulus package needs to be repaid by the next General Election is not an economically watertight assertion. It is a politically expedient goal for the Conservatives (less so for the Liberal Democrats) but as the majority of the debt is in the form of government bonds that do not need to be repaid for approximately 14 years there is not the urgency to embark on the most drastic round of cuts to public expenditure in the modern era. The Labour Party was, at the General Election, committed to reducing the deficit by £70 billion which is approximately half of the total amount and significant reductions are required because the British economy has not historically operated with such levels of debt – the equivalent of 43 per cent of GDP. Added to this is the point that such a deficit reduces both investor and consumer confidence, although the UK did not forfeit its triple AAA international credit rating. As Carl Emmerson of the Institute for Fiscal Studies made clear in his briefing the day after the Comprehensive Spending Review:

> As a result the cuts to total public spending over the four years starting next April are, after economy-wide inflation, set to be the deepest since World War II and the cuts to spending on public services will be the deepest since the four years beginning in April 1975 when the then Labour Government was trying to comply with the IMF austerity plan. (Emmerson, 2010: 2)

Therefore, one must draw the conclusion that there is more to the Comprehensive Spending Review than economic necessity, but what?

The 'Big Society' or the Retrenchment of the Social Democratic State?

Cameron argued before the General Election that what was needed was reform of Labour's 'big state' and that it ought to be supplanted by the 'big society'. The present economic crisis facilitates an argument to reform the welfare state and the traditional notions of state-funded public goods. The 'big society' narrative is not merely a call to greater volunteerism and an encouragement to the nation to be 'better citizens' or specifically to be more community-minded, that is hardly controversial and few would object to such exhortations from a Prime Minister. However, the 'big society' does sound more benign and apolitical than it is. It is asserted here that the 'big society' ought to be viewed as the ideological agenda for a set of reforms driven by the financial measures outlined in the CSR. In essence, the deficit is the immediate problem but, for these two sets of liberals, the more entrenched problem is the practice of perpetuating an embedded social democratic state. The CSR and the welfare reforms are both *means* to secure the wider ideological *end* – the 'big society', but they are also *ends* in themselves. Some might ask 'what is wrong with this?' and on one level they are right – there is nothing wrong with a government enacting radical public policy reform that it believes is required. Nonetheless, the complexity of the economic and political context has muddied the waters of comprehension on these issues. The 'big society' is not purely a vision for greater civic virtue through a programme of public policy reform; it is a plan to roll back and unpick the welfare state in a manner reminiscent of the unfulfilled aspiration of Thatcher. As Cameron made clear in his 2008 party conference speech:

> The central task I have set myself and this Party is to be as radical in social reform as Margaret Thatcher was in economic reform. That's how we plan to repair our broken society. (Cameron, 2008: 9)

It needs to be understood as a renewed neoliberal challenge to the social-democratic state. Whilst few voters disagree with reducing the deficit, contributing more to their pensions and greater levels of volunteerism, far fewer would vote for a substantial retrenchment of the welfare state and its role in guaranteeing essential public goods and services. Furthermore, because this neoliberal challenge of Cameron's and Clegg's is couched in relatively anodyne terms the full scale of the reforms outlined are often overlooked. Therefore, what the CSR and the 'big society' will mean for the normal activity of the social democratic state is nothing short of a paradigm shift. Cameron may well think that individuals, community groups, voluntary associations and social enterprises are at times more responsive and effective than much of the public sector at providing goods and services. He might also think that it empowers non-state stakeholders and engenders a common culture of altruism and service. Furthermore, he evidently sees the merit of reducing the financial burden of the state. But it is argued here that what is driving the 'big society' narrative is neoliberal ideology. Of the 'big society' Cameron says:

> The old way of doing things: the high-spending, all-controlling, heavy-handed state, those ideas were defeated. Statism lost . . . society won. That is what happened at the last election and that is the change I believe we can lead. From state power to people power. From unchecked individualism to national unity and purpose. From big government to the big society. The big society is not about creating cover for cuts. I was going on about it years before the cuts. It's not about government abdicating its role, it is about government changing its role. It's about government helping to build a nation of doers and go-getters, where people step forward not sit back, where people come together to make life better. (Cameron, 2010: 8)

But if government is supposed to change its role, this requires a change to the idea and ethos of public services and the welfare state. The generally accepted notion of communal public services free at the point of delivery, provided by professionally trained and accountable public practitioners, is under threat from the philosophy of the 'big society'. So if the state is to be rolled back, what will replace it? The market. Though not just a free market of private providers but a plurality of third sector organizations, social enterprises, private firms and perhaps a residual public form of local provision. In welfare, in education, in health care such diverse markets will replace state-mandated provision of goods and services. It is a new form of privatization, but instead of a private firm purchasing a nationalized industry or company, the role of the state as sole provider is removed or reduced to one of many possible service providers. One of the ideational drivers in the 'big society' is that individuals know what goods and services they need and have a right to acquire them. In short, consumerism is the absolute good. The reasoning goes that consumerism maximizes freedom and empowers individuals whereas the state often prevents choice and is the enemy of freedom.

Conclusion

As students of British politics are we any nearer to understanding the politics and ideology of the Coalition? The Comprehensive Spending Review appears to provide ample supporting evidence that despite the political moderation of Cameron's Conservatives on the environment, international aid and NHS funding, their commitment to neoliberal *means* and *ends* appear to trump other competing concerns. At the core of the liberal Conservatives and the supporters of Clegg is more or less a Joseph–Thatcher economic perspective which declares the primacy of the market over the welfare state, champions the private government of individuals over public government and reduces the efficacy of public administration to mere cost-benefit analysis. Cameron's neoliberal credentials have certainly come to the fore and in his partnership with Clegg and other liberals from the Manchester tradition, a robust liberal perspective has once again surfaced in the policies of the British centre-right.

Liberalism is therefore very clearly *en vogue* and restored to a leading position in the ideological discussions of British politics. The nub of the debate between the Coalition and the Labour Party is an argument between neoliberals and social democrats. They espouse competing diagnoses of the causes of Britain's economic woes and advocate divergent remedies. The intellectual battle continues over the purpose, size and funding of the state. It is at root an animated and often ill-tempered conversation about the most important questions that free people can ask: 'What is the good society and how do we achieve it?' In this post-New Labour era, the Conservative Party are in the ascendant and alongside their Liberal partners they look to the traditions of classical and neoliberalism as the Labour Party (though recently more confident of their social democratic aspirations) currently search for inspiration.

References

Beech, M. (2009) Cameron and Conservative Ideology. In S. Lee and M. Beech, *The Conservatives under David Cameron: Built to Last?* (Basingstoke: Palgrave Macmillan).

Beech, M. (2011) British Conservatism and Foreign Policy: Traditions and Ideas Shaping Cameron's Global View. *British Journal of Politics and International Studies*, published online onlinelibrary.wiley.com/doi/10.1111/j.1467-856X.2010.00445.x/pdf, 15 February, pp. 1–16.

Cameron, D. (2007) A Liberal Conservative Consensus to Restore Trust in Politics. Speech, Bath. www.conservatives.com/News/Speeches/2007/03/Cameron_A_liberal_Conservative_consensus_to_restore_trust_in_politics.aspx.

Cameron, D. (2008) Speech to Conservative party conference, Birmingham, 1 October.

Cameron, D. (2010) Together in the National Interest. Speech to the Conservative party conference, Birmingham, 6 October.

Cameron, D. and Clegg, N. (2010) Foreword. In *The Coalition: Our Programme for Government*, (London: HM Government).

Clegg, N. (2008) Speech on the reform of public services, Liberal Democrat manifesto conference, London School of Economics, 12 January. news.bbc.co.uk/1/hi/uk_politics/7187852.stm.

Crawford, R. (2010) Where Did the Axe Fall? *Institute for Fiscal Studies 2010 Spending Review Briefing*, 21 October, www.ifs.org.uk/publications/5311.

Crosland, A. (1956) *The Future of Socialism* (London: Jonathan Cape).

Emmerson, C. (2010) Opening Remarks. *Institute for Fiscal Studies 2010 Spending Review Briefing*, 21 October. www.ifs.org.uk/publications/5310.

HM Treasury (2010) *Spending Review*, Cm 7942 (London).

Lee, S. (2007) *Best for Britain? The Politics and Legacy of Gordon Brown*, (Oxford: OneWorld).

Marshall, P. and Laws, D. (2004) *The Orange Book: Reclaiming Liberalism* (London: Profile Books).

Miliband, E. (2010) Speech to Labour's leadership conference, Birmingham, 28 September. www.bbc.co.uk/news/uk-politics-11426411.

Minford, P. (2010) 'Just Keep off the Sofa', *Parliamentary Brief*, 13(2), November: 5–6.

Index

Compiled by Sue Carlton

281